THE COMMUNITY TOURISM GUIDE

THE COMMUNITY TOURISM GUIDE
Exciting Holidays for Responsible Travellers

Mark Mann

for

TOURISM**CONCERN**

Earthscan Publications Ltd, London

First published in the UK in 2000 by Earthscan Publications Ltd

Copyright © Tourism Concern and Mark Mann, 2000

A catalogue record for this book is available from the British Library

ISBN: 1 85383 681 8

Typesetting by PCS Mapping & DTP, Newcastle upon Tyne
Printed and bound by Thanet Press, Margate, Kent
Cover design by Susanne Harris
Cover photos: Guy Marks/Tribes Travel, Paul Miles, Dominic Lever,
   Julian Matthews/Discovery Initiatives, Patricia Barnett, Mark Mann

Tourism Concern
Stapleton House, 277–281 Holloway Road
London N7 8HN, UK
Tel: +44 (0)20 7753 3330
Fax: +44 (0)20 7753 3331
Email: info@tourismconcern.org.uk
http://www.tourismconcern.org.uk

For a full list of publications please contact:

Earthscan Publications Ltd
120 Pentonville Road
London N1 9JN, UK
Tel: +44 (0)20 7278 0433
Fax: +44 (0)20 7278 1142
Email: earthinfo@earthscan.co.uk
http://www.earthscan.co.uk

Earthscan is an editorially independent subsidiary of Kogan Page Ltd and publishes in
association with WWF-UK and the International Institute for Environment and
Development

This book is printed on elemental chlorine free paper

'The quest of the responsible traveller should be to learn, to be understanding, to share, to contribute – rather than to act as a consumer who seeks maximum gratification at minimum expense.'

Rolf Wesche/Andy Drumm, from *Defending our Rainforest*

'The fact that indigenous people want to insert themselves in the market does not mean that they disappear as peoples.'

T Tapuy, coordinator of RICANCIE, Ecuador

'When we speak of ecotourism, we speak of us – our people, our lives and the way we do things. This is what ecotourism means to us.'

Edgar Boyan, Lokono community member, Guyana

'When you enter our lands, you become part of us. The land, the creatures, the forest, you and I become one.'

Stanley Sam, Ahousaht elder, Canada

'The raw material of the tourist industry is the flesh and blood of people and their cultures.'

Cecil Rajendra, human rights activist, Malaysia

CONTENTS

SECTION ONE: COMMUNITY TOURISM – THE ISSUES AND PRINCIPLES

SECTION TWO: HOLIDAY DIRECTORY

SECTION THREE: USEFUL INFORMATION

FOREWORD:
TOURISM CONCERN – PUTTING PEOPLE IN THE PICTURE

So you're planning your next holiday. It's been a fraught and busy year; you've thought it over and decided that even though the money's tight, you deserve to spoil yourself a bit. Yes, this is the year you're actually going to do that long-postponed big adventure – no holds barred.

In this delicious frame of mind, the last thing in the world any of us wants is to have our dream planning interrupted by some squeaky, small voice of conscience whispering: What about the environment? What about human rights? What about the poverty? Don't you care that *you* might be making things worse by going *there*?

In truth, you probably do care. But, you rationalize, there's nothing you personally can do about any of that stuff, and staying away won't stop anyone else from going, so you might as well go anyway. That's where Tourism Concern can make the difference. For a decade it has pursued two big aims: firstly, to get the tourism industry to recognize that it is creating serious problems and should be doing something about them; and secondly, to tap into tourism's huge potential in order to spread its benefits far more even handedly.

Tourism Concern was founded in 1989 on a simple premise: our holiday destination is always somebody else's home, and the people who live there are not merely part of the scenic backdrop to our fabulous holiday experience. They matter.

It's a very basic notion. And if you turn it around, it makes instant sense. How many of us have caught ourselves cursing inconsiderate tourists congregating in coachloads in a narrow high street, lengthening the lunch-time queues at busy bank counters or ticket offices, booking out the one hotel you always stay in on the bank holiday weekend, marching up and down your local beauty spot until the path is as busy as a motorway and twice as ugly?

Local people matter. Yet the failure to recognize it has sparked local protests and campaigns the world over against tourism development. So Tourism Concern has been trying, since its inception, to fill in the seductive but empty images of paradise in the travel brochures by putting people back in the picture. We do this through a mixture of research, education, lobbying, campaigning, tackling the industry head-on, and getting together with like-minded people. And after ten years our work is producing results. The industry and even governments are starting to take the problems of tourism much more seriously. Some of the ideas we've pioneered – such as fair trade and educational videos for holiday-makers – have been taken up by bits of the industry. We are no longer a lone voice. Voluntary Service Overseas (VSO) and Action for Southern Africa (ACTSA) have both run campaigns to highlight how little of the money we spend on our holidays benefits the local people whose areas we visit. The first of our two aims, then, is showing signs of being realized – today there is much broader recognition of tourism's tendency to create problems. We have even started to tackle the tricky bit: finding solutions.

TOURISM CONCERN'S ORIGINS

Tourism Concern started life in 1988 as an informal network run from my home in Newcastle. I'd become interested during the 1980s in the work of some churches based in Bangkok. They called themselves the Ecumenical Coalition on Third World Tourism (ECTWT), and they wanted to promote a new kind of tourism, which would lead to 'just, participatory and sustainable development'.

We wanted to do something practical by creating a British group to support and publicize what the ECTWT was doing. We began contacting people in Britain who might want to join in a fresh critique of the tourism industry, and Tourism Concern was officially launched as a membership organization in September 1989.

The fledgling organization instantly ran into an image problem. This was 1989, and the green movement was riding the crest of a wave of public popularity. It was hard to convince people that this wasn't yet another campaign hitching a ride on the environmental bandwagon. Actually, we would have had an easier time if we *had* limited ourselves to campaigning for rare animals and plants threatened by tourism's heavy footprint.

Yet we have always been clear that our definition of environment is much broader than that: it includes people, their environments, economies, cultures, societies and their basic rights. (And, in any case, experience has shown that environmental solutions rarely work if the people who actually live in that particular environment are not consulted and involved.)

In ten years Tourism Concern has grown from a small group of individuals into a national organization with over 1000 members. Members include teachers and students, academics and journalists, people from the tourism industry and development workers – and, of course, people who live and work in holiday destinations. We hold an annual conference, have a quarterly magazine, and run debates and seminars for our members and the public. We have produced affordable audio-visual and education materials for teachers and students to help them understand the key issues in tourism. Our website is up and running and we have a vast library of books, papers, magazines and other documents.

The voluntary coordinator who started out running the whole show from her home has over the years given way to a full-time director and specialist staff generously housed by the Business School of the University of North London.

PART OF A GLOBAL NETWORK

Tourism Concern is a small voice. But it is not alone. When it was set up, groups across the world were already challenging the conventional view of tourism as a 'passport to development'. Individual groups have come and gone, but the global network remains a reality and a source of real strength.

People from all over the world find their way to our office, to share their experiences and to ask for our advice and support. On occasion, we've been lucky enough to play a hand in the birth of local campaigns. Goa was one such case. Tourism Concern was set up just when the Indian state of Goa was receiving its first charter flights from Europe, carrying unprecedented numbers of package tourists. For our first campaign, we decided to highlight this development. Local Goan groups were already sounding alarm bells about what uncontrolled package tourism might mean. They asked us to raise the issue with tour operators and people in Britain.

We have developed strong links with Goan organizations and have relayed their worries and views to the UK tourist industry and public. While we can't claim total success, we have generated publicity and awareness in Britain, which has added weight to local efforts to challenge damaging projects.

NOT AN ANTI-TOURISM CAMPAIGN

Although we are often called up by journalists when they want an 'anti-tourism' quote, Tourism Concern is not campaigning against tourism. Most of our members became involved precisely because they love travelling, so it would be hypocritical of us to tell others not to travel. In any case, we realise that people will still go on holiday, whatever a small organization such as Tourism Concern says.

What we *are* about is developing a more responsible, sustainable and fair tourism industry – one that benefits local people just as much as ourselves and doesn't degrade environments – and we seek to work *with* the tourism industry rather than against it. We don't believe that considering the welfare of local people has to mean a 'worse' holiday. Indeed, the whole message of this book is that, in the right circumstances, tourism *can* support local people, cultures, environments and economies, while still being exciting and enjoyable for us.

OUR OTHER ACTIVITIES

The tourism industry

One example of our work within the industry is the Himalayan Tourist Code (see 'Responsible tourism codes' in Section Three). We produced the code in

1991, working with the Annapurna Conservation Area Project and most UK trekking operators. The code provides low-impact responsible travel advice for trekkers and is still used by many travel companies.

Public awareness campaigns

If only bad practice could be turned into good simply by holding a friendly and frank discussion around a table! But you can't always shift opinions that way – especially when large commercial interests are at stake. The holiday industry exists to give people a good time and to make profit out of doing it. Tourism Concern exists to point out what's happening to people on the receiving end of tourism and to change the terms so that tourism becomes more just, sustainable and participatory. So for us, public campaigning is essential, not least because public opinion matters increasingly to the well-being of private companies.

Human rights

Human rights is a big part of our work. In particular, we are trying to persuade the Government that it should have an ethical tourism policy relating to other countries (it doesn't even have a single department responsible for outbound tourism, let alone a policy).

Fair trade

We are examining this idea through some substantial research, in order to see how far it might solve the classic problems of tourism development. We believe it could be the way forward, and that fair trade will probably form the basis of our work in the next ten years. Our hope is that Tourism Concern will help define a new way of doing tourism which shares its benefits more equably between travellers, the tourism industry, governments of the countries we visit – and, above all, the people among whose homes we take our holidays. Only then will they take their place at the centre of all those pictures of paradise.

Alison Stancliffe
Founder and original coordinator, Tourism Concern

Tourism Concern

Stapleton House, 277–281 Holloway Road, London N7 8HN
Tel: +44 (0)20 7753 3330 Fax: +44 (0)20 7753 3331
• www.tourismconcern.org.uk • info@tourismconcern.org.uk

INTRODUCTION: STRANGE BIRDSONG IN THE JUNGLE

This guide contains two of the best holidays I've ever been on. The first was in the Australian Outback, about 300 kilometres from Uluru (or Ayer's Rock, as it used to be called). If nowhere has a middle, this was it, with no major town for thousands of kilometres in any direction. The vast night skies were filled with shooting stars and the desert was alive with plants and animals, drawing on the unseen water reserves buried beneath the flaming red earth. Secret waterholes made perfect swimming pools to cool off in during the heat of the day.

The second was in the middle of the Ecuadorean Amazon, deep inside the world's greatest rainforest. There was certainly no shortage of water here. On one occasion we even found ourselves up to our necks in soupy brown flood-water, as we tracked a herd of wild boar through the forest. At night, we spread our sleeping mats on an open wooden platform and drifted into sleep to the sounds of crickets and frogs and strange birdsong.

Two dramatic, and dramatically different, settings. What links them is that both holidays were run by the local aboriginal/indigenous communities: people who still live in remarkable natural places and who still feel and understand the rhythms of nature. Through them, I learned to see places I would other-wise have regarded as wildernesses as *homes*. Places where people have lived for thousands of years.

I also realized that a 'responsible' or 'ethical' holiday didn't have to be boring. Instead, these community-run tours were a great way to get closer to the people and cultures I was visiting. A chance to step off the tired tourist tread-mill for a few days. And they showed me that a 'tour' didn't have to mean being stuck with 30 other tourists, herded in and out of places I didn't really want to see anyway. Instead, I found myself with a few like-minded visitors, with time to relax, to appreciate our surroundings and to get to know our hosts.

Since then, I've discovered that these two holidays are part of a new but growing movement: a movement that lacks a clear name but which is most commonly described as 'community tourism'. These holidays permit us to visit wonderful places in ways that benefit the people who live there and help preserve the natural beauty that attracted us in the first place. They get beyond the bland facade of mainstream tourism and offer us a real insight into local life. They show us living cultures instead of the fake, out-of-context 'cultural shows' served up with dinner in tourist hotels. And they take us to some of the most beautiful places on the planet.

WHAT ARE COMMUNITY-BASED HOLIDAYS?

Gone are the days when a 'politically correct' holiday meant listening to a lecture on tractor production statistics in a Cuban workers' cooperative. Tour operators (and local communities themselves) have realized that people don't go on holiday to listen to lectures about poverty. Instead, the trips in this guide offer you a chance to *do* something positive while still having a rewarding, enjoyable, fun... holiday.

In fact, our directory contains an incredibly diverse range of holidays in over 40 countries, linked by a common thread of local involvement and benefit. Most are small-group tours or small, locally run lodgings. They allow you to get to know local people in a way that package tourism and big hotels don't. Many trips take you to beautiful wilderness areas. There are drumming holidays in Senegal, language schools in Central America and Kenya, treks in Nepal, horse riding in Arizona, sea-kayaking or snorkelling in the South Pacific, and much more. And, as it happens, our directory *does* contain holidays in Cuba, but ones that focus on the island's fabulous musical wealth and vibrant culture.

Nor does community tourism have to mean sleeping in mud huts and not washing for a week. There are tours and lodgings here to suit all comfort levels and budgets, from backpacker trips for £5 a day to £200-a-day luxury safari lodges.

Finally, the guide includes holidays you can book before you leave home and tours that you can easily arrange locally. For each entry in our directory, we provide details of how to book or get more information.

WHAT TYPE OF HOLIDAYS WILL YOU FIND IN THIS BOOK?

- Tours that have local grassroots involvement and benefits.
- Holidays with a high level of interaction with local people and cultures.
- All budget and comfort levels, from roughing it to luxury.
- Many 'green' tours featuring wildlife, wilderness regions, etc.
- Small-group travel, not mass package tours.
- Tours you can book before leaving home and tours you can arrange locally.
- Tours lasting from half a day to three weeks.
- Village stays with indigenous and rural communities in the developing world.
- Community-run campsites, lodges, hotels, museums, cultural centres, etc.

HOW THIS BOOK IS ORGANIZED

Section One of this book introduces the issues and principles of community tourism. It also includes a chapter, 'Being there', that describes visits to a few community tourism projects. Section Two is a directory of community-based holidays. This is divided into tour agencies in the UK and other Western countries ('Responsible tour operators') and tours, guesthouses and lodges in individual destination countries ('Locally based tours by country'). A Holiday-finder Index is included to help you match holidays to your own interests. Section Three contains a directory of responsible tourism organizations and resources and some guidelines for responsible tourism, in case you would like to know more about the issues raised in this book.

INDEPENDENT TRAVEL OR PACKAGE TOUR?

As well as complete holidays, the Holiday Directory features local tours and guesthouses that you can visit while travelling independently. Each directory entry includes contact details, and most are easy to arrange locally. Even if you generally prefer to travel independently, a few days spent in a community on one of these community-based projects can add an extra dimension to your holiday – and bring more benefit to local people.

ACKNOWLEDGEMENTS

Many people have helped to make this book a reality. In particular, I wish to thank Zainem Ibrahim for her invaluable editorial support and Patricia Barnett, Tourism Concern's Director, for supporting this project. I'd also like to thank Sue Wheat, Lara Marsh, Stuart Hume, Rod Leith, Barbara Gehrels and Christine Franklin at Tourism Concern for their encouragement, advice, enthusiasm and for generally making Tourism Concern an enjoyable place to work.

Many other people provided information on individual countries and regions. They included Deborah McLaren (US); David Lovatt Smith (Kenya); Judy Bennett (Kuna tourism in Panama); Rolf Wesche and Andy Drumm (Ecuador); Ron Mader (Mexico); Chris McIntyre (Namibia); Paul Miles (Solomon Islands); Roger Diski and Liz Dodd (southern Africa) and Dominic Hamilton (Venezuela). Jane Taylor helped solve a minor editorial crisis. None of these people are responsible for any errors of fact or judgement in this book.

My thanks to the following for permission to reproduce articles and codes in the 'Being there' and 'Responsible tourism codes' chapters: Chris McIntyre, Paul Morrison, Belinda Rhodes, Mike Gerrard, David Peterson/Dorobo Safaris, *The Times*, *The Independent on Sunday*, *Wanderlust*, *Traveller*, Survival and the International Porter Protection Group.

DISCLAIMER

These tours have been researched through a mixture of personal visits, email, the internet and Tourism Concern's many contacts among travellers, journalists, academics and travel-industry professionals. We've tried to check that the tours we include genuinely benefit local communities, but it would be virtually impossible to inspect every tour ourselves. Even if we did have the time and resources to visit all of these projects, deciding exactly what is beneficial to local people can still be complex and contentious. We cannot *guarantee* that we've got it right in every case.

Tourism Concern neither endorses nor condemns tourism *per se*. If tourists are going to visit the developing world or indigenous territories, we believe that community-based tourism is a better alternative to mainstream tourism. But there are real dangers in this form of tourism, as in any other: if tours are not carefully planned in consultation with local people, then people and cultures can become just another marketing commodity, helping tourism to invade remote corners of the globe. And even the most worthwhile projects bring changes and have costs – even if it's only the pollution created by a long-haul flight to get there in the first place.

For these reasons, **inclusion in this guide does not constitute an official Tourism Concern 'seal of approval'**. (This disclaimer applies to both editorial listings and advertisers.) As an independent organization, Tourism Concern does not represent any interest within the tourism industry and does not officially endorse *any* tour operators. No tour operator may claim to be supported, endorsed or recommended by Tourism Concern. Finally, all prices are for guidance only and no responsibility or liability is accepted by Tourism Concern as a result of reliance on information in this guide.

SECTION ONE

COMMUNITY TOURISM – THE ISSUES AND PRINCIPLES

TOURISM AND THE
DEVELOPING WORLD

THE GLOBAL ECONOMY

One day soon, somewhere deep in a rainforest in South America or Borneo or Central Africa, a few nervous men and women will step into a muddy clearing in the jungle. Cautiously, they will accept the steel machetes or cooking pots being held out by a government-sponsored anthropologist, before hurrying back into the safety of the forest.

The encounter will not be marked by any great fanfare. It will probably not make the news. Yet it will be a significant landmark in human history. The last 'uncontacted' tribe on earth will have been caught in our global web, and an era of exploration, invasion and global integration that began when Columbus first set eyes on the Americas will be over. For the first time, the entire human race will be connected in one giant, all-embracing cultural and trading network.

As this era of human history comes to a close, we are left with a dominant social and economic system that ignores human and environmental costs. A system that destroys communal life because of its demand for a mobile labour force. That creates mental illnesses and stress by sucking people into huge, anonymous cities. That discourages people from growing their own food because doing so doesn't involve selling anything (and therefore doesn't show up as profit in economic statistics). A system that puts a greater value on a pile of dead wood than on a living forest.

Beginning with the triangular colonial trade in slaves and sugar, a Western-dominated global economy has imposed itself on the world. This is the so-called 'free market': imposed by deceit and force, from the brutality of the conquistadors and the gunboat diplomacy of the British Empire to CIA-backed coups and the financial bullying of the International Monetary Fund.

The engine that drives this system is trade. Almost all human societies have engaged in some form of trade, but the global economy is unique in its scope and the way it aggressively destroys local self-sufficiency and replaces it with global trade relationships that defy common sense. These are trade relationships in which an apple transported half-way around the world via a massive infrastructure of expensive planes, airports, trucks and roads can still cost less than the same apple grown a few miles from your home.

Until the last few decades, many rural and indigenous communities in the developing world remained on the periphery of this global economy, living largely self-sufficiently. But now, because of massive improvements in modern communications, even the most remote tribe is being forced into the global marketplace. Many once-isolated communities face the end of self-sufficiency. Many of these communities now have no choice but to become involved in trade. But the terms of this trade are heavily weighed in favour of the West, which controls the capital that oils the system. Almost all of the world's major banks and stock markets are found in the West (or Japan), as are most of the shareholders of the increasingly dominant transnational corporations.

This global economy shapes – distorts – all exchange between the 'developed' and the developing world. It explains why it is *us* visiting *them*. Why *we* have the money and the consumer choice and *they* don't.

Tourism is a form of trade. It is a part of the global economy and thus bound to reproduce the inequalities and distortions of the larger system. This book aims to highlight a more positive type of holiday – one that brings benefits to local communities. However, as long as tourism takes place within this unreformed, Western-dominated global economy, even the best community tourism projects will never be perfect.

ESCAPING ESCAPISM

'Escape to the sun.' 'Leave your worries behind.' 'Get away from it all.' The marketing clichés of the tourist brochures sell us holiday fantasies cut off from real life: a parallel universe where everything bad is magically suspended for two weeks. But, for the people we visit, tourism can be anything but an escape. We can walk away from the problems that tourism creates, but they can't. It may be our holiday, but it's their home.

We need to forget tourism's escapist fantasy and accept that our holidays take place in the real world – and have a real effect on real people.

Letting go of this fantasy can also be an opportunity – not only to help the people we visit, but for ourselves as well. Community tourism can still be an escape; the holidays in this book can take you to truly beautiful places, and about as far from the daily grind of offices and traffic jams as it's possible to get. And many of these trips feature nothing more demanding than lying on a tropical beach or taking photographs of wild animals. But going on holiday, with our eyes open, to the real world also helps us to make friends across cultural divides; to engage more fully with the places we visit; to understand the lives of the people we visit. In short, to explore this endlessly complex and fascinating world in which we find ourselves. Escaping from 'escapism' allows us to move beyond the superficial fantasies of the tourism industry towards richer – and ultimately more rewarding – holidays.

THE WORLD'S BIGGEST INDUSTRY

Tourism is, or will soon be, the world's biggest industry. It is estimated to provide one in every ten jobs on the planet. If tourism were a country, it would have the second largest economy in the world after the US. Behind the escapist fantasies, tourism is big business.

It's a complex industry too: a hydra-headed monster that embraces the large and the small, from huge corporations such as British Airways to family-run guesthouses or women braiding tourists' hair on a beach. Tourism can mean anything from rambling in Snowdonia to family trips to Disneyland, sun'n'booze packages to Spain or Greece, middle-class villas in Tuscany, all-inclusive Caribbean resorts, skiing in the Alps, wildlife safaris in Africa, or jungle tours in the Amazon.

Although Tourism Concern as an organization also examines tourism issues in Europe and Britain, this particular book is mainly about tourism to the developing world,[1] which accounts for approximately a fifth of global tourism. A fifth of the world's biggest industry is still big business and still very complex. A rainforest tour in Borneo, for instance, raises different issues than an all-inclusive resort in Barbados.

A recent phenomenon: a brief history of tourism

There have always been explorers, adventurers and traders, but modern tourism might be said to have begun with the 'Grand Tour' of Europe in the 18th century, when it became fashionable for young aristocrats to spend a year or so taking in the monuments, art and salons of continental Europe. For the working classes it was the industrial revolution of the 19th century, with railways and paid holidays for factory workers, which provided their initial chance to travel, although right up until the 1950s a holiday for most working class people generally meant a 'day out' in the country or at the seaside.

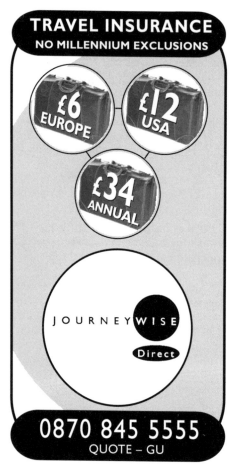

In 1841, Thomas Cook, the 'father of package tourism', organized his first train excursions in the Midlands, taking tee-totallers to meetings of the Temperance Society. In the 1850s, he branched out into rail trips to the continent. For most people, however, holidays still meant the British seaside or countryside. It wasn't until the advent of cheap air travel in the 1960s that the age of mass international tourism really began, with the first modern holidays in the sun to Mediterranean destinations such as Majorca or the Costa Brava in Spain. In the 1960s, too, small numbers of hippies and adventurous travellers set off with their backpacks to explore more exotic destinations such as Indonesia, Nepal and India, where you could live for next to nothing and find inexhaustible supplies of cheap dope. The 'Hippie Trail' was perhaps the first example of modern tourism in the developing world. While the number of Western travellers was small, they often had a disproportionate impact on local economies and cultures because of their high visibility and (relative to local people) high spending power.

Where hippies and backpackers blazed a trail, mainstream holiday development soon followed. The island of Ko Samui in Thailand, for instance, went from being an 'undiscovered' hippie hangout in about 1980 to a package tour destination with an airstrip and modern hotels by the end of that decade. The same thing happened in Hawai'i, Ibiza, Goa, Bali, Sumatra, Mexico's Yucatán peninsula, Guatemala, Fiji, the Sinai, Kenya, Peru and elsewhere. Today, it is happening in Kerala in southern India, in Zanzibar and in many other places.

Two developments – apart from the general post-war increase in disposable income in the West – have fuelled this growth in developing world tourism. One was the falling cost of air travel and the introduction of a generation of faster, wide-bodied planes in the 1970s. These permitted the extension of cheap charter flights and package holidays beyond the Mediterranean to such developing world destinations as Mexico, the Caribbean or The Gambia.

The second was that the tourism industry began to get involved in independent travel. Agencies such as Trailfinders and STA began selling cheap, convenient round-the-world air tickets that took much of the risk and uncertainty out of independent travel. Guidebooks such as the *Lonely Planet* series allowed visitors to get by in almost any country, with little or no knowledge of the local language or culture.

Tourism to the developing world has grown so rapidly over the last three decades that it's easy to forget many older people in these new tourist destinations grew up without ever seeing a white person. Many are still struggling to understand this strange intrusion into their lives.

And the future? The World Tourism Organization (WTO) predicts that international tourist numbers will rise to 1.5 billion by 2020 – a threefold increase from 1996. It predicts that a quarter of all these holidays will be taken in the developing world.

INTERNATIONAL TOURIST ARRIVALS: 1950 TO PRESENT					
WORLD TOURIST ARRIVALS (MILLIONS)					
1950	1960	1970	1980	1990	1997
25.3	69.3	159.7	284.8	425	610
TOURIST ARRIVALS IN DEVELOPING COUNTRIES (MILLIONS)					
1950	1960	1970	1980	1990	1997
–	–	–	50.3	–	186

Source: World Tourism Organization[2]

Who travels?

International travel remains the preserve of a few. The World Tourism Organization estimated that, in 1996, only 3.5 per cent of the world's population travelled abroad. Approximately 80 per cent of these international travellers came from just 20 countries – 17 European nations plus the US, Canada and Japan.[3] The emerging middle classes in such countries as India and Mexico are also beginning to take holidays in increasing numbers, but tourism is still largely a Western pastime.

Looked at from the opposite direction, while internal tourism *is* a factor in countries such as Mexico, most tourism development and planning by developing world governments still targets high-spending Western tourists rather than local travellers. Luxury hotels, all-inclusive resorts, golf courses, airports, safari parks and theme parks all cater predominantly for the demands of rich Westerners.

Who works in tourism?

Jobs in tourism are typically badly paid and insecure, with notoriously poor conditions – in the developing world and in Western countries such as the UK. Because tourists need attention around the clock, tourism often requires long and antisocial working hours. Of course, there's the benefit of free travel for some, but most tourism workers don't even get to travel: they work in hotels, bars, restaurants, amusement parks, car-hire offices and the like. Many jobs in tourism are seasonal, with many workers only employed during a high season that lasts just a few months.

In the developing world, local people may be employed for a year or two in the construction of a new resort, but only a few of them will be kept on once the resort actually opens – and then mainly in low-skilled, low-status roles such as porters, maids, waiters and cleaners. Most management jobs are filled by Westerners or other outsiders. People need training to manage a hotel or resort, and it's usually cheaper for the resort company to bring in someone who is already trained.

As in other industries, women working in tourism earn less than men and are heavily concentrated in part-time, low-skilled jobs. They are less likely to be promoted or trained for management roles.

Who profits?

Next time you go on holiday, ask yourself who owns your hotel or the airline or the tour agency who booked your holiday, or who supplied the drink with your dinner. Who is making money from your holiday? Much of what we spend on holiday – even in the developing world – ends up back in Western countries. This is known as leakage. Most tourists stay in hotels owned by a Western company. They drink imported spirits, beers and soft drinks. They eat food imported to cater for Western tastes. If they are staying in an 'all-inclusive' resort they may not leave the hotel complex during their entire stay. If they do, it may be on a half-day sightseeing trip in an imported, hotel-owned coach.

Leakage means that your holiday probably generates more money for Western companies than for people in the country you visit. The World Bank estimates that, on average, 55 pence out of every £1 you spend on holiday in a developing country returns to the West.[4] Much of the rest goes to business-people in developing world capitals. Little 'trickles down' to the people who live in the rural and seaside villages in which you are actually staying.

Power and ownership in tourism is increasingly concentrated in the hands of a small number of transnational corporations. Four companies (Thomas Cook, Airtours, First Choice and Thomsons) account for roughly 80 per cent of British package tourism. The table below shows the main subsidiaries owned

THE 'BIG FOUR' IN THE UK TRAVEL INDUSTRY			
	THOMSONS	AIRTOURS	FIRST CHOICE	THOMAS COOK
High street travel agents	800+ shops (Lunn Poly, The Travel House, etc)	1200 shops (Going Places, Advantage Travel, Travelworld, etc)	650 shops (Travel Choice, Bakers Dolphin)	800 shops (Thomas Cook)
Tour operators	Thomson Holidays, English Country Cottages, Blakes, Chez Nous, Simply Travel, Jetsave, Crystal, Tropical Places, Austravel	UK Leisure Group, Aspro, Tradewinds, Eurosites, Cresta, Bridge, Panorama	Sovereign, 2wentys, Meon Villas, Skibound, Hayes and Jarvis, Inijet, Suncars, Rainbow Holidays	Thomas Cook Holidays, Sunset Holidays, Time Off, Club 18-30, Sunworld
Airlines	Britannia Airways	Premier Air, Air Belgium, Airtours International	Air 2000	Flying Colours, Caledonian

Source: *Travel Weekly*, 9th August 1999

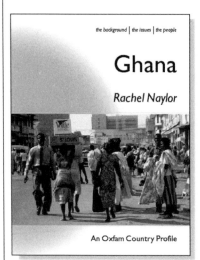

GLOBAL AIRLINE ALLIANCES			
ONE WORLD	WINGS	QUALIFLYERS	STAR
British Airways	Continental	SwissAir	Lufthansa
Quantas	KLM	Delta	SAS
American	North West	Austrian	United
Canadian	Alltalia	Turkish (plus: CrossAir,	Thai
Cathay Pacific	Braathens	Sabena, Lada, TAP,	Air Canada
FinnAir		AOM, Tyrollean)	Varig
Iberia			

Source: Travel Weekly, March 1999. Delta also had a separate alliance with Air France.

by the 'big four'. Thomas Cook (which has a 10 per cent stake in First Choice) is itself 50.1 per cent owned by the giant German tourism company, Preussag. At the time of writing, Airtours was waiting for an EU ruling on its bid to take over First Choice.

If you go into a Lunn Poly shop and book a holiday with Austravel, flying out to Australia with Britannia Airways, in reality you would be dealing exclusively with Thomson. This phenomenon, where one company is involved at every step of your holiday, is known as vertical integration. And it's a similar pattern worldwide, with an estimated 13 giant transnational (but mainly US) corporations controlling a large share of the global tourist market.

Within the airline business, too, a recent spate of mergers and 'alliances' (in which airlines agree to integrate their flight networks, share planes on certain routes and so on) has left four giant partnerships controlling much of the world's air travel.

* * *

Tourism is an industry dominated by a few increasingly powerful corporations, almost all of whom are based in the West. This industry caters for a market of tourists largely drawn from 20 Western countries. Tourism – and especially international travel – is a Western pastime.

NEGATIVE IMPACTS OF TOURISM

Tourism can promote respect for different cultures and encourage us to care about what happens to people in faraway countries. It can create jobs and put money into local economies. It can help rural and indigenous communities preserve their cultures. These potential benefits are explored in the next chapter.

Too often, however, tourism to the developing world only adds to the difficulties facing local people. Here are some of the ways that tourism can affect local people.

Displacement

Images of local and indigenous people – especially 'exotically' dressed tribal people – are commonly used in tourist marketing to sell destinations. Pick up a brochure for holidays in Kenya and the chances are that it will contain a picture of a few Maasai tribespeople in 'traditional dress', probably jumping up and down. Yet Maasai communities in Kenya have been evicted from their land to make way for the country's famous national parks, such as Amboseli. Most environmentalists now agree that their presence wasn't harming the wildlife. The Maasai themselves feel they were forced to move because they were 'in the way' of tourist development that benefited the Kenyan government and businesspeople in Nairobi, but didn't benefit the Maasai.

The Maasai are not unique. All over the world, poor rural communities standing in the way of profitable tourist development have been thrown off their land. In Tanah Lot in Bali, farmers claim that the government forced them to hand over their farms for a golf course and hotel by shutting off irrigation to their fields. In Goa, developers of hotel complexes persuaded the government to compulsorily acquire land in several villages, from people who had previously refused to sell.

On the other hand, in the 1980s in the Peruvian Amazon, communities of Yagua Indians were coerced by tour operators to move in the opposite direction, *closer* to tourist lodges, so that tourists could photograph them more conveniently. Removed from their traditional hunting land, the Yagua have become dependent upon tourism.

In Malaysia, 29 shop owners on the coastal road near the jetty at Kuah were forced to move because the Tourist Development Committee considered them an eyesore. A tourist shop and restaurant were built in their place.

In Burma, thousands of people were forcibly relocated by the governing State Law and Order Restoration Council (or SLORC: now renamed the State Peace and Development Council or SPDC) to clear the way for tourist development in Pagan, whose monumental collection of temples was seen by the regime as one of the country's big tourist draws.

Individually, these may not sound spectacular. A few insignificant villagers moved on here or forcibly bought out there. That's just the point: that poor local people are regarded as insignificant when they stand in the way of tourist developments that will generate money for governments and business interests. And these are not isolated examples: there are thousands of similar stories.

Cultural degradation

Tourism may encourage begging and 'hustling', or transform traditions of hospitality into commercial transactions, stripped of the kindness and generosity of spirit they once contained. Locals may aspire to Western lifestyles and adopt the materialistic values of their Western visitors. Tourism may reduce cultural traditions to meaningless tourist attractions. Sacred dances become after-dinner shows in luxury hotels. Such shows might, in theory, keep cultural traditions alive, but they are all too often stripped of meaning and significance to become parodies of the real thing.

Tourism can encourage prostitution, as it has in Thailand. In a study of 100 schoolchildren in Kalutara, Sri Lanka, 86 children had their first sexual experience aged 12 or 13 – the majority with a foreign tourist. In Thailand, impoverished families, often from the northern hilltribes, sell their daughters into prostitution, largely to cater for the sex-tourism industry.

Distorting local economies and social structures

Tourism may lead to dependence on income from Western tourists. A farmer may neglect his crops because he can earn more money by guiding tourists. However, unlike farming or hunting, tourism does not in itself produce food to feed people or materials to clothe and house people. Tourism is a service industry that depends upon fashions and trends in distant countries. Local people in the developing world have no control over the global tourist market. Fashions change. A kidnapping in another part of their country may frighten tourists away. What does the farmer do then, if he hasn't prepared his land – or if he sold his land to invest in his new tourist business?

Tourism can also undermine established social structures. If a young boy can earn more guiding backpackers to cheap hotels than his teacher earns from teaching, will his teacher still command respect? Similarly, a young tourist guide may find himself the richest person in his village simply by mastering a smattering of English and taking a few tourists for a walk. He can distribute money or gifts and hand out jobs as porters and cooks, for instance. Will he – and the rest of his village – still defer to the traditional chief or elders, who may have little economic power in this new world? These traditional community authorities may be bypassed by the hustle of free-market tourism.

Environmental degradation

Air travel is extremely polluting. Air traffic is growing fast and scientists predict that, by 2015, half of the annual destruction of the ozone layer will be caused by air travel. This is partly because fuel emissions at high altitude (specifically, nitrogen oxide) have a far greater effect on the ozone layer than emissions at sea level. Even responsible tourism – green or community-based holidays – has to face the fact that, if it involves plane travel, it will have an environmental cost. To be truly 'green', holidays would have be taken as closely as possible to home with the minimum amount of travel.

At a localized level, the best defence of many 'unspoilt' wilderness regions has been their inaccessibility: a new road or airstrip to service a remote 'eco-lodge' may threaten this. New infrastructure such as roads or airstrips opens up regions for incoming colonists and other destructive activities, such as logging and farming.

Hotels often dump untreated sewage into rivers and oceans. In the Sinai, hotels dump rubbish in the desert, out of sight of the tourists. Trekkers and trekking companies dump their litter as they go – as has happened at Everest Base Camp or along the Inca Trail in Peru. Coral is damaged by clumsy snorkellers or by tourist boats dropping their anchors. Deforestation and soil erosion occurs in Nepal as already scarce trees are cut down so that trekkers can have hot showers. It is estimated that the average trekking group uses as much firewood in two weeks as a local family uses in six months.

Around 350 new golf courses are built worldwide each year, many in holiday destinations such as Thailand or Goa. It's estimated that golf courses in such countries need around 1500 kilogrammes of chemical fertilizers, pesticides and herbicides each year. Building golf courses usually means clearing away well-adapted native species and replanting imported grasses, which often have no defence against local diseases and therefore require extra pesticides. The health of local people can be affected by drinking water or eating fish from rivers contaminated by toxic run-off from golf courses.

Diversion of scarce resources upon which local people depend

The development of hotels, or other tourist facilities such as golf courses, may divert scarce resources away from local people. For example, it's estimated that a single golf course in Thailand can use as much water as 60,000 rural villagers. Golf courses may draw so much water from the local water table that it is severely depleted. Village wells run dry and villagers – usually women – have to walk for hours to fetch water for their own use. (As with many of these negative tourism impacts, the extra burden tends to fall disproportionately on women.)

All-inclusives – hotels which contain all the facilities that tourists need within their grounds – not only exclude most local people from a share of the profits, but also deny them access to land and beaches from which they may once have swum or fished themselves, or where their children used to play.

Disease

With remote tribal groups, visitors risk introducing diseases to which the tribe has no immunity. In extreme cases, tribal people have died from contact with Western tourists.

* * *

If you'd like to know more about these issues, see Tourism Concern's website at www.tourismconcern.org.uk.

ACCEPTING THE TRUE COST OF OUR HOLIDAYS

We all do it. We tell opinion polls that we want better social services, then vote for tax cuts. We say we want organic food, then buy the cheaper stuff on the next shelf. And we talk about more socially responsible, environmentally friendly holidays… then book the cheapest package tour we can find.

It's hard to resist a bargain. But cheap holidays, like cheap food and lower taxes, mean that corners have to be cut. Hotels are built without proper sewage treatment plants. Rubbish is dumped in fragile areas, rather than carried out. Staff are underpaid and laid off out of season.

The tour operators argue that they have no choice. They say that holiday prices have been driven down by less scrupulous competitors. If they invest properly in being 'green' and in making sure they don't disadvantage local people, then they will have to charge more for their holidays. But (the tour operators argue) consumers are only interested in the bottom line. If a company raises prices to pay its workers a better wage, then customers will simply switch to another operator who *has* cut corners to keep prices down.

Many people in the tourism industry privately acknowledge that cut-price tourism is unsustainable. It degrades each destination before moving on in search of the next 'unspoilt' paradise. But tourism is growing rapidly. If it causes problems now, what will it be like in 50 years' time, with four or five times the present number of tourists?

Is it possible to imagine a type of tourism that leaves a place just as beautiful as it finds it? Where tourists can keep on coming, year after year, without degrading the local environment and undermining local cultural values? A tourist industry that is non-destructive and sustainable?

Tour operators argue that it's up to us to prove that we are willing to actually pay more for sustainable holidays. Only then will the mainstream tourism industry begin to take notice and put more emphasis on behaving responsibly. The holidays in this directory are small scale and may not, in themselves, have much impact on global tourism statistics and problems. But they may be a way in which you can demonstrate that there is a demand for more responsible, less damaging, holidays.

NOTES

1   See the glossary at the end of this book.
2   Note, however, that WTO figures are for all international travel, including business travel, but exclude domestic tourism. (Domestic tourism – holidays taken in someone's own country – is hard to measure but has been estimated at three to five times greater than international tourism.)
3   Most of these travellers were heading for other Western countries. According to the WTO figures, the top six destination countries for British tourists in 1996 were, in descending order: France, Spain, Ireland, US, Greece and Italy.
4   Studies for individual countries have put the figure for leakage at 40 per cent in India, 60 per cent in Thailand, 70 per cent for Kenyan beach holidays and up to 80 per cent in the Caribbean.

COMMUNITY TOURISM: AN
ALTERNATIVE

COMMUNITY TOURISM DEFINED

The idea of community tourism is simple: you can help local people and still have a good holiday, simply by going on tours that involve local communities. In other words, it is mutually beneficial trade. In practice, however, there is no one single model for community-based tourism and the projects in our directory are owned and managed in a variety of ways. Rather than lay down a rigid set of rules for community tourism, this chapter discusses the general principles that lie behind such holidays.

Who and where?

This guide is mainly about tourism to the developing world. Of course, the principles of community tourism (local benefit, consultation, sustainability) apply everywhere, but the impact of tourism – for good or bad – is arguably greater in the developing world, where many countries are coming to depend upon tourism as one of their main foreign currency earners. In any case, it's much harder to talk about 'communities' in Western countries, with their mobile and largely urban populations.

Most of the tours and projects we list are rural. Although many people in the developing world now live in cities, the idea of community is hard to apply in an urban context. Few tourists want to spend their holiday in developing world cities anyway, so urban tours are pretty thin on the ground.

While also including non-tribal tours, this book places a special emphasis on tribal people. This is not because tribal people are any more special than non-tribal people. However, as tribal people are more likely than non-tribal people to live communally (that is, after all, what 'tribal' means[1]), it's not surprising that they feature strongly in a book about communally organized tourism. They are also, on the whole, more vulnerable to the impacts of tourism. Tourism sees tribal culture as a selling point. Tourists seek out tribal people whether or not tribal people want to to be visited – for example, on 'hill-tribe treks' in northern Thailand. Tribal communities often find it hard to cope with the volume of tourists trying to visit them. Tribal peoples are also more likely to live in 'ecotourism' destinations such as rainforests or deserts: 'ecotours' often enter tribal land without permission. And because tribal communities often live very differently from Westerners, tourists are more likely to disrupt local life or give offence than in more acculturated communities. Tourism Concern recommends that you only visit tribal territory on tours that are run by – or have been authorized by – the communities themselves. We include tribally and indigenously run tours even in Western countries such as the US (see box below).

FIRST NATIONS

First Nations is a collective term for Native Americans in the US and Canada, Australian Aboriginals and New Zealand Maoris. Why are they included in a directory of developing world tourism? Because, in many ways, they have more in common with indigenous people elsewhere than with the European societies who have colonized their lands. They often suffer developing world levels of poverty – one recent study reported that Australian Aboriginals had the worst health statistics of any ethnic group on earth. Like other indigenous people, many First Nations still live in 'wilderness' areas; still live in tribal communities; still preserve close ties with the land. They also face similar obstacles when starting businesses: lack of education and business experience, discrimination by governments and white society. And tourists want to visit them for the same reasons that we want to visit indigenous people elsewhere: to experience non-Western attitudes, customs, spirituality, etc.

What is a community?

In this book, a 'community' means a mutually supportive, geographically specific, social unit such as a village or tribe where people identify themselves as community members and where there is usually some form of communal decision-making. The breakdown of such traditional, locally based communities in the West and the urban developing world – largely due to the global economy's demand for a mobile labour force – is one of the reasons why this book is mainly about the rural developing world, where most people still spend most of their lives in one village or tribe.

What is a community-based tour?

The obvious definition would be: 'tours owned and run entirely by local communities'. At present, however, this is too limiting: some of the most successful projects involve non-community partners such as non-governmental organizations (NGOs) or commercial tour operators. Others may be set up by individual community members: sometimes this works well and sometimes it creates divisions within the community. For these reasons, we've adopted a broad definition of what counts as community-based to include anything that involves genuine community participation and benefits. (I'll discuss what these benefits might be later in this chapter.)

PRACTICALITIES

What sort of holiday can you expect?

Community tours tend to be small-group trips run by small specialist operators. You won't find mass package tours where you travel in large groups and stay in identikit hotels. These are holidays for people who want to get away from the crowd, not be part of it. Many of these tours are nature based. Others emphasize local life and culture. Many combine both. They allow you to experience different lifestyles and to meet local people in a relaxed, unhurried atmosphere. And they are extremely varied. There are beaches in Brazil, wildlife in Kenya, drumming in Senegal, dancing in Cuba, Spanish lessons in Guatemala, trekking in Nepal, sea-kayaking in Samoa, horseriding in Arizona, yak-trekking in Mongolia, and much more. The 'Holiday-finder index' in Section Two of this guide will help you find a holiday to suit your interests.

Mud hut or luxury lodge?

The directory includes a wide range of comfort levels. Some of the safari lodges in Africa, for instance, are about as upmarket and luxurious as it gets. Other trips involve sleeping in mud huts or under the stars. Some communities have comfortable guesthouses; in others you do as the locals do – even if that means heading off into the bushes when you need the toilet. Prices vary accordingly. Individual directory entries indicate the level of comfort, price and facilities you can expect.

Efficiency

Some trips will run smoothly. Others can be less reliable. Many travellers find that a degree of unpredictability is 'all part of the fun', but you may disagree if you're on a tight schedule. Usually, the more you pay, the more efficiency and punctuality you can expect. You can reasonably assume that a tour which has a UK agent, fax, email and website is more likely to run punctually than a tour that you reach by throwing a stone across a river to attract attention. But many people want to visit remote rural and indigenous communities precisely to get away from things like efficiency and punctuality. You can't have it both ways. So take a moment to decide what sort of holiday you really want.

BETTER HOLIDAYS FOR YOU

Let's be clear. The holidays in our directory are definitely that. Holidays! Of course, if all you want is sex, sun and booze without too many annoying foreign people, then maybe Club 18-30 or Ibiza would be better choices. But if you've read this far, you probably see a holiday as an opportunity to discover new places and explore different cultures. If so, community tourism offers some special rewards.

Cultural contact

Meeting people from different cultures can be one of the pleasures of travel. Community-based tours provide more opportunities than mainstream tours to get closer to local culture and to spend time with local people in a relaxed, unhurried atmosphere. You will have more time to develop friendships and see what life is really like for your hosts. These tours are a way to get beyond the artificial 'cultural shows' that you find in tourist hotels, or the typical 20-minute coach tour stop in a local village to buy handicrafts. And you can expect a warmer welcome because local people know that they are benefiting from your visit. Even backpackers will find that a few days on a locally booked community tour can provide an extra degree of insight into local life and culture, often for little more than it costs to travel independently.

Exciting destinations

Our directory lists hundreds of tours in over 40 countries. Many take you to beautiful natural places: rainforests, deserts, tropical beaches and coral reefs, towering mountain ranges and African plains. You can visit remote tribal communities in the Amazon rainforest or experience everyday life in rural Asian villages. You can see mighty ruins of ancient civilizations and some of the most amazing wildlife on earth.

Alastair Sawday's
Special Places to Stay

Want to support rural economies in Europe when you travel? And find cultural authenticity? And eat locally produced or organic food? YOU CAN!

Alastair Sawday's *Special Places to Stay*

- The *Special Places to Stay* series, (covering Britain, France, Ireland, Italy, Spain & Portugal), is the perfect antidote to Europe's chain hotels and mass tourism.
- Organic food and producers are encouraged and in many cases visitors provide essential income to rural communities.
- Owners are encouraged to commission environmental audits of their houses and increase bicycle and rail transport usage.
- Each book is stuffed with an eclectic selection of properties.

Alastair Sawday's *Special Places Walks*

The philosophy behind *Special Places Walks* in **Andalucia, Tuscany/Umbria** and the **Pyrenees,** is to *'leave fainter footprints'*. In other words, to enjoy travel without damaging or impacting adversely upon the environment and indigenous population. And each *Special Places Walks* helps sustain local communities.

Alastair Sawday Publishing, 44 Ambra Vale East, Bristol BS8 4RE

To order a *Special Places* **Book or find out more information about the** *Special Places* **Walks, call (++44) 0117 9299921 e-mail: specialplaces@sawdays.co.uk or visit our website: www.sawdays.co.uk (Freephone USA: 1800 367 0303)**

Local knowledge

You'll have the privilege of seeing these places in the company of the people who know them best – the people who live there. For instance, tours run by indigenous communities often make a feature of their traditional knowledge of local wildlife or medicinal plant uses: knowledge built up over thousands of years of living in that particular environment.

Helping the people you visit

There is satisfaction in contributing to the efforts of local people to build a better life for themselves: a feeling of solidarity and shared ideals. It may be intangible but, as many 'community tourists' have discovered, it could be the thing that makes your trip truly memorable.

An 'indigenous message' for us

The tours in this book illustrate that (apart from Antarctica) there are few truly uninhabited regions of the planet. Most of what we think of as wilderness

– rainforests and deserts and so on – has been home to people for thousands of years. These areas are, in fact, managed environments. In many cases, the indigenous people who live in these places have simply managed their environments better than we in the West, using them productively yet preserving their natural beauty and richness. If we in the West are to relearn a less destructive way of life, then we must learn from their example. Community tours to indigenous communities can be a source of inspiration. They can show Western visitors that a 'sustainable lifestyle' and 'living with nature' are practical realities, not just utopian concepts.

An attitude to travel

This book is more than just a list of tours. It is also about an attitude to travel. Even if you prefer to travel independently, the principle of community tourism can point you towards richer and more rewarding holidays. The idea is mutual benefit – better holidays for you and better holidays for local people. By contributing more, you get more yourself.

HOW COMMUNITY TOURISM DEVELOPS: UNPLANNED AND PLANNED

Community tourism tends to develop in one of two ways, each of which raises slightly different issues.

Unplanned

In the first, unplanned, scenario, an area is 'discovered', first by adventurous backpackers and then by commercial operators who notice the emerging market. At first, local communities may be bemused by this invasion, reacting to tourism rather than planning and controlling it. They offer accommodation because tourists and tour operators ask them for this facility and because of traditional rules of hospitality: as a result, a variety of informal arrangements spring up between tourists, operators and local people. As local people start to understand what tourists want (and how much they really pay), they begin to seek more control of tourism in their territory. In this scenario, community tourism develops as a response to tourism. Often communities will develop partnerships with those operators who make the effort to consult them properly.

We might also call this scenario 'demand-led', because local tourism is driven by consumer demand. Community tourism projects that develop in this way have few marketing problems, since backpackers are turning up anyway. But a local pattern of exploitative, disruptive tourism may already be established and hard to change.

Planned

The alternative, planned, scenario typically involves an NGO (or the community itself, or occasionally a commercial operator) who identifies tourism as a potentially sustainable source of income for a community that is engaged in a more environmentally harmful activity (for instance, overfarming poor soil, logging, etc). The NGO/operator/community tries to develop a community-based tourism project before the backpackers and commercial operators move in.

These projects aim to preempt the harmful impact of unplanned tourism. But because both local community and NGOs may lack experience in tourism, they can struggle to deliver an attractive product to the tourist. Prices are often set wishfully high. Inexperienced guides don't understand what tourists want. Things don't run on time.

We might also call this scenario 'supply led'. The supply (the tour) is there before the demand (the tourists), hence the second problem for these projects – attracting tourists. Planned/supply-led projects often aim to bypass the low-paying backpacker market in favour of a more upmarket clientele, who will bring more money with less disruption. Reaching this market requires high initial investment in installing upmarket accommodation and infrastructure, plus glossy advertising and marketing deals with upmarket travel agents. All this is expensive and may lie outside the experience of the NGO.

TEN PRINCIPLES FOR COMMUNITY TOURISM

1 Community tourism should involve local people. That means they should participate in decision-making and ownership, not just be paid a fee.
2 The local community should receive a fair share of the profits from any tourism venture.
3 Tour operators should try to work with communities rather than individuals. Working with individuals can create divisions within a community. Where communities have representative organizations these should be consulted and their decisions respected.
4 Tourism should be environmentally sustainable. Local people must benefit and be consulted if conservation projects are to work. Tourism should not put extra pressure on scarce resources.
5 Tourism should support traditional cultures by showing respect for indigenous knowledge. Tourism can encourage people to value their own cultural heritage.
6 Operators should work with local people to minimize the harmful impacts of tourism.
7 Where appropriate, tour operators should keep groups small to minimize their cultural and environmental impact.
8 Tour operators or guides should brief tourists on what to expect and on appropriate behaviour before they arrive in a community. That should include how to dress, taking photos, respecting privacy.
9 Local people should be allowed to participate in tourism with dignity and self-respect. They should not be coerced into performing inappropriate ceremonies for tourists, etc.
10 People have the right to say no to tourism. Communities who reject tourism should be left alone.

BETTER HOLIDAYS FOR LOCAL PEOPLE

While community tourism has much to offer tourists, the uniting principle is the idea of local benefit. Here are some ways in which these holidays can help local people.

More of your money stays in the local economy

This is the most obvious benefit. It may mean that your guide or porter is paid more. It may mean that you (or your tour operator) pay a fee into a community fund. It may mean local people own the tour company. It may mean that tourists provide a market for other small local businesses, such as carvings, clothes, crafts, jewellery, snacks or restaurants. Such businesses may also open up new employment opportunities – especially for women, since working part-time from home or within their village often fits well with childcare and other responsibilities. Thus, community-based tourism can give women more economic and social independence.

Even so, the chances are that local people will see only a fraction of the money you spend on your holiday. They do not get any of your airfare, which is most people's single largest holiday expense (but see **North-South Travel** in the chapter on UK/General Tour Operators). If you book with a UK-based agency, much of the cost of your trip inevitably goes on marketing, administration and UK office staff. Yet even a few extra pounds paid locally could be the difference between poverty and security to someone in rural Peru or Zimbabwe.

Not harming the environment: beyond ecotourism

When used by tour operators to sell their tours, ecotourism can be a vague concept. It can simply mean looking at trees or animals. In practice, most so-called ecotours do little to protect the environment – and little or nothing to improve the well-being of local people.

In fact, such nature tours ('ecotourism-lite', as they've been dubbed) tend to simply ignore local people. Look at the brochures of many ecotour companies – or even trips run by some non-profit environmental organizations – and you'll notice a strange absence of people. Instead, ecotourism operators sell images of exotic animals and empty landscapes, or present indigenous people as if they were another exotic species of wildlife to be pointed at and photographed. Notions of sustainability and responsible tourism are understood in terms of preserving the environment or wildlife, rather than in terms of helping local people.

In reality, the two go together. Few 'wildernesses' are really as devoid of people as the brochures suggest and if ecotourism ignores the human presence it is of little use as a conservation tool. Such tourism simply puts extra pressure on fragile areas, using up scarce resources and leaving more rubbish. Community-based ecotourism, on the other hand, allows local people to benefit from conservation and can be a valuable conservation tool. Here's why.

A sustainable economic alternative for local people
In parts of Africa, local people have killed elephants for their ivory, or rhino for their horns, because they have no other income. In the Amazon or Borneo, local communities have logged (or sold logging rights) or signed deals allowing oil companies to drill for oil on their land. In Brazil, communities clear land to farm by burning forest. These people understood the harm they were doing...

> ## COMMUNITY TOURISM OR ECOTOURISM?
>
> The US-based Ecotourism Society defines ecotourism as: 'responsible travel to natural areas that conserves the environment and improves the well-being of local people'. Many of the tours in this directory fit this definition. But community tourism is a distinct (if overlapping) concept: it means 'tourism that involves and benefits local communities'. Community tourism doesn't have to be nature-based. Communities may offer cultural tours or simply run local guesthouses. In general, community tourism puts the emphasis on people, while arguing that it is only by putting people at the centre of the picture that true conservation solutions will be found.

but everyone has to eat. Community-based tourism may offer local people a more environmentally sustainable alternative.

Indigenous land rights can protect 'wilderness'
Many indigenous communities, in particular, still live in areas rich in plant species and wildlife. These wilderness regions are now threatened by a host of 'development' pressures, from oil companies, loggers, miners and ranchers to tourism or governments desperate for hard currency to fund debt repayments to Western banks. Indigenous people have a claim to ownership of their traditional lands, based upon the simple fact that they have lived there for centuries. These indigenous land rights (if accepted by governments, who usually dispute them) can block harmful development. Without the presence and resistance of indigenous people in the Ecuadorean Amazon, much more of that country's rainforest would have been destroyed.

But most indigenous communities are no longer able to live self-sufficiently. If conservationists want them to say 'no' to harmful development, they must offer them an alternative means of feeding their families. Tourism may be that alternative. In many places, tourism is a central pillar of emerging alliances between local communities and conservation organizations.

Supporting tribal / communal structures

Tourism can easily disrupt complex communal relationships, especially in tribal and indigenous cultures. While change may be inevitable, tour operators should work within existing social structures to allow communities to change on their own terms. And operators have a responsibility to ensure that any tourists they bring into communities also understand and respect these social structures.

This demands a long-term commitment from tour operators. Internal community relations may be hard for outsiders to grasp, and decision-making may be slow and complex. Many indigenous people are being forced to adapt quickly to new situations and concepts (such as a money-based economy), while the very future of their culture may depend upon the choices they make. In these circumstances, people should not be rushed into quick decisions. Traditional decision-making within indigenous cultures is often a slow process: people may have to walk for hours or even days to attend a meeting and debates may be loosely structured and last for days, involving many meetings and rituals (to consult ancestors and guiding spirits, for instance).

Community consultation can therefore be frustrating, expensive and time consuming for a tour operator. It may result in a less profitable tour. A tour operator may be impatient to get things moving and be tempted to work with a few cooperative individuals – even if they do not represent the whole community. It is a test of a tour operator's commitment to community tourism that it takes consultation seriously.

The reason that most of the communities in this guidebook have turned to tourism is that they realize they have to adapt. Across the globe, development means traditional self-sufficiency is rarely possible. Even many remote tribal communities must now become involved in the market economy.[2] Without a source of local income, community members will have to move to cities to look for work, joining the ever-increasing army of underemployed squatters in the makeshift shanty towns that surround most developing world capitals. If too many people leave, the community will disintegrate. Its former members will be cut off from their roots, culture and support networks. This has already happened in much of Europe and North America, and it may be one reason why depression, stress and mental illnesses are on the increase in the West despite our material prosperity. Community tourism may help keep communities together.

Allowing local people to participate in tourism with dignity and pride

This means not being pressured into performing inappropriate rituals for tourists. It means being able to put local viewpoints to tourists. It ensures that local people are not seen as tourist exhibits or photo opportunities. It means children seeing their parents involved in decision-making and working as teachers and guides rather than as porters or beggars. Self-respect, although intangible, can make a real difference to the quality of people's lives.

Many indigenous communities have been subjected to years of propaganda from governments, educators and missionaries, telling them that their traditional culture (animism, hunting, etc) is primitive, inferior and even evil. Meeting tourists who are interested in, and respectful of, their culture can be a surprise to many indigenous people. It can encourage them to reevaluate their own attitude towards their traditions. The 1997 ToDo! Awards report for the Shawenequanape Kipichewin – an Anishinabe camp and cultural centre in

Canada – notes that: 'Thanks to the visitors' high regard for traditional First Nations culture, young Anishinabe have become conscious of their own values, which is the greatest achievement of the project.'

Defending community land rights

There are countless cases of people being forced off their land so that governments, rich businesspeople and Western corporations can move in and exploit its natural and mineral wealth. Sometimes people are forced out to make way for tourism itself, as we saw in the previous chapter.

Publicizing a community's presence

Community tourism can assert a community's land rights simply by making its presence more widely known. Tourists who have visited a community are more likely to take a continued interest in what happens to its people, and advertising a community's presence in tour brochures makes it harder for governments to pretend a community does not exist.

Giving communities an economic value

Governments look at wild areas and, instead of seeing natural beauty and richness, they see economic vacuums. Even when people are living sustainably in these areas, governments see no money changing hands, no profit, no export earnings. A tourism project at least registers on the economic statistics. It attracts tourists, who bring in foreign exchange and go on to visit other parts of the country. For the same reason, governments are also more likely to tolerate indigenous culture if it attracts tourists.

DIFFICULTIES AND DANGERS

A job in tourism may sound glamorous – a chance to travel. But for people in poor developing world communities, it's not like that. For a start, tourism to them doesn't mean the chance to travel. Many of these communities see tourism not as a glamorous adventure, but as the least harmful option open to them. Even the best community-tourism project will cause some disruption and bring change. But we have to ask: 'would the alternative have been better'?

Practical difficulties

Rural and indigenous communities face practical problems in running their own tourism projects. To overcome these, they often work with a commercial tour operator or an NGO. These are some of the practical problems.

- They lack capital: to invest in infrastructure, advertising, training, etc. Therefore their 'product' may not match that of commercial rivals. Their guesthouse may not be as comfortable, their boats not as fast.
- They may not be used to Western business practices: the need to keep accounts, to reinvest profits, to advertise, to work to precise timetables.
- They may not understand tourists: after all, what is the point of tourism? Why do we want to visit their village? What do we want to do, now that we're here? Many local people may not realize that our societies are very different from theirs, and are amazed that we are willing to pay to watch them catch a fish or carry out some other everyday task.
- They lack access to tourist markets: based in remote parts of the developing world, how do these communities reach tourists in Europe or North America? (This book is intended to help them do just that.)

Potential dangers

All change is unpredictable. There are many pitfalls for communities who get into tourism. Even a successful project can create new problems. Tourism inevitably involves exposure to Western people and Western ideals and this will inevitably change traditional and indigenous cultures. Even development agencies may impose Western values – insisting, perhaps, that women participate in activities from which they were traditionally excluded. Should we force cultures to change practices we dislike?

Even as well-intentioned tourists, we may still bring our Western values and hang-ups: the value we place on money and material gain; our cynicism; our secular scepticism; our belief in individual freedom over communal obligations; our liberal attitudes towards sex and drugs, and so on. And tourists, with their gadgets and self-confidence, can be unwitting propagandists for a Western lifestyle. People who can afford exotic foreign holidays are, in a way, the 'successes' of Western society. The people we visit don't see the 'failures' – the alcoholics, the addicts, the homeless, the people in prisons and psychiatric institutions.

Tourism can also remove self-sufficiency. People may neglect other tasks, such as tending the fields or going to school, to focus their energy on their successful tourism scheme. But tourism depends on Western consumer trends. If tourists stop coming – maybe because of a changing exchange rate or a terrorist threat – the community may have nothing to fall back on.

There is also the danger that tourism will turn once practical cultures into fossilized tourist attractions. Rituals and survival skills may lose their meaning if they become simply tourist shows. When ritual becomes divorced from functionality, a practical way of life is on the way to becoming a dead 'museum culture'.

DEGREES OF COMMUNITY PARTICIPATION

Responsible tours

These are tours run by commercial tour operators who behave responsibly towards local communities. A share of the profits may be given to local community projects. Local people are trained as guides and properly paid. While better than most commercial trips, they are still controlled by outsiders. Responsible tours are often ecotours, with more emphasis on wildlife and nature than on culture.

Partnership tours

Here, tours run in partnership between the local community and an 'external partner' – maybe a responsible commercial operator or an NGO. This covers a variety of arrangements in which the local community has some say in – but not total control over – planning and managing tours. The external partner cushions the impact of tourism on the community and provides business or marketing skills that the community lacks. But, like responsible tours, they depend on the good faith of the external partner. These tours are likely to offer tourists more cultural insight than normal holidays.

Community tours

These are tours set up, owned and run entirely by the local community. This is the 'purest' type of community tourism, but not all communities are able to run their own tours. They may have problems with marketing or understanding what Western tourists want. Even a sudden influx of cash can create problems in a community unused to the cash-economy. Some community-owned ventures employ an outside manager to overcome these problems.

Lastly, tourism can destabilize a community. It may give individuals an influence that clashes with traditional structures. It may create jealousies and resentment. After all, money can be destabilizing even for us – and we're used to dealing with it.

Is it genuine... and who decides?

Does a new village school or health centre make up for the loss of traditional knowledge of culture? What if increased income leads to more materialistic, less communal values? Weighing up the benefits and costs of a community tourism project is a subjective and contentious business.

Who makes these decisions? Ideally, it should be the community itself. But communities are often internally divided. In such circumstances, *what* we hear about a project may depend on *who* we talk to. In many cases, our information comes from commercial tour operators who work with local communities. While most of these operators are undoubtedly sincere, a few may be using the pretence of community involvement to sell purely commercial tours. In Kenya and South Africa, white ranch-owners have converted their farms into game reserves which they claim to be 'community projects' simply because they employ local people. Some of these reserves may genuinely involve the local community and bring real benefits to local people, but others are simply perpetuating the old colonial order of a white land-owning elite and low-paid black workers.

How do we decide what is genuine and what is a sham? All we can do is gather as much information as possible about each project, from as many people as possible, and make a judgement. The line between genuine community tourism and tokenism can be a fine one, and we may have made mistakes in compiling our directory. That is one reason why we don't officially 'recommend' any tours. We welcome your comments, good or bad, on any tour we list.

* * *

Community tourism won't save the world. But it might help some local communities improve the quality of their lives. It might help protect fragile natural regions until we develop a saner approach to the environment. And it might help to demonstrate a consumer demand for fairer, more sustainable holidays – a demand that could eventually change the mainstream tourism industry too.

NOTES

1   See the glossary at the end of this book.
2   In the few cases where tribal communities are still able to live self-sufficiently, they usually show little interest in tourism and we recommend that you don't visit them.

BEING THERE

So much for Theory. But what are community-based holidays like in practice? These articles might give you a better idea of what it's like to be a tourist on a community-based tour. All of these trips are featured in the Holiday Directory.

ECUADOR: AT HOME IN THE AMAZON

This article of mine appeared in *The Times* in March 1997. It describes a visit to a **Siecoya** community on the Aguarico River in the Ecuadorian Amazon. This exact tour no longer runs, but the same community still take visitors. (See **Pirana Tours**, Ecuador.)

What is Ramiro thinking about, I wonder, as we crash clumsily along the rainforest path behind him. For us, our walk reveals a thousand new sensations: giant tree trunks, insects camouflaged as leaves, the sounds of birds and frogs and crickets, splashes of colour among endless shades of green – scarlet flowers, strange yellow fruits, white fungus on rotting logs, electric blue butterflies.

But Ramiro has walked this way a thousand times before. This is where he grew up. So maybe he is thinking about his wife and three young children. Or of rebuilding his house, which burned down last week while he was out hunting. Or is he thinking of the oil company Occidental, who want to build an oil well where we now stand? Ramiro says he will die fighting rather than let the oil workers move in.

Ramiro, a stocky 28-year-old dressed in T-shirt and football shorts, is a Siecoya Indian. This beautiful stretch of primary rainforest along the Aguarico ('rich water') river in the Oriente, Ecuador's part of the Amazon, is Siecoya land. The Siecoya have fished, hunted and farmed here for centuries. Today, like the neighbouring Cofan and Siona, the once-feared Huaorani and the Achuar, they number less than 1000. (Two other indigenous groups, the Shuar and Quichua, are slightly more numerous.)

Ramiro still hunts and fishes, but nowadays he is also a tourist guide. He has little choice. Since the 1970s, oil companies, loggers and settlers have seized huge tracts of forest. The hunting is poorer and the Siecoya's freedom to move through the forest is gone. Increasingly, they have to find alternatives. Most, such as working for the oil companies or logging, involve destroying the forest. Only tourism seems to offer a sustainable future.

Although Ecuador has many jungle tours, few involve or benefit the indigenous Indians, the rightful owners of the forest. It's our loss, too, since the Indians – who know the rainforest better than anyone – have much to teach us. But this trip is different. It is run by the Siecoya themselves.

The itinerary is much the same as for other 'jungle tours'. We see macaws and toucans and monkeys swinging through the canopy. We travel in dugout canoes at night to spot caimans. We fish for piranha. We learn about the different ecosystems in the forest (of which 'jungle' is only one – the dense growth along riverbanks or in clearings left by fallen trees). It is not so much the details as the overall feel that is different. The feeling of being not in a wilderness, but guests in someone's home, with children and pets running around your feet, women cooking, neighbours visiting.

We learn how the Siecoya use the forest. For instance, they have controlled their own population with a plant that is a contraceptive in small doses and makes women sterile in larger amounts. They can stitch wounds with a particular type of ant. Holding it so that it pinches the wound shut, they break off the body, leaving the head and pinchers fixed in place.

But this is no fantasy trip to a make-believe paradise. We also learn about the politics of the forest and the pressures on the Siecoya to abandon their traditional life. In fact, the ultimate aim of these tours is to help the Siecoya maintain their way of life and remain in the forest – not only by generating income, but also by encouraging the children to value their culture, by seeing outsiders eager to learn about it too. Alongside the economic pressures, for example, well-funded missionary groups such as the Summer Institute of Linguistics have undermined respect for traditional ways by teaching that shamanism and hunting are primitive and evil.

It's not just the Siecoya's future at stake. It's vital for the forest itself that it continues to be inhabited by people who value it and know how to manage it sustainably. The Indians' presence is a major factor keeping the oilmen out of Ecuador's remaining primary forest. But the situation is precarious. Occidental recently persuaded the Siecoya's president to sign a contract to build their oil well, with a road connecting it to the town of Coca, in return for five outboard motors and a well. Luckily, he was able to retract his signature in front of lawyers, but no one thinks Occidental will give up. Yet Ecuador's oil reserves will barely see out the century.

It was time for us to go. Ramiro and his wife Betty waved to us from the little beach in front of their home. As we set off in the motorized canoe, they were soon swallowed up by the endless wall of living green forest, mirrored in the brown waters of the Aguarico.

Despite their problems, I left with a sense of hope. I'd learned that the Amazon is neither uninhabited nor a wilderness. People have lived here for millennia (evidence of settlement dates back to at least 5000BC) and humans are as much part of the rainforest as are birds and insects. The forest

has its dangers, of course, but the 'savage jungle' of Western imagination is more a reflection of our own mistrust of nature – an attitude that has led us into environmental crisis. Seeing the forest as the Siecoya do, as a home, a provider of food, shelter, materials and medicines, reminds us that there is another way. Man can live harmoniously with nature, without having to destroy it. And that, ultimately, is worth more than any holiday photos or exotic souvenirs.

(Sadly, the community leaders *did* subsequently sign an agreement – in controversial circumstances – with the oil company allowing exploratory oil drilling on their land, which they are now trying to retract.)

FIJI: FIJI GIRL SMART IN SEX

This is another article of mine, which was published in *The Times* in December 1996. It describes a trip to **Navala** village in the hills of Vitu Levu, where the village takes in visitors for overnight stays.

There are three Fijis. The palm-fringed tourist beaches are one. Navala, where I was headed, belongs to the second: a traditional Fijian village tucked away in the hills of Viti Levu, Fiji's main island.

To reach Navala, you must go through a third Fiji – bustling coastal towns full of the Indian migrants who now comprise half the population. The town where I changed buses, Ba, could be in India, with the scent of aromatic spices drifting from the shops, Indian sweet stalls beside the road, women in sarees, curry houses and signs in Hindi and Urdu.

Leaving Ba, the old British Leyland bus roared off in a cloud of dust and exhaust fumes. It struggled up steep inclines, tilting at alarming angles. The sugar plantations of the hot coastal plains gave way to rugged hills, with cliffs of black volcanic rock jutting out of dry yellow grass. And then, in a valley over a last hill, was Navala.

The village, on a grassy sloping riverbank, is one of the few in Fiji still built entirely of *bures* (pronounced boo-rays). About 60 of these thatched huts stood in neat rows, surrounded by flowers, coconut palms and vegetable patches. Children ran between them. Some youths played touch rugby. Men carrying machetes returned from the sugar fields, and fires burned in the surrounding hills – part of a wild boar hunt. It looked beautiful, a self-contained world.

Guests traditionally stay with the chief. I was shown inside his *bure*: one room, the floor covered in palm mats, empty except for a bed and a wardrobe. On the wall were family photographs and pictures of the Fijian prime minister and the Pope.

The chief was rotund and greying, in jeans and sweatshirt. He invited me to drink some 'grog'. Grog, or *yaquana* – made from the ground root of the kava plant (*Piper Methysticum*) – is the traditional Fijian brew, drunk mainly by men. It is slightly narcotic and numbing. I'd heard that too much causes one to lose all muscular control, so I was disappointed to find we were still coordinated when diner arrived – a tasty stew of wild pig, fresh from the hunt. I slept on a mattress on the floor, as did the chief's son, John, his wife and their child. I guess I wasn't important enough for the bed, which remained empty.

Next morning, everyone went to church "cos we catholics, see' (most Fijians are protestant). Having heard that visitors are often asked to deliver a sermon, I explored the village instead, accompanied by the inevitable entourage of skipping and giggling children. A woman invited me into a *bure* full of about 20 girls – 'the village netball team'. They were large girls – they could have been the wrestling team – with equally big laughs. They all had wild, electric-shock, Don King hairstyles, as if they'd been plugged into the village generator. The conversation soon reached a familiar stage.

'You married?'

'No.'

'Oh.' A pause. 'Single?'

'I have a girlfriend.'

In developing world villages, people go by the principle that any single Western gentleman, presumably in possession of a good fortune, must be in want of a wife. For solo travellers, a girlfriend or boyfriend is a necessary fiction. Mine wasn't working.

'Your girlfriend in Fiji?'

'No, she's in England.'

'You take girlfriend in Fiji?'

'But I'm only here for one night.'

'You take Fiji girlfriend for one night. You take (pointing to a quiet girl in the corner) Alessi.'

I must have appeared hesitant, for she persisted.

'Fiji girls smart in sex, you know.'

I think she was joking. (Fiji is not, I should point out, a sex-tourism destination.) Still, I wasn't entirely sure, so I declined politely and escaped to the river to teach the children to skim stones.

For once, Fiji is a place where the colonial legacy seems positive. Christianity ended years of rampant cannibalism. The British never invaded but were asked to take over the islands in the mid 19th century by the fearsome Chief Cakabu (said to have personally killed and eaten 80 men) to stop bloody intertribal warfare. They initially turned down the offer.

The first governor, Sir Arthur Gordon, decreed that no land could be sold to a non-Fijian and no native labour could be used on the new sugar plantations. He also left the traditional village chief system in place. As a result, Fijian culture is the best preserved in the South Pacific.

The other side of Britain's laudable decision not to exploit native labour was the importation of Indian workers. Someone had to keep the sugar mills supplied and Sir Arthur wasn't about to do the job himself. Denied access to land, the Indians in Fiji developed an industrious business ethic and now run the economy.

Two more contrasting cultures are hard to imagine. The Indians are hard-working, eager to make money and keen for progress. The Fijians are relaxed and conservative. The Indians can only rent land from Fijians, which they resent: they complain that they work hard while the Fijians do nothing but drink grog and live off the profits.

The British also installed an abiding affection for two of their favourite upper-class institutions, the royal family and rugby, both almost obsessions in Fiji. The most common questions I was asked (after 'Where you from?' and 'You married?') were: 'You play rugby?' and 'How is Princess Di?'

In the morning I left. I caught a bus down the pot-holed road to the Indian supermarkets and saree shops of Ba, and then back to my tourist paradise. In two days I'd learned just a little about Fiji, but it was more than I would have in a month on the beach.

AUSTRALIA: SYDNEY'S FORGOTTEN ABORIGINAL HERITAGE

This unpublished article of mine describes a day trip in Sydney with an Aboriginal guide, Rodney Mason, who operates **Dharawal Tour**.

'My ancestors', says Rodney Mason, 'were standing right here watching old Captain Cook when he arrived. They were here to meet that old bugger Captain Phillip too, when he landed – shook 'im by the leg, an' all. The "first contact" – that was us, mate. And we're still here today.'

We are standing on the shore of Botany Bay, now a suburb of southern Sydney, looking across to the flagpole on the far shore that marks the spot where Cook made that historic landing. The houses behind us, says Rodney, are the homes of his people, the Dharawal. The same Dharawal who watched Captain Cook sail his strange ship into this very bay, over two centuries ago.

'This was all Dharawal country', Rodney continues, 'from Sydney Harbour right down the south coast. Now most of us live here. Too bloody expensive up in near the city. People think you only find Aboriginal people out in the desert, painted in ochre or whatever. But you don't have to go to no bloody desert to find Aboriginals. We're right here in Sydney, mate.'

Rodney is a tall, tough-looking, tattooed Aboriginal man, with a beard last seen on tour with ZZ Top and oil on his jeans from fixing his van.

'Getting a flash new one next month', he tells me, 'Did my heavy vehicle licence the other day.'

Rodney runs Dharawal Aboriginal Tours. His aim is to introduce tourists to Sydney's forgotten Aboriginal history. When the first Europeans arrived there were people living in every part of Australia, not just in the remote deserts. However, persecution that at times amounted to ethnic cleansing, European diseases and the sheer volume of white immigrants quickly overwhelmed the Aboriginals in places such as Sydney. Today it is easy to overlook their presence. To do so would be like visiting London and ignoring everything that happened before Queen Victoria.

In fact, Sydney was home to a number of Aboriginal tribes, divided into three language groups – the Ku-ring-gai on the northern shores, the Dharug on the western plains towards the Blue Mountains and the Dharawal on the southern coast. Each of these subdivided into smaller clans, bound together by a complex system of relationships and obligations.

Today, most Aboriginals in Sydney do not belong to any of these groups. They migrated into the city from other parts of Australia, having been driven off their traditional lands by settlers or forcibly separated from their families. For years in the middle part of this century, government policy was to remove Aboriginal children from their parents and place them with white foster parents. The Dharawal of Botany Bay, on the other hand, have probably been here for thousands of years and, even as the suburban sprawl of southern Sydney enveloped them, they have managed to keep alive their connection with their traditional land.

Rodney runs trips from Bondi Beach, deep in the heart of tourist Sydney, to Botany Bay and into the Royal National Park, an area of bushland immediately south of Sydney. It's a unique opportunity to learn about Aboriginal culture, on the doorstep of the nation's biggest city.

We start off by looking at some Aboriginal rock art on the cliffs overlooking Bondi Beach. (There is Aboriginal rock art to be found throughout Sydney.) Whales and fish are etched into the rock on the cliffs overlooking Bondi Beach. These figures represent both signposts – 'supermarket signs' as Rodney calls them – indicating the types of fish or animals to be hunted in the area, and also include totem animals. Each Aboriginal clan would have had a totemic animal, connected to an ancestoral creation story. (A clan had certain responsibilities for protecting its totem animal, ensuring that they were not overhunted.) The Dharawal, according to Rodney, are 'whale people', because whales migrating along the coast would have their babies in the waters just off Bondi, within their territory.

Next stop is Botany Bay to see where Cook and Phillip landed, as well as a French expedition which spent six weeks camped in the Bay. Rodney says that many Dharawal families still have artefacts that were given to their ancestors by the original settlers – watches, spoons, plates, jewellery, coins or swords. Ironically, perhaps (since the settlers no doubt thought they were giving away worthless trinkets), these have now become valuable antiques, and Rodney says he sold a couple of old muskets to buy his van. They have been handed down through the years and kept in mint condition, and there are plans to establish a Dharawal museum at Botany Bay to display them and to tell the history of the community. Rodney relates some of these stories, handed down through the generations, of settlers and sailors from the first fleet who jumped ship and married into the Aboriginal community.

Then we drive down towards the Royal National Park. The road south follows the ridge of a hill. The route, Rodney says, is an older Aboriginal track. This would have once been a well-worn path through the bush, used by people moving up and down the coast. Such tracks are known as 'dreaming tracks' or 'songlines' and are part of a vast network of tracks that criss-cross the whole of Australia. Dreamtime stories describe the landmarks along these paths, acting as oral guidebooks that allow a traveller to find his or her way around the country. Rodney claims his great-grandfather walked to Sydney from Arnhemland (which is like walking from London to Cairo) to marry into the Dharawal clan.

Our final destination, the Royal National Park, is the second oldest national park in the world and protects an area of rivers, waterfalls, coastal cliffs and red-gum bushland. This coastal woodland is a reminder of the landscape of Sydney as it was before the arrival of Europeans. Here, away from the skyscrapers and traffic, we can see the natural environment in which traditional Aboriginal culture developed. It's very beautiful, with cool swimming holes and waterfalls hidden in the forest.

Rodney shows us 'bush tucker'. In fact, the word indicates more than just food. 'Aboriginals divide plants into four classes', he explains. 'You've got food, fibre, medicine and weapon plants. In the old days, your survival depended upon that knowledge.' Next, he takes us to a high outcrop of flat rocks. This, Rodney says, was a sacred site.

'People get the wrong ideas about sacred sites, see. Really, they're just places were Aboriginals can come and perform their ceremonies. Look at this place: you can see for miles all around. Once you understand the land, it's obvious why someone would pick it.' He was right. It was exactly the sort of spot that called out to you to have a rest and take in the view.

Sitting here, I can imagine how Dharawal life must once have been: living off the land and hunting, gathering, fishing. Retelling mythical stories around the campfire – stories that contained vital information about where to find food and shelter. Walking along 'dreaming' trails that led to water holes and rivers, pathways worn through the dense bush by thousands of years of repeated use. A life deeply tuned into nature and the land.

But it's time to head back to Bondi and off into the urban jungle. And I find myself thinking that, while Sydney is undoubtedly a beautiful city, the land on which it stands must have been much more beautiful when it was still all Dharawal territory.

NAMIBIA: FRUIT FROM THE DESERT

This is an article by Chris McIntyre, from the February/March 1998 issue of *Wanderlust*, about **Damaraland Camp** in Namibia. (Damaraland is marketed in the UK by **Sunvil**. For information about *Wanderlust*, call 01753-620 426 or email: paul@wanderlust.co.uk.)

'I applied for a job as a guide, but I was good at entertaining guests – and so trained for the bar. But I still want to be a guide, so I've built a small water bowl near my tent. I watch the birds, and learn to identify them from a book.'

Franz Coetzee's bird-bowl seemed a long way from the Savoy, where a waiter filled our glasses as we listened for the British Guild of Travel Writer's Silver Otter award to be announced. I wondered if all this pomp would make any difference to Damaraland Camp, or Franz's rural community there that ekes out its living on the fringes of the Namib desert.

The trip to London had certainly affected Franz, who had seldom stopped smiling. Until now, his longest journey had been as a child, when his parent's community had been displaced from South Africa and trekked into Namibia. They settled in the arid, semi-desert region of Damaraland. 'It was good that we came to Damaraland', he said. Despite entering an area already occupied with Damara people, 'We mixed with those people, and we accepted each other,' he assured me. Franz and his family stayed on, when most returned to South Africa, two years ago. 'We won our land back, but my parents wanted to stay in Namibia. I don't know anything more. So I stayed also.' After finishing school, he searched for a job. 'I went to town, with no luck. To Walvis Bay, as my sister was there. There is a really big problem with unemployment. I decided to go back to Damaraland to concentrate on farming.'

Like most of his community, Franz lived by tending cattle, sheep and goats. Damaraland may be spectacularly beautiful, but its land is poor for farming. Rocky hills and minimal rainfall mean a difficult life. There is game around, and sometimes he would hunt springbok, or even zebra, kudu or oryx. Occasionally he would glimpse the area's desert-adapted black rhinos – but elephants were a different story. 'They visited the water points during the night and our vegetable gardens on the farm. I remember once, a month before the harvest, a lot of elephants came, damaging the farm. The dogs barked, and we became nervous. We just stood. You can do nothing to an elephant. You can't even chase him away. You just clap your hands, but stay out of the way.' Though rare, these desert elephants meant nothing to Franz when compared to his vegetables.

Then things started to change. A government survey visited farms, explaining how they could benefit directly from the wildlife and tourism. Eventually the 70 households in Franz's community established themselves as custodians of the land, forming the Ward 11 Residents Association – with its own constitution and membership. They then sought investors, and after two years of tortuous negotiations, involving the whole community, they settled on an agreement with Wilderness Safaris – one of Southern Africa's best safari operators. Wilderness would build Damaraland Camp, and train local people as staff to run it. The community gets the jobs, and 10 per cent of the profits. After ten years, ownership of the camp will revert to the community.

Franz is enthusiastic about the benefits, and to date the community has N$57,000 in the bank.

'We will try to renovate our local clinic, and have donated N$2,000 to the school for a photocopier. At first it was just a loan, but later we said, "Just donate it." It's for our children.' But he recognizes that the next challenge is to decide how to use the increasing revenues. 'Farms which have had windmills damaged (by elephants seeking water) will be the first to get help. And there are other problems – predators like jackal catch goats and sheep.'

Gradually, attitudes towards wildlife have changed. Now Franz tells stories about elephants over breakfast, before guests go out on safari. The community knows how to deal with them, and nobody kills wild animals to eat – they're worth more alive as attractions for visitors.

Almost two years since it started, Damaraland Camp is now one of the most popular camps in Namibia. Except for two managers from Wilderness, all the staff are from the community – and next year two will start training to replace the existing managers. Franz explained that his work of 'entertaining guests' meant 'telling them about yourself – visitors usually want to know about our traditions.' With a ready smile and a disarming line in chat, it's clear why he was perfect for this.

Later that evening, the winner was announced: the city of Dubrovnik, for its restoration work. Damaraland Camp was highly commended, followed by Madikwe Game Reserve, in South Africa, which has a similar approach to conservation. Franz's smile never wavered – clearly the award would make no difference to that. But why was this project so special? Surely all camps should be run like this?!

PHILIPPINES: KINGS OF THE SWINGERS

This article by Belinda Rhodes, about an indigenous **Aeta** community's own 'jungle survival tour' appeared in *Traveller* magazine in 1997. (*Traveller* is a magazine for members of Wexas Travel Club, 020-7581 4130.)

As we glide over Subic Bay towards its languid little airport, a vast, tropical forest slides into view, its foliage creeping snug to the edge of a placid turquoise sea. From above, I can only guess at what the forest holds, but its apparent impenetrability hints at wild animals and vicious reptiles.

Just a few hours later I am strolling towards an opening in the dense forest wall. 'Do you have bug juice?' asks Pepito Tabradillo, my jungle guide. I envision blood-thirsty mosquitoes lurking behind every gentle palm frond and every innocent leaf, and obediently smear myself with repellent. When I offer some to the diminutive Pepito he simply chuckles, 'Oh, they've bitten us too much already!'

Entering the deep, dark underworld of the rainforest unarmed and without a map is clearly not going to be the leap into the unknown for Pepito and his partner Gary Duero that it is for me. Their scanty preparations consist of putting a handful of rice into the leg-pockets of their camouflage trousers and sliding sharp hunting knives under their belts.

Tribesmen of the Philippines' Aeta cultural minority, Pepito and Gary walk nonchalantly in the direction of the jungle, weaving rope from stringy tree bark as they go. To them, this rich forest on the west coast of the island of Luzon represents a bountiful wellspring of food, water, shelter and equipment. It contains every item they could possibly need, and they are about to share these secrets with me.

Subic Forest, 10,000 hectares of lush, lofty jungle, lies inside the old perimeter fence of the former US naval base at Subic Bay, 160 kilometres north-west of the Philippines capital Manila. Because the land was off-limits to Filipino hunters and loggers for the five decades the Americans held the base, the forest has remained virtually untouched. Meanwhile, roughly three-quarters of the rainforest, which used to cover the rest of the Philippines, has been lost to the ravages of the tropical hardwood industry. There is virtually no virgin forest left in the country and environmental groups are struggling to preserve what little remains.

One reason the US navy kept Subic Forest intact was in order to use it for jungle survival training. Infantry preparing to serve in the Vietnam War came here to learn potentially lifesaving lessons from the Aeta tribesmen. They could have had no better teachers: the Aeta have lived in the region's forests for centuries and consider it their ancestral domain. Many a pilot returned to Subic from the Vietnam War to thank the Aetas for teaching him how to find fresh water, catch birds, treat snakebites and recognize the 'compass tree' whose leaves always show which way is south.

But now that the former naval base has been turned over to the Philippines for civilian use, the fun-loving Aetas show tourists the ropes – including the type that Tarzan swung from. Jungle tours, which can be custom designed to be as easy or difficult as visitors require, are proving immensely popular amongst a local population previously unaccustomed to taking an interest in their natural environment.

'Subic Forest provides people from urban areas their first chance to see a real rainforest,' says attorney Mary Mai Flor, legal officer at the Subic Bay Ecology Centre. 'Nowhere else in the Manila area is there anything like this. When visitors go inside, they're pretty impressed. Not many Filipinos knew that the Aetas trained the marines, so now tourists are flocking to see those demonstrations,' she adds.

Swinging their hunting knives about their heads, Gary and Pepito beat a path through thick vegetation, constantly glancing back to check that I am following. When they see me stooping and wriggling through the small tunnel they have cut between the lianas and spiky shrubs, they let out hoots of laughter. 'The trail is only Aeta-size!'

Small, athletic and as fleet-of-foot as Zola Budd, these spirited people find constant amusement in the fact that their Caucasian visitors are twice their size and certainly more than twice as clumsy. 'White men walk like buffalo, breaking everything and scaring the animals!' they laugh. They scamper lightly through the forest on bare feet, now and then shinning up a tree trunk to survey the forest canopy.

Pepito gives the first lesson in jungle lore: how to make an 'emergency hat'. He skilfully folds two large bangaba leaves, pins them with a twig and puts the creation over my head. 'Princess hat!' he chuckles, watching every-thing but my chin disappear. It will protect me from insects and camouflage my white skin which might otherwise alarm the wildlife. Next we must find fresh water inside the hollow chambers of a bamboo trunk. By carefully slicing just beneath one of the solid bands around the trunk, and a few inches above, he carves out a cylindrical cup full of clean, cool water.

Lessons follow in how to make traps for different kinds of animals – a sprung noose for a feral chicken, a pit trap for a boar – and tips on how to detect where the animals live. 'Even if you know how to make a trap, you'll have no food if you don't know the tactics of the animals,' says Pepito.

As we walk, the Aeta teach me to identify trees, vines and ferns – some for fun and some for their nutritional or medicinal value, from soup and edible berries to poultices and headache cures. The bark of one of the tall elegant dipterocarps which dominate the forest can be scraped off to make what Gary calls an 'Aeta band-aid'. Held over a wound for half an hour, it will stop the bleeding. The trunk of the *Ficus nota*, locally known as the tibig tree, holds gallons of fresh water. The bark of a tough shrub can be used to make improvised shoes.

The value of this forest, one of the few remaining large stands of triple-canopy rainforest in the Philippines, was acknowledged long before the Americans handed it over in 1992. Filipino botanists and zoologists could hardly wait to delve into its leafy depths and see whether it still held natural secrets long since destroyed in other parts of the Philippines.

The Subic Ecology Centre is now working on an inventory of the flora and fauna in the forest. Preliminary results have revealed 292 plant species, some of which are endangered and some of which are only found in one or two other places in the country. It is thought there are some species in the forest which have never before been identified in the Philippines. 'This highlights the importance and urgency of preserving the forest,' says attorney Flor.

Amongst the birds, mammals and reptiles often seen in Subic's jungle are wild pigs, civet cats, parrots, owls, eagles, vipers and pythons. The Aeta have reported seeing a red-and-black striped snake, whose identity has not yet been established. Monkeys (Philippine macaques), which used to loiter at the roadside ready to ambush American picnickers, have been encouraged to return to their natural lifestyle and now forage and breed in the dense forest canopy.

The wildlife did, however, suffer badly during the massive eruption of Mount Pinatubo in 1991. Ashfall from the volcano, 30 kilometres north-east of Subic, was dumped on the forest destroying the canopy and making the ground soil sandy and dry. Although rainforest vegetation is fast growing, it will take some time for the forest to make a full recovery.

Just after noon Pepito and Gary lead me to a clearing by a waterfall where we stop for lunch. While huge ochre-coloured butterflies bat around our heads, I am treated to a masterful demonstration of the versatility of bamboo and the dexterity of the Aeta with hunting knives. In what seems like seconds they carve cooking pots, plates, knives and forks from bamboo trunks, make a water carrier and a shelter from bamboo poles and create fire with bamboo tinder.

Gary comes leaping up from the river bank with pieces of greenery and a handful of what look like small brown stones, and a few minutes later we are served fern and snail soup in bamboo cups. Over lunch Pepito recalls his terrors during the eruption of Mount Pinatubo. The volcano is the Aetas' god and the resting place of their ancestors' spirits, so the tribespeople were deeply shocked when it apparently turned its wrath on them. Pepito was at work on the naval base when the sky went black and the earth began to tremble with the earthquakes which accompanied the eruption. He walked 20 kilometres through the ashy darkness to be with his family during the catastrophe.

When the dust settled, the Aeta found that some of their number had been lost in the explosion. Because there was no mention in the Aetas' oral history of Pinatubo being a volcano, thousands of them were living on its upper slopes where they practised slash-and-burn farming. Many hundreds were forced to flee to evacuation camps in the lowlands and have not yet been able to return. It is feared that these Aeta will eventually forget their traditions, tribal rituals and knowledge of the rainforest.

This makes it all the more vital to practise and preserve the ways of the forest, say Gary and Pepito. Although even they watch the odd TV show, drink the occasional Coca-Cola and don't actually live in the forest most of the time, they are proud in the knowledge that they have the survival techniques born in the jungle. 'Believe it or not, my family once stayed in there for three whole years. The American marines used to get mad in the jungle sometimes; they wanted to go downtown. But this is our home, and we want to take care of it.'

MOROCCO: WINDS OF CHANGE

The following is an extract from an article by Paul Morrison in the August/September 1999 issue of *Wanderlust* magazine. It describes a trip to the **Rif Mountains** of Morocco. This project is marketed in the UK by Tribes Travel. (For information about *Wanderlust*, call 01753-620 426 or email: paul@wanderlust.co.uk.)

Abdu's brother and his wife had been unlucky in a way that was hard to imagine. 'Their first five children died,' he told me with a shrug. 'They just got sick.'

Their latest baby had made it, so far at least, though problems in labour had meant his four brothers had had to carry his sister-in-law on a blanket for three hours to reach the road that led into town for medical help. I had started by asking Abdu why he had left his village in the northern Rif Mountains, and ended by wondering why anyone would stay. But he was the only one in his village to go to school, and it was this education that was his passport to life in the city and a job in tourism.

'I am intelligent!' he declared with a grin, and he was. He was also smart enough to know how lucky he was. Here in the High Atlas Mountains, to the south of his new home in Marrakesh he could appreciate what a difference a lucky break can make.

I was travelling in a party of three, along with Abdu, as guide and interpreter, and Rhazi, the visionary director of a unique Moroccan tour company – Tizi-Randonnées. What makes Tizi-Randonnées so different is its concern to regenerate remote communities such as the one where Abdu grew up. They still offer their clients the kind of outdoor and cultural experiences that Morocco has in abundance, but behind the scenes the philosophy is refreshingly different.

'I wanted to ensure that the funds that visitors spent went to the local community,' Rhazi explained as we stood on the roof terrace of the guesthouse overlooking the village of Aroumd. The clouds had parted to reveal the mountains, dusted in snow, towering over a fertile valley where women stood in the river beating colourful clothes against the dark volcanic boulders. And at first glance this apparently timeless scene could be another rural community caught in the past. It's the satellite dishes that give it away.

Aroumd was like many remote villages in the Atlas. Trekkers sometimes pass through on their circuits, or parties of seasoned skiers visit as they head to the slopes of Toubkal further up the valley. But this was not enough to keep the youngsters from leaving for the city – like Abdu. What turned it around in Aroumd was a project initiated by Tizi, but with local people in control, that sought to breathe life back into the village. With a promise of materials secured from a development association in Rabat, it was up to the villagers to raise the balance of funds. All 200 households gave what they could. In 1997 electricity was brought to every home, and seven freshwater fountains were installed, fed by a small reservoir above the village.

'Before we had big problems for water,' Mohammed explained. 'When it snowed we would heat snow, but when there was no snow the women would go with a donkey to collect water from the river down in the valley, or from a spring much higher up the hillside.'

Mohammed was born in the village, where he lives with his wife and five children, and makes a living as a guide. A true Atlas man, he speaks only Berber, a tongue of which Arabic Moroccans like Abdu have little knowledge. Rhazi (who spoke French, but no English) bridged the gap, and between the four of us we were able to have a slow but revealing conversation.

'People are now very happy and feel healthier as the water is purified – we already have fewer problems of sickness for children.' I thought of Abdu's brother's family and looked again at Mohammed, who grinned at us from beneath his black woollen hat with Chicago emblazoned on the front. This symbol of the outside world somehow complemented his brown striped *djellaba* (the traditional robe) and, like the satellite dishes on the mud-walled homes, hinted at the changes in the village.

'My wife likes action films,' declared Mohammed.

But TV was not killing the art of conversation in Aroumd for the simple reason that there were no programmes in Berber, so no one could understand what was being said. Instead, it offered a glimpse, however unreal, of an outside world. 'I recently spoke with an 80-year-old man in the village,' said Rhazi, 'who had never been beyond the mountains. "Before I was blind, but now I've seen things!" he told me.' Mohammed told us he believed his children would now stay in the village, whereas in the next valley most of the village teenagers leave for the city.

Tourism, even on a small scale, is playing a part in keeping Aroumd alive. They have rebuilt the school, reworked irrigation channels, and even bought their own bull (the previous two, being shared with other villages, died from overwork). And a similar project is underway in the north, in Abdu's village.

But Rhazi realizes that he couldn't sell tours to foreign visitors just on the strength of the projects. People come to Morocco for a good time, and in the High Atlas this means walking through magnificent scenery. So after lunch we took off along a pilgrims' trail to a holy shrine in the mountains. The path twisted upwards towards the distant peak of Toubkal, and the sun burned our faces through the cloud cover. On the way we passed straggles of bizarrely clad skiers picking their way between the rocks with their poles as they returned from the high-country lodge. In their bright skiwear and clompy boots they looked like spacemen who'd missed their landing site. Their sport is not the only hazard in the mountains – in the summer of 1995 a flash flood swept hundreds to their deaths in this valley, but the atmosphere was peaceful on that warm March afternoon. The scenery was stark and magnificent, with a feel of the Himalayan foothills. As we strolled back into the village at the end of the day it was hard to comprehend how close we were to Europe.

Facilities for travellers are still fairly simple, and not for someone who insists on a hot shower in an ensuite bathroom. But the scenery and insight to local life more than compensated. Our *gîte* was comfortable enough, and the local food was excellent. Lunch and dinner centred upon the *tagine* – a stew of vegetables, herbs, spices and meat cooked in the traditional clay vessel of the same name. And despite warnings in the guidebooks to the contrary, my vegetarian equivalent was easily obtained and equally delicious. All meals were followed by 'Moroccan whiskey' – a teeth-tormenting sweet tea made from a stew of Chinese tea leaves and fresh mint, supplemented by a fistful of sugar. It's a taste I found myself getting to like after a few days, though noticing the brown stains on the teeth of many Moroccans, I was pleased that the habit was short lived.

Like all the mountain settlements I saw, Aroumd was made from the earth and stone around it, giving the impression of having been hewn out of the rock. From the air these settlements must be virtually invisible, blending into the landscape in perfect camouflage. Where the rock was red with iron, so were the houses, but Aroumd was made of a dull grey-brown volcanic stone, which would have made the village seem sombre were it not for its spectacular setting. One morning I woke early and walked along its narrow paths across to the eastern side, where the morning sun was driving the chill from the air and wafts of rising smoke caught the dawn light. Here I witnessed the decoration of the village in a flash of colours guaranteed to wake up the senses.

Although most villagers in the High Atlas are devout Muslims, theirs is not a faith that requires dressing down and covering up. Berber culture predates the Arab invasion 13 centuries ago and is strongest in the mountains of Morocco. Here, the women wear bright dresses and scarves, with their faces usually uncovered, revealing a rosy flush to the cheeks that seems to typify mountain people the world over. This sense of colour clearly extends to the home – as I walked out that morning onto the sunkissed side of the village I was greeted by the scene of women spreading out rugs and bedcovers on their rooftops and hanging them from windows. The patchworks of reds and greens and pinks and blues gave the village a festive air. A flock of red-beaked choughs was performing aerial displays above the rooftops, the birds cawing to each other as they circled upwards on the morning thermals.

On our final evening in Aroumd, Abdu announced that we would have visitors after dinner. The tables were dragged to the walls and the chairs rearranged in the centre. Moments later, figures appeared in the doorway and soon the small room was alive with chatter as half a dozen local men assembled around the fire to warm the skins of their tambourine-shaped drums and argue about nothing in particular. The atmosphere of the room was transformed into a lively bar, but there was no alcohol fuelling the spirits, just sweet tea. Mohammed served the guests, as four young girls filed in and took their seats against the wall. The teenagers sported brightly coloured cardigans and chattered away quietly, turning to smile at us at intervals with their eyes down. The guys puffed their chests out and assembled on the other side of the room.

One fellow, Barim, was the joker in the pack, sending his companions into convulsions of laughter with a single phrase; yet as it turned out he was also the nearest the musical group had to a leader. Holding his drum in front of his mouth, he started to sing an improvised rant that led to a chanting refrain by the men, followed by a response from the girls – a sort of vocal tennis match, as each side threw choruses back and forth. The girls' high voices and harmonies made them sound almost oriental. The men played their drums in a variety of rhythms with their fingers and palms. Mohammed sat behind and joined in by banging a saucepan with a pair of spoons.

The sound soon attracted more faces at the doorway and Barim decided that it was time to take to the floor. He enticed a reluctant girl to join him, and before I had a chance to resist I was there as well, partnered by young Mina from the house next door, who was trying to contain her laughter as she tutored me in the steps. It looked easy, just a shuffle back and forth, but then she shook her shoulders in a manner and speed that I could only comically imitate. At ten o'clock the music ended, the girls disappeared without a word, and the room returned to normality.

As we drove out of the mountains the next morning I reflected on life in Aroumd and was satisfied that our incursion into this remote community had brought benefits that travel does not always bestow. It wasn't just the project that was making a difference, but also the policy of Rhazi's company, which meant, for instance, that everyone involved gets a fair wage. Tourism can be a fiercely competitive game and it is often those on the ground who feel the squeeze. But Tizi pays everyone, from porters to guides, at the top end of the local going rate for the job.

TANZANIA: DOROBO SAFARIS

Dorobo Safaris is a safari company in Tanzania that works closely with local communities. Although not describing an actual tour, this extract from one of their newsletters, written by David Peterson (a Dorobo director), captures the way that interaction with local people can add an extra dimension to our experience of a place.

One day near the beginning we were hunkered around one of those everlasting acacia fires in the crisp dawn of South Maasailand. The 'old man', pushing 80 and with eyesight shuttered by cataracts, turned to Thad and Daudi and said, 'We're low on water, you guys better go down and fetch some from that pool in the riverbed.' That sounds pretty straightforward but you've got to imagine the racket that was emanating from that pool. For the last several hours, camp music had been lions' throaty growls punctuated by buffalo bellows and the volume was high.

'But there's lions down there,' we said.

'So what, we need water, just walk down there assertively and fetch some.'

So we did walk down there assertively until at 30 metres we were faced by eight very feisty, vocal and aggressive lions, whose tails were ramrod stiff and thrashing the bushes, a clear prelude to a charge. 'When the tail stops, the charge starts.' At that point our assertive walk while still facing the lions somehow changed direction and we ended up back in camp.

Without water!

'Where's the water?'

'Those lions are right next to the water, are very aggressive and won't give way.'

'No excuse. You guys backing off like that are teaching those lions bad manners. You can't let them get away with it. Now you walk in there assertively and get that water!'

Three times we walked assertively and three times we found ourselves back in camp with no water. The old man was totally disgusted and disappointed. Now, it's true we needed water. We didn't even have enough for a second round of morning *chai*. And we did trust and respect the old man and felt pretty badly about letting him down. But facing that moving wall of growling lion just felt too much like forever foregoing another cup of tea anywhere.

The decision to move camp and look for alternative water was painful but at this point obligatory. As we were packing up, we saw another Dorobo man approaching camp, still out of the old man's vision. We quickly went out to meet him to get a second unbiased opinion. 'What do you do if lion are very aggressive and keep you from getting water?' we asked. Without hesitation the Dorobo answered. 'You walk in there assertively until they back off.' 'Show us,' we said, and he replied, 'Let's go.'

Despite the second corroborating opinion, our assertive walk was accompanied by some inner trepidation. We walked right into the waterhole without raising a single growl. We kept walking to where the lions had been thrashing with their tails. No lions. They had just left, which explained why the growling stopped just after we left camp. There in the middle of a patch of trampled grass and broken bush lay the horns, skull and vertebrae of an old buffalo bill. He had been a worthy adversary for several hours of bellowing resistance until he continued his journey through the food chain.

Although we will always wonder what would have happened if the lions had not finished feeding and left before we finally walked in there, the old man taught us a lot and we have on several subsequent occasions walked assertively in our encounter with lions. Mike and Daudi on two separate Mzombe River walks ran into what was almost certainly the same very tenacious lioness who had cubs. While her cubs and cohorts slipped away, she faced our large group of clients and porters with continuous growling and repeated half-way charges. Every slow hominid step backwards only brought her several quick steps forward. Five minutes of this scenario brings one close to adrenaline depletion and in the end it was the old man's assertive walk which, at closer than 20 metres, finally led her to slink off with a throaty backward glare to join her cubs and companions.

This story is a roundabout way of introducing the 'old man' who played a primary role in the naming and defining of Dorobo. The old man's name was Mzee Mori. An Iraqw tribesman by birth, he was a Dorobo by inclination and lifestyle. By the time we met him in the mid 1970s, he was kind of 'king of the Dorobo' within a large area of south Maasailand in that he'd taught most of the younger Dorobo the art of gathering wild honey and was respected by being tithed a portion of honey each season. He died in 1984, well into his 80s, in his sleep and most likely after partaking of a healthy gourd of well-brewed honey beer.

The old man left us with an intimate relationship to a particular piece of God's real estate. He showed us all the elephant highways, the important larger waterholes, the springs and river courses, baobabs that held water cisterns, baobabs that consistently attracted wild bees to their natural cavities, hollowed baobabs and rock overhangs one could escape to for shelter. Based on Aldo Leopold's definition that 'the best ownership of land is knowledge of land', we 'owned' some 20,000 square kilometres of South Maasailand. When we imagine heaven for the old man, baobabs, waterholes and elephant are very prominent.

Just as importantly, or more so, the old man with his unique perspective of looking and feeling left us with a spiritual, aesthetic and playful relationship with country and its critters. Whenever we'd come to a waterhole, the old man would scoop up a handful of water, look, taste and smell the water and give his assessment. 'This water's too dirty for elephant; it's only fit for buffalo.' Then we'd proceed to circuit the waterhole and analyse track and spoor, which invariably confirmed his earlier assessment.

One time, we filled a jerry can with water from a particular raunchy seepage and brought it back to camp where the old man was tending the fire. We brewed tea and laced the cups with more than normal amounts of milk and sugar to mask the water flavour. The old man took a sip and broke out with a huge grin. 'Buffalo piss, much better tasting and much healthier than cow piss.'

There were 500 to 800 elephants drinking at one of the big waterholes and the bush and woodland all around were totally thrashed. As we approached the waterhole we saw lovely unscathed *Acacia tortilis* trees ringing the edge. 'Don't tell me elephant don't have a sense of aesthetics. Look how they've left those acacia untouched.'

One night sleeping around the fire, we woke to a persistent birdcall. We asked why that bird was calling in the middle of the night. 'God put that bird there to fill the heads of people alone in the bush so they wouldn't go crazy with their own thoughts.'

Dorobo is a collective name for hunter-gatherer peoples found in remnant groups scattered throughout both Kenya and Tanzania Maasailand. It is likely that before the advent of Bantu and Cushitic agriculturists and Nilo-Hamitic pastoralists, the land was sparsely peopled by hunter-gatherers. These early folk were either assimilated by or pushed out by agriculturists but were able to coexist as hunter-gatherers within the production mode of extensive pastoralism as practised by the Maasai.

All Dorobo, regardless of ethnic background, have been culturally influenced in varying degrees by the stronger, dominant Maasai culture. So, for example, the Dorobo the old man hung out with have lost all vestiges of their own language and speak only Maa. They live as poor Maasai within Maasai kraals except when they are off on their honey gathering forays. Most have no wives as poor Maasai men marry available Dorobo women. The future of these Dorobo as a group is pretty clear. Further south, where Maasai expansion occurred later, there are groups of Akie Dorobo who still speak their own language, but only in private amongst themselves; otherwise they speak Maa. These Dorobo live in their own kraals and practice a mix of hunting and gathering, livestock and agricultural economic options.

Although Dorobo are within the greater Maasai cultural and economic sphere, they and their lifestyles are openly and disparagingly considered inferior by Maasai. Yet the Maasai depend upon Dorobo to perform cultural rites of circumcision, for provision of honey to brew beer for ceremonial occasions and as a fallback in times of drought, disease and famine. Many Maasai survived the great rinderpest cattle plague in the early 1890s by running to, and living with and as, Dorobo hunter-gatherers.

Our relationship with the old man and his Dorobo associates was an important reason why we chose the name Dorobo for our safari business. The fact that Dorobo is not one ethnic group but rather many unified by a common lifestyle – a lifestyle characterized by fitting in with and working as part of natural systems – was also a compelling reason. Lastly, we hope in some small way that our name and philosophy of doing business has or will help some Dorobo folk to stand with dignity as Dorobo.

EGYPT: WIND, SAND & STARS

This article by Mike Gerrard appeared in *The Independent on Sunday* in June 1997. It describes a tour to the Sinai desert in Egypt with UK operator **Wind, Sand & Stars**.

'You mean we're not staying in a five-star hotel?' Louise asked. Louise, aged 66, had never slept in the open before and wasn't expecting to do so on the first night of our trip to the Sinai desert. 'Much better,' said our Egyptian guide, Aswani. 'Tonight you have a five-million-star hotel.'

We set up camp in a sheltered desert valley inland from the airport at Sharm el Sheik. The night before it was Gatwick and now we are sleeping under the stars. While we clean our faces and wonder about the toilet arrangements, the Egyptian drivers are building a bonfire and making the first of a thousand cups of tea. The smell of roasting chicken soon follows, and we gather around the flames for a briefing from the British tour leader, Tamsin Clegg. This needs to be done before the stars emerge, as three people in the group are deaf and it's hard to read sign language in the dark.

Rachel Mapson, of the Royal National Institute for Deaf People, is the group's interpreter and will soon be signing Tamsin's instructions, her face as expressive as her gestures as she copes with the signs for snakes and scorpions, the problems of dehydration, camels and suntan cream, and explaining the toilet arrangements. A desert journey is down to earth in more ways than one. Ladies to the left, gents to the right, find yourself a handy rock, bury the waste and discreetly dispose of the paper in the rubbish bags provided. Later I ask Rachel what's the most difficult thing she's ever had to interpret. 'A pantomime,' she says. 'Can you imagine having to sign "zip-a-dee-doo-dah"?'

The group is more concerned about what might pop up in the desert at night, but Tamsin soon puts our minds at rest. 'There are a few creepy-crawlies around,' she says and Rachel signs, 'but they won't harm you. There's the odd snake or scorpion but it's unlikely you'll see one, though it's best not to unroll your sleeping bag before you want to go to bed, just in case something takes a fancy to crawling into it.'

There is a particular reason why this mixed group of deaf and hearing people has come to the Sinai, besides its stunning scenery and the chance to camel trek for a few days accompanied by the local Bedouin from the Mezaina tribe. This tribe suffers from congential deafness, worsened by its tradition of intermarrying. 'It is on the increase too,' Aswani tells me. 'Deafness has always been common in the Bedouin because they intermarry. But lately it has been getting worse so that now it is common to have two deaf children in a family of seven or eight children. But here it is not seen as a disability. They are just different.'

Deafness is so common that almost everyone knows some sign language for talking to friends and relatives. Although sign languages vary from country to country, there's enough in common to make communication between deaf visitors and the Bedouin much easier than between people who share no language at all.

'Deaf people are used to thinking visually and in symbols,' Rachel tells me, 'so that also makes communication easier. Most cultures do have many symbols in common. For example, to gesture behind you is to indicate the past, and in front of you indicates the future, except for some North American Indian signing systems where the past is in front of you, because you can see it, and the future behind you.' What was in front of us was four days of trekking through the lands of the Mezaina tribe, once we had been given the permission of Sheikh Hamid to do so.

'Sheikh Hamid is the ruler of one family within the tribe,' explains Tamsin, 'and he's a very good man. The sheikh is responsible for the whole group and must look after their welfare, which he does, making sure that, for example, the camel trekking is divided up fairly between all the men in the tribe in turn. It's the men who look after the camels, the women and girls have always traditionally looked after the sheep and goats. The women are a very important part of the Bedu life. Men and women have different responsibilities but each is vital and therefore respect is mutual. The women are lively and funny, and I've had some entertaining evenings with them when it's been women only. The women have great parties together.'

We collect our camels from Sheikh Hamid and set off into the desert, all 12 of us, with the elderly Sabali and half a dozen young Bedu men to guide, cook and help us get on and off the camels. Being tall I'm given a large camel, a handsome white one called Abden, who is good-tempered by camel standards and doesn't even react when, one day, another camel bites him on the bum. It could have been nasty if Abden had decided to race off into the desert.

We plod through the sand past sculpted sandstone rocks. It's the ultimate Lawrence of Arabia fantasy and we see no one but each other and a few Bedouin encampments for the next four days. The sun blazes down with a blowtorch heat. The apparently limited palate of the desert has infinite variety.

Only someone who has never been there could call the desert landscape boring. We head for what seems to be a solid rockface, only to find that a narrow crack leads into a secret zigzag red-rock canyon, through which the camels tread single file, ripping at the occasional acacia tree with their rasping tongues.

When the sun is at its highest we seek shade beneath overhanging rocks, or beside some trees, and picnic on chickpeas, humous, feta cheese, olives, halva and, always, freshly baked bread.

The Bedu boys produce flour and water, a plastic bowl to mix them in, a flat stone and an old jar to roll out the dough, and the top of an oil drum to heat in the flames and cook the bread on. If time allows, and there's enough wood, they build up a fiercer heat and bake a thick bread under the fire in the charcoal ashes. After lunch, while the camels graze, we sit around and talk, sleep or sign. The biggest of the boys is Mohamed. 'Were you born deaf?' Rachel asks him, using the graphic sign for someone being born, a gesture that Mohamed understands. 'Yes,' he nods. He is 17, will get married in three years and has three sisters and five brothers, one of whom is also deaf.

'I feel I've got to know Mohamed quite well,' says Christine, one of the deaf travellers. When sorting out the camels, Mohamed immediately took two of the deaf visitors and put them on his two camels, so he could walk beside them.

'Its easy to sign on a camel when Mohamed's walking alongside,' Christine explains, 'and he's told me a lot about his family and his life. He was very interested in my hearing aid. He said to me that sometimes he shouts to me and I turn round, and sometimes I don't. I told him that I don't always have my hearing aid switched on. He tried it but it was just a jumble of noise to him. He doesn't need one here, because everybody signs.'

Everybody signs to such an extent that, one day, Mohamed was signing with two of his friends and when he walked away to do something, the friends carried on signing instead of reverting to speech.

It was speech, though, that conveyed to me the immensity of this experience for everyone. It was one of the most enjoyable weeks of my life. And as we scrambled up a mountain side, to look at a cave high up in the rock face, seeing more and more of the vast desert panorama as we climbed, Louise paused to get her breath and turned to Tamsin who was helping her struggle up. 'I think I must be dreaming,' she said. 'I just can't believe I'm here. I'm so happy.'

SECTION TWO

HOLIDAY DIRECTORY

RESPONSIBLE TOUR OPERATORS

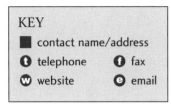

KEY
■ contact name/address
📞 telephone   📠 fax
🌐 website   ✉ email

This is a directory of responsible tourism companies in the UK, Europe, the US, Canada and Australia. Contact details for these operators are updated regularly on Tourism Concern's website at www.tourismconcern.org.uk.

UK-BASED COMPANIES

International dialling code +44.
Tribes Travel and **Discovery Initiatives** offer global tour programmes that feature a high degree of community involvement. Most of the other operators specialize in one particular country or region.

Bear Print International
Bear Print produce *AIM4Awareness*, the magazine of the American Indian Movement, and published *The Trail of Many Spirits* by Serle Chapman, a highly praised book about the history and contemporary culture of Native America. They also run tours to Native American lands and communities. (See Locally based tours by country: US.)

■ PO Box 244, Cambridge CB5 8YL

📞 01924-840 111

✉ bearprint@bun.com

Caledonia Languages Abroad
Language courses in Spain, Italy, Peru, Ecuador, Costa Rica, Japan, China, Russia, etc. They also run two-week holidays to Cuba, which combine classes in Spanish language and Cuban dance (son, rumba and salsa) in Santiago de Cuba in the south of Cuba. (see Locally based tours by country: Cuba.)

■ The Clockhouse, Bonnington Mill, 72 Newhaven Road, Edinburgh EH6 5QG

📞 + 📠 0131-621 7721/2 📠 0131-621 7723

🌐 www.caledonialanguages.co.uk ✉ info@caledonialanguages.co.uk

Language holidays worldwide

Spanish in Spain, Cuba, Costa Rica, Peru, Ecuador and Mexico. **French, German, Italian, Greek** and **Portuguese** in Europe. **Russian, Japanese** and **Chinese**. Spanish and latin dance in Cuba and Malaga. Italian, French and German plus skiing. French and watersports. All levels, all ages, all year round. Accommodation and cultural activities included.

Caledonia Languages Abroad

The Clockhouse, Bonnington Mill, 72 Newhaven Road, Edinburgh EH6 5QG
Tel: 0131 621 7721/2. Fax: 0131 621 7723
info@caledonialanguages.co.uk
www.caledonialanguages.co.uk

Discovery Initiatives

Small-group trips with a conservation and/or community element. Discovery Initiatives work in partnership with local conservation organizations in the South and offer both conventional holidays and short-term volunteer holidays on conservation projects. Destinations include Bolivia, Peru, Ecuador, Dominica, Tanzania (and Zanzibar), Zambia, South Africa, Botswana, Kenya, India, Pakistan and Mongolia. Holidays include wildlife lodges and safaris in Africa, rainforest tours in the Amazon and Borneo, trekking in the Karakoram mountains of Pakistan, tropical beaches and Swahili culture in Zanzibar, horse-trekking in Rajasthan and Mongolia. See their website or get their brochure for full details. Also customized itineraries. ATOL bonded.

■ Julian Matthews: 21 The Bakehouse, 119 Altenburg Gardens, London SW11 1JQ

☎ 0202-7978 6341 ✆ 0202-7738 1893

🌐 www.discoveryinitiatives.com ✉ enquiry@discoveryinitiatives.com

Earthwatch Institute (Europe)

Paying volunteer holidays with conservation projects. Their focus is mainly conservation, archaeology and wildlife, but a few projects involve local communities.

■ 57 Woodstock Road, Oxford OX2 6HJ

☎ 01865-311 600 ✆ 01865-311 383

🌐 www.earthwatch.org ✉ info@uk.earthwatch.org

Full Moon Night Trekking

Trekking holidays to Baltistan in northern Pakistan, with stunning scenery and fantastic trekking opportunities among the mighty Karakoram and Himalayan mountains. (see Locally based tours by country: Pakistan.)

■ 9a Avonmore Mansions, Avonmore Road, London W14 8RN

☎ 020-7603 9893

🌐 www.fmntrekking.com ✉ info@fmntrekking.com

Insight India
Arrange tours to the scenic Kulu Valley near Manali in Himachal Pradesh, and Haryana in the Himalayan foothills. Tours include visits to villages and development projects.

■ Kishore Shah/Vasanti Gupta: 33 Headley Way, Headington, Oxford OX3 0LR

☎ 01865-764 639

📧 kishorevasanti@msn.com

IntoAfrica
'Fair-traded' adventure treks, wildlife safaris and mountain climbing in Kenya and northern Tanzania. The company is African with a UK partner. The emphasis is on providing insights into local life, environment and cultures as well as seeing the wildlife and famous national parks. (See Locally based tours by country: Kenya and Tanzania.)

■ Chris Morris: 59 Langdon Street, Sheffield S11 8BH

☎ 0114-255 5610

🌐 www.intoafrica.co.uk 📧 enquiry@intoafrica.co.uk

■ IntoAfrica Eco-Travel: PO Box 50484, Nairobi, Kenya

Karamba Ltd
Music and dance holidays to Cuba and Senegal. (See Locally based tours by country: Cuba and Senegal.)

■ Gary Newland: Ollands Lodge, Heydon, Norwich, Norfolk NR11 6RB

☎ + 📠 01603-872 402

🌐 www.karamba.co.uk 📧 karamba@gn.apc.org

Muir's Tours

A non-profit tour operator offering trekking and mountain-based adventure travel (eg mountain-biking, white-water rafting, skiing, climbing) to Nepal and the US South-West. They also arrange trips to Bhutan, Ladakh, Pakistan, Mongolia, India, Yunnan, Tibet, etc, including cultural tours. Set up by a charity called the Nepal Kingdom Foundation. Profits go to charities and local development projects.

■ Maurice Adshead: 97a Swansea Road, Reading RG1 8HA

t 0118-950 2281 f 0118-950 2301

w www.nkf-mt.org.uk e info@nkf-mt.org.uk

The Nepal Trust

A Scottish charity that works with local communities in Nepal to develop health, education and other community projects. It runs treks which combine hiking with work on these community projects. (See Locally based tours by country: Nepal.)

■ PO Box 5864, Forres, Moray IV36 3WB, Scotland

t + f 01309-691 994

w www.thenepaltrust.demon.co.uk e admin@thenepaltrust.demon.co.uk

North South Travel

A non-profit, flight-only travel agency that offers competitive discount flights with profits going towards community projects in developing nations. Projects they've supported include Children of the Andes, Tools for Self-Reliance in Mozambique, Oxfam and the Zimbabwe Workcamps Association.

■ Brenda Skinner: Moulsham Mill, Parkway, Chelmsford, Essex CM2 7PX

t + f 01245-608 291

e brenda@nstravel.demon.co.uk

Rainbow Tours

Tours and self-drive itineraries to South Africa, plus Zimbabwe, Mozambique, Lesotho. Tours include a 16-day general introduction to South Africa, plus shorter trips. Also customized trips, including South Africa's superb wildlife parks, undeveloped Indian Ocean beaches and visits to local communities and development projects. Rainbow works closely with a number of community-based lodges, hotels and local businesses. ATOL bonded. Brochure available.

■ Roger Diski: Canon Collins House, 64 Essex Rd, London N1 8LR

t 020-7226 1004 f 020-7226 2621

e rainbow@gn.apc.org

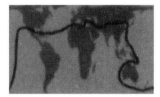

Simply Tanzania Tour Company

Tailor-made 4WD tours run by an ex-VSO field director for Tanzania, combining wildlife safaris with off-the-beaten-track destinations and visits to communities and development projects. From £1400 for a two-week tour. Shorter trips available.

■ Tony Janes: 54 Cotesbach Road, Clapton, London E5 9QJ

✆ + 🖷 020-8986 0615

🆆 www.simplytanzania.freeserve.co.uk

🅴 tjanes@simplytanzania.freeserve.co.uk

Specialist Trekking

Trekking holidays in Nepal. (See Locally based tours by country: Nepal.) Also trips to Bhutan and Tibet. Passenger Protection bonding. Brochure available.

■ Chapel House, Low Cotehill, Carlisle, Cumbria CA4 0EL

✆ 01228-562 358 🖷 01228-562 368

🆆 www.specialisttrekking.com

🅴 trekstc@aol.com

Sunvil Discovery

A UK travel company which works with local communities on some tours and is one of the more responsible and community-aware mainstream operators – in particular on their southern Africa programme. This features a number of projects listed in the 'Locally based tours by country' section, including Damaraland Camp, Lianshulu Lodge and Tsumkwe Lodge in Namibia, Jack's and San Camps in Botswana, and Kawaza Village in Zambia. ATOL bonded. Brochure available.

■ Sunvil Discovery, Sunvil House, Upper Square, Old Isleworth, Middlesex TW7 7BJ

✆ 020-8232 9777 🖷 020-8568 8330

🆆 www.sunvil.co.uk 🅴 africa@sunvil.co.uk

Symbiosis Expedition Planning

A tour operator specializing in small-group tours and customized itineraries to South-East Asia, including community-based projects in Thailand, Indonesia, Malaysia and the Philippines.

■ 205 St John's Hill, London SW11 1TH

☏ 020-7924 5906 ✆ 020-7924 5907

ⓦ www.symbiosis-travel.co.uk ⓔ info@symbiosis-travel.co.uk

Travel Friends International

Travel Friends don't actually organize trips, but they act as an information source for the following projects (all listed in the 'Locally based tours by country' section): Woodlands Network, Sri Lanka; the Green Hotel, India; Mitra Bali Foundation, Indonesia; plus Kololi Inn and Paradise Inn in The Gambia and similar organizations in Bulgaria, Poland, Greece and Slovakia.

■ Ted Finch: St Clare, The Street, Pakenham, Bury St Edmunds, Suffolk IP31 2JU

☏ + ✆ 01359-232 385

Tribes Travel

An excellent global programme of small-group tours featuring community tourism projects. Destinations include Belize, Botswana, Canada, Ecuador, Egypt, Peru, Nepal, US, Guatemala, India, Indonesia, Kenya, Tanzania, Morocco

and Jordan. Types of holiday include trekking, rainforest trips, wildlife viewing, cultural tours, camel trekking or horseriding, etc. Customized itineraries possible. Bond Plus protection. Brochure available.

■ Amanda Marks: 7 The Business Centre, Earl Soham, Woodbridge, Suffolk IP13 7SA

☎ 01728-685 971 ✆ 01728-685 973

ⓦ www.tribes.co.uk ⓔ ctg@tribes.co.uk

Wind, Sand & Stars

Trips to the Sinai with local Bedouin communities. Trips include camel treks and desert hiking in the Sinai's mountainous interior. Also customized itineraries, plus trips for schools, a student summer expedition and special interest tours (eg biblical, wildlife, etc). Helps fund local educational and health projects. British Airways Tourism for Tomorrow Awards, highly commended 1996.

■ Emma Loveridge/Janina Macdonald: 2 Arkwright Road, London NW3 6AD

☎ 020-7433 3684 ✆ 020-7431 3247

ⓦ www.windsandstars.co.uk

ⓔ office@windsandstars.co.uk

Zanzibar Travel

A UK-based 'responsible' tour operator that uses locally owned hotels and operators, and includes village tours, meals with families, etc.

■ Michael Sweeney: Reynards House, Selkirk Gardens, Cheltenham, Gloucestershire GL52 5LY

☎ + ✆ 01242-222 027

ⓔ sweeney@cotswoldgroup.demon.co.uk

US-BASED TOUR OPERATORS

International dialling code +1.

Conservation International

An NGO that is helping to develop community-based ecotourism projects in various developing countries, including Bolivia, Brazil, Guatemala, Suriname, Guyana, Botswana, Ghana, Madagascar, Indonesia, Papua New Guinea, Philippines and Solomon Islands. Although not a travel agency as such, their website gives details of the tours. Some of these are listed in the individual country listings.

■ 2501 M St NW, Suite 200, Washington, DC 20037

☎ 202-973 2219 ✆ 202-887 0193

ⓦ www.ecotour.org ⓔ j.sweeting@conservation.org

Cross-Cultural Solutions

Three-week (and longer) volunteer placements with local NGOs in India, Ghana and Peru. Typical costs: $1850 for three-week Ghana placement. Volunteer roles include English teaching, healthcare, arts, computing, etc. Also tours of India focusing on women's issues.

■ 47 Potter Avenue, New Rochelle, NY 10801

☎ 914-632 0022 (1800-380 4777) 📠 914-632 8494

🌐 www.crossculturalsolutions.org ✉ info@crossculturalsolutions.org

Dreamweaver Travel

Small 'responsible' tourism company run by an ex-Peace Corp volunteer, which specializes in adventure travel to Cameroon, Niger and Togo in West Africa. Activities range from camel treks in Niger to whale watching in Togo. The company pays a visitor fee to local communities and includes homestays, participation in daily village activities, etc.

■ Dudley Parkinson: 1185 River Drive, River Falls, WI 54022

☎ 715-425 1037 📠 715-426 0829

🌐 www.dreamweavertravel.net

🌐 www.greentravel.com/xnet/search.tcl ✉ dparkins@pressenter.com

Global Exchange

Non-profit making organization that runs 'reality tours', which they describe as 'people to people' tourism. Trips feature meetings with local activists and community leaders. Destinations include Cuba, Guatemala, Haiti, Dominican Republic, India, Indonesia, Mexico, Ireland, Israel, Senegal, South Africa and Vietnam.

■ 2017 Mission Street 303, Suite 303, San Francisco, CA 94110

☎ 415-255 7296 📠 415-255 7498

🌐 www.globalexchange.org/tours ✉ info@globalexchange.org

IVEX (International Volunteer Expeditions)

Short-term volunteer holidays on sustainable development projects (environment, agriculture, construction), including Native American communities, Dominica, East Africa, Mexico, Philippines, Indonesia, etc.

■ Volunteer Co-ordinator: IVEX, 2001 Vallejo Way, Sacramento, CA 95818

🌐 www.espwa.org/ivex.html ✉ oakland2@ix.netcom.com

Rethinking Tourism Project

An indigenous peoples' tourism campaign that also runs 'reality tours' to Mexico and Alaska (see Locally based tours by country: Mexico (CICE) and US (Yukon River Tours)).

■ Deborah McLaren (Director): PO Box 581938, Minneapolis, MN 55458-1938

☎ + ❶ 651-644 9984

🌐 www2.planeta.com/mader/ecotravel/resources/rtp/rtp.html ✉ RTProject@aol.com

Tread Lightly

Small-group ecotours run in partnership with local conservation organizations using local guides and staff. Destinations include Belize, Borneo, Brazil, Chile, Ecuador, The Falklands, Guatemala, Honduras, Panama, Venezuela, etc.

■ Jim and Audrey Patterson: 37 Juniper Meadow Road, Washington Depot, CT 06794

☎ 800-643 0060; 207-853 2632 ❶ 860-868 1718; 207-853 2367

🌐 www.treadlightly.com ✉ info@treadlightly.com

Wilderness Travel

Wilderness Travel is a well-established ecotour operator that offers trekking, wildlife safaris, cultural tours, sea kayaking, sailing, etc, including some community-based projects in Africa, Alaska, Antarctica, Arctic, Asia, Europe, Latin America, Middle East and the Pacific.

■ 1102 Ninth St, Berkeley, CA 94710-1211

☎ 510-558 2488 (1800-368 2794) ❶ 510-558 2489

🌐 www.wildernesstravel.com ✉ info@wildernesstravel.com

Wildland Adventures

Ecotours to Latin America and Africa, including some community tours.

■ Kurt Kutay, director: 3516 NE 155 Street, Seattle, WA 98155

☎ 206-365 0686 ❶ 206-363 6615

🌐 www.wildland.com ✉ kurt@wildland.com

EUROPE-BASED TOUR OPERATORS

Associazione RAM

Italian NGO working for fair trade and responsible tourism. They also run trips in Nepal, India, Thailand, Bangladesh and Italy.

■ Renzo Garrone: Via Mortola 15, I-16030 San Rocco di Camogli (GE), Italy

☎ + ❶ (+39)185-773 061

✉ ramcatrg@rapallo.newnetworks.it

Multatuli Travel

Dutch company running tours to Indonesia (with Bina Swadaya), Philippines, Tanzania, Nepal and South Africa.

■ Freek ten Broeke: Max Euweplein 24, 1017MB, Amsterdam, The Netherlands

☎ (+31)20-627 7707 ☏ (+31)20-627 4886

ⓦ www.multatuli.com ⓔ travel@multatuli.nl

AUSTRALIAN-BASED TOUR OPERATORS

International dialling code +61.

Community Aid Abroad Tours

The tour agency of Community Aid Abroad (Oxfam in Australia). Their tours aim to provide grassroots contact with local people and include visits to development projects, meetings with progressive and indigenous organizations and stays with local communities, as well as conventional tourist sights and activities. Destinations include Aboriginal communities in South and Central Australia, Brazil, Guatemala, India, Laos, Madagascar, Mongolia, Solomon Islands, Tibet, Vietnam, Zambia and Malawi. Brochure available. Prices from $1000 to $3000, with trips of one to three weeks. IATA accredited.

■ Brian Witty: PO Box 34, Rundle Mall, South Australia 5000

☎ 08-8232 2727 (1800-814 848) ☏ 08-8232 2808

ⓦ www.caa.org.au/travel ⓔ info@tours.caa.org.au

Ecotour Travel

'Green' travel agents who also book some Aboriginal tours and overseas community projects.

■ Janet Southern: 447 Kent Street, Sydney, NSW 2000

☎ 02-9261 8984 ☏ 02-9261 8425

ⓔ southern@acon.com.au

LOCALLY BASED TOURS BY COUNTRY

This directory lists locally based tours, lodges, guesthouses, etc by country of destination. Contact details for these projects are updated regularly on Tourism Concern's website at www.tourismconcern.org.uk.

KEY

ACCOM	accommodation only (camping, guesthouse, lodge, etc)
ACCOM+	accommodation plus activities (cultural displays, etc)
AGRI	'Agritourism' – ie learning about local farming methods and lifestyles
BUDGET	no-frills, backpacker-style facilities
CENTRE	visitor centre or museum
DAY	day tours or shorter
RAINFOREST	rainforest lodges, tours
LUXURY	upmarket, luxurious
ORG	NGO (non-governmental organization), marketing organization, trade association, etc: sources of more information about local community tourism
SAFARI	wildlife tours, lodges
SAFARI+	wildlife tours, lodges, which also feature cultural tours
SCHOOL	language or other school
TOUR	multi-day tours, complete holidays
VOL	volunteer work placements

Cost

A cost per day indicates an all-inclusive price including accommodation, food and tours. A cost per night indicates accommodation only. Prices are per person, usually based on sharing a double room. All prices are approximate, subject to change and for guidance only: contact each tour/project for exact prices. All dollar prices refer to US$ unless indicated.

■ contact name/address   ❸ telephone   ❶ fax   ⓦ website   ❸ email

Telephone codes

When dialling internationally, drop the initial zero from local numbers. In a few cases, we were unsure whether a number had an initial zero when dialled locally. If a number doesn't work as listed, try redialling with or without an initial zero.

English-speaking?

Some Latin American tours are in Spanish only. Check with the tour operator. Unless specified, tours in other countries are in English, or can provide English-speaking guides.

HELP US UPDATE

If you know of similar community tourism projects or changes to these listings, please email Tourism Concern on info@tourismconcern.org.uk.

INDEX OF COUNTRIES

Australia – Aboriginal tourism
Belize
Bolivia
Botswana
Brazil
Canada – First Nations tourism
Costa Rica
Cuba
Ecuador
Egypt
Ethiopia
Fiji
The Gambia
Guatemala
Honduras
India
Indonesia
Kenya
Kyrgyzstan
Malaysia
Mexico
Morocco
Namibia

Nepal
New Zealand – Maori tourism
Nicaragua
Pakistan
Palestine
Panama
Peru
Philippines
Russia
Samoa
Senegal
Solomon Islands
South Africa
Sri Lanka
Swaziland
Tanzania
Thailand
Uganda
US – Native American tourism
Venezuela
Zambia
Zimbabwe

AUSTRALIA – ABORIGINAL TOURS

International dialling code +61. Prices are in Australian dollars.
Aboriginal Australians endure some of the poorest living conditions in the world. In many Aboriginal communities, health and education facilities are almost non-existent and the life-expectancy of Aboriginal Australians is fully 25 years less than white Australians. Aboriginal imagery – Aboriginal painting, boomerangs, didgeridoos, rock art, 'Dreamtime' myths, etc – features heavily in Australia's tourism marketing, although few Aboriginal people see the benefit from this tourist trade.

Of an estimated 200 Aboriginal tourism businesses in Australia, most take place in the vast Outback (which starts once you cross the Blue Mountains, three hours west of Sydney and stretches across to the Indian Ocean) or in the Top End – the tropical region near Darwin, including Arnhemland. These areas are far from the big cities where most white Australians live. It's in these places that you'll find the most 'traditional' Aboriginal culture. Although none are entirely unaffected by white Australia, there are communities where people still speak their own language, gather food from the bush and preserve ties with the land.

The Australian Outback is one of the world's special places. A so-called 'empty' land that bursts with life. A land of brilliant colours and light, huge distance, wide horizons, incredible scenery and amazing starry skies.

Aboriginal people have lived here for thousands of years and their culture and spirituality is deeply connected to the land. Seeing the Outback with Aboriginal guides is totally different from a standard nature tour. Aboriginal society is one of the most conservation-minded in the world, and learning about the Aboriginal attitude to the environment is a lesson in what it means to truly respect nature.

Aboriginal tours typically feature gentle bushwalks to learn about Aboriginal use of plants for food and medicine ('bushtucker'), plus explanations of Aboriginal culture, spiritual beliefs and 'Dreamtime' stories. There's usually a chance to buy paintings and crafts.

Aboriginal Arts and Cultural Centre   CENTRE/TOUR
ToDo! Award winner
Aboriginal-owned art gallery and didjeridoo school in Alice Springs that also arranges cultural tours.

■ 86 Todd St, Alice Springs, NT 0870

t 08-8952 3408 **f** 08-8953 2678

w www.aboriginalart.com.au **e** aborart@ozemail.com.au

Anangu Tours/Uluru Cultural Centre   CENTRE/DAY

Based in the impressive new Cultural Centre, Anangu Tours offers short (two-hour, half-day) Aboriginal-guided walks near Uluru (Ayer's Rock). Bushtucker, medicinal plants, Dreamtime stories. A$39.

■ Uluru Cultural Centre, Yulara, NT

☎ 08-8956 2123

Australian National Tourism Office   ORG

Has a department developing Aboriginal tourism. The page on their website has details of various Aboriginal tours, including some listed here.

■ Nature-based and Indigenous Tourism Regional Development Branch,
   Department of Tourism, PO Box 9839, Canberra ACT 2600

☎ 02-6213 7014 ☎ 02-6213 7096

Ⓦ www.tourism.gov.au/publications/talent/start.html Ⓔ info.tourism@isr.gov.au

Darlngunaya Backpackers   ACCOM/BUDGET

Charming Aboriginal-owned hostel in a historic building in Fitzroy Crossing in the Kimberley.

■ PO Box 169, Fitzroy Crossing WA 6765

☎ 08-9191 5140

Darngku Heritage Tours   DAY

Based in Fitzroy Crossing. Aboriginal-owned boat-trips to Geikie Gorge.

☎ 08-9191 5355 ☎ 08-9191 5085

Desert Tracks   TOUR

Excellent community-owned tours to a Pitjantjatjara community 200 kilometres south-west of Uluru (Ayer's Rock). Trips depart from Yulara (the Ayer's Rock resort), and include a tour of Uluru and Kata Tjuta (the Olgas). Tours include walking sections of 'Dreaming' tracks, learning about Outback ecology and bushtucker, visiting rock art sites, and the chance to see contemporary Aboriginal life in the central desert. The Outback scenery is memorable. Tours from two to eight days. There is an annual dance festival. Seven-day tours: A$2400.

■ PO Box 1285, Byron Bay, NSW 2481

☎ 02-808 566 ☎ 02-808 567

Ⓦ www.yoni.com/cronef/deserttracks.shtml Ⓔ dsrttrks@nor.com.au

Dharawal Aboriginal Tours   DAY
Day tours and overnight camping trips (A$45 and A$90) from Sydney's Bondi Beach to Botany Bay and the Royal National Park, exploring Sydney's little-known Aboriginal heritage. The Dharawal are the traditional inhabitants of the south Sydney region.

■ Rodney Mason: Dharawal Education Centre, 15 Murrong Place, La Perouse, NSW 2036

☎ 02-9661 1226

Ecotour Travel   ORG
'Green' travel agents who also book some Aboriginal tours.

■ Janet Southern, 447 Kent Street, Sydney, NSW 2000

☎ 02-9261 8984 ✆ 02-9261 8425

✉ southern@acon.com.au

Guluyambi River Trips   DAY
Aboriginal-run two-hour boat cruise on the scenic East Alligator River in Kakadu National Park, near the Border Store and the famous rock-art site of Ubirr. A$25.

☎ 01800-089 113

Kooljaman   ACCOM+
A Bardi community at the tip of the Dampier Peninsula, 200 kilometres north of Broome. Camping or cabins. Beautiful deserted beaches and pristine wilderness location. Bushwalks, mudcrabbing, snorkelling, swimming, fishing, boat charters and scenic flights over the Buccaneer Archipelago. 4WD access only. Four-person cabins: A$90 per night. Camping from A$8.

■ PMB 8, Cape Leveque via Broome, WA 6725

☎ 08-9192 4970 ✆ 08-9192 4978

✉ leveque@bigpond.com

Landscope Expeditions   TOUR
Non-profit study tours run by the West Australian Department of Conservation (CALM) – programme varies each year and sometimes includes Aboriginal cultural tours. Brochure available.

■ University of Western Australia, Perth: University Extension

☎ 089-380 2433 ✆ 089-380 1066

Lombardina ACCOM+

An Aboriginal community on remote and beautiful coast on the Dampier Peninsula north of Broome. Crafts, mudcrabbing, guided bushwalks, deserted beaches, boat tours, fishing trips, birdwatching and wildlife. Access by air or 4WD. Cabins from A$35 per day.

■ PO Box 372, Broome, WA 6725

✆ + ☎ 08-9192 4936; 08-9192 4116

📧 lombo@comswest.net.au

Manyallaluk TOUR

Award-winning Aboriginal-run campsite and tours near the famous Katherine Gorge. There is a four-day 'walkabout' in the Nitmiluk (Katherine) National Park, plus shorter tours exploring Aboriginal culture and the park. Rock art, swimming holes, magnificent landscapes, explanations of bushtucker, etc. Tours: A$99 per day. Camping: A$15 per night.

■ Murray Dennis: Manyallaluk, PO Box 1480, Katherine, NT 0851

✆ 089-754 781; 089-754 727 ☎ 089-754 724

Mimbi Caves DAY

Aboriginal-run day trips to newly opened limestone caves near Fitzroy Crossing in the Kimberley. May–Oct. A$85.

■ Fitzroy Crossing Tourist Bureau

✆ 08-9191 5355

Minjungbal Cultural Centre CENTRE

An Aboriginal cultural centre at South Tweed Heads in northern NSW. Museum, dance performances, short walks, crafts.

■ Kirkwood Rd, South Tweed Heads, NSW 2486

✆ 07-5524 2109

National Aboriginal Cultural Centre CENTRE

An Aboriginal crafts shop and dance theatre in Sydney's Darling Harbour.

■ Darling Walk, 1-25 Harbour St, Darling Harbour, Sydney

✆ 02-9283 7477 ☎ 02-9283 7488

🌐 www.bujiri.com 📧 dreaming@amaze.com.au

Peppimenarti   TOUR
A three-day tour from Darwin to a Ngangikuranggur community on the Daly River, south-west of Darwin. Remote Top End scenery, waterfalls, billabongs, wildlife. A$315 fly-in or $199 excluding flight.

■ Aussie Adventure Holidays, PO Box 2023, Darwin, NT 0801

☏ 08-8981 1633 ☏ 08-8941 1016

✉ larcdu@ibm.net

Sydney Aboriginal Discoveries   DAY
Day-tours of Sydney exploring its Aboriginal history, including a two-hour harbour cruise, plus half- and full-day coach tours.

■ PO Box Q507, QVB, Sydney, NSW 1230

☏ + ☏ 02-9571 8283

Tiwi Tours   TOUR
Community-owned and -run tours to the Tiwi Islands, via light aircraft from Darwin. Mudcrabbing, bushwalks, Aboriginal art, etc. One-day trip A$240; two days A$460.

■ PO Box 2023, Darwin, NT 0801

☏ 08-8981 1633 ☏ 08-8941 1016

■ Aussie Adventure Holidays: PO Box 2023, Darwin, NT 0801

☏ 08-8981 1633 ☏ 08-8941 1016

✉ larcdu@ibm.net

Umorraduk Aboriginal Safaris   TOUR
Tours to a Gummulkbun community in Arnhemland, 365 kilometres north-east of Darwin. The area is beautiful wilderness and rich in rock art. A$450 per day.

■ Brian Rooke, Brookes Australia Tours: PO Box 41086, Casuarina, NT 0811

☏ 08-8979 0218 ☏ 08-8948 1305

ⓦ www.tourism.gov.au/publications/talent/umorraduk.html

Wadda Safaris   TOUR
Tours to the Nqkalbon community in Arnhemland. Experience daily life, bushtucker walks, wildlife, rock-art sites, bush scenery, swimming in hidden waterholes, etc.

■ Darwin YHA, 69 Mitchell Street (Postal: PO Box 2556), Darwin, NT 0801

☏ 08-8981 2560 ☏ 08-8981 7222

BELIZE

International dialling code +501.
Culturally, tiny Belize is more a part of the Caribbean than Central America, with a laid-back atmosphere and an English-speaking black majority. However, Hispanic immigrants from Guatemala are slowly bringing the country closer to its Latin neighbours. In tourist terms, Belize is very much an ecotourism destination. A string of islands and the world's second-largest Barrier Reef are the main tourist attractions, and islands such as Ambergris Caye can be quite touristy. The mainland coast is prone to hurricanes and less developed for tourism, with long stretches of mangrove swamps rather than beach. Inland, tracts of lush rainforest hide rivers, waterfalls, caves and Mayan ruins.

Belize Audubon Society   ORG
Helps develop community tourism projects.

■ 12 Fort St, (Postal: PO Box 1001), Belize City

❶ 02-35004; 02-34987 ❶ 2-34985

Ⓦ www.belizeaudubon.org ⓔ base@btl.net

Bermudian Landing Community Baboon Sanctuary   DAY
A locally-run conservation and tourism project sponsored by the Worldwide Fund for Nature (WWF) and the Belize Audubon Society. Local farmers have agreed to farm in ways that do not harm wildlife. Good birdwatching, wildlife, guided hikes, canoe trips and homestays. The 'baboons' are actually black howler monkeys.

■ Contact the Belize Audubon Society (above) for more details

Toledo Ecotourism Association   TOUR
ToDo! Award winner
Organizes village stays and ecotours around Punta Gorda in southern Belize to 13 local Garifuna (Black Carib), Mayan and Kekchi villages. Profits from tourism go to community projects including schools, healthcare, etc. Visitors are limited to eight per village and tours can be tailor-made for individuals or groups. The area has some of Belize's best-preserved rainforest, with excellent birdwatching, wildlife, caves and rivers. Basic prices are $40 per night, including an overnight village stay and two half-day tours. These include canoeing, horseriding, fishing, arts and crafts lessons, music, story-telling. A three-day itinerary spends one night each in a Garifuna, Mayan and Kekchi village. Punta Gorda is also accessible by ferry from Livingston in Guatemala.

■ Chet Schmidt/Reyes Chun: Vernon and Front Street, (Postal: PO Box 157), Punta Gorda

❶ 07-22096 ❶ 07-22199

Ⓦ www.plenty.org/TEA.html ⓔ ttea@btl.net

BOLIVIA

International dialling code +591.
Bolivia is sometimes called the Tibet of the Americas: the western half of this poor, landlocked country is a dry high-altitude plateau called the altiplano. It's here, in one of the most inhospitable inhabited environments on earth, that you'll find the hardy Quechua and Aymara campesinos. The altiplano landscape can be dramatic, from beautiful Lake Titicaca and the 6000m-plus peaks of the Cordillera Real to the surreal Salar de Uyuni – the world's largest salt flat – and the 'coloured lakes' of the far south. La Paz is the world's highest capital with a spectacular setting inside a vast canyon. Further south, Potosi and Sucre are historic colonial cities. Bolivia has the highest indigenous population of any South American nation and offers magnificent trekking, especially around Coroico and Sorata in the Cordillera Real. The eastern half of the country – accessible by light aircraft or some of the world's most hair-raising bus-rides (see my book, *The Gringo Trail* (Summersdale, 1999), for a description of one such road) – is quite different, consisting of low-lying Amazonian rainforest. Many backpackers take jungle tours from Rurrenabaque, while the remote national parks of Noel Kempff Mercado and Madidi offer even more pristine – but more expensive – wilderness experiences.

Chalalan Lodge/Madidi National Park   RAINFOREST
Madidi is a remote, pristine park in primary Amazon rainforest, accessible by light aircraft, with over 300 types of bird, 1200 butterfly species and monkeys, capibara, jaguar, tapir, caiman, etc. **Chalalan Lodge** was set up in the park by the American organization Conservation International in partnership with the local Quechua-Tecana community of San Jose de Uchiapiomaoas, with local guides drawn from the community.

■ In the UK: Discovery Initiatives (see Responsible tour operators)
■ In the US: Conservation International (see Responsible tour operators)

Villa Amboro Ecotourism Project   TOUR

Tours in tropical forest, run by a community of 43 campesino families on the edge of **Amboro National Park** near Santa Cruz. Guests stay in a simple camp. Guided walks in the forest to look at wildlife, medicinal plants, etc. Good birdwatching and wildlife. The project is contactable via an NGO: **Probioma**. It has been supported by the British aid agency, Christian Aid Abroad and profits go towards community projects.

■ Probioma

❶ 03-431332

❷ probiama@roble.scz.entelnet.bo

BOTSWANA

International dialling code +267.

Botswana, to the north of South Africa, is the size of France with a population of 1.3 million. Its most famous attraction is the vast Okavango Delta in the west, a huge wetlands wilderness of 16,000 square kilometres with thousands of tree-fringed islands and plentiful wildlife. Travel in the delta is by dugout canoe along narrow reed-lined waterways.

To the south of the Okavango lies the Kalahari Desert, traditional home of the San Bushmen. There are roughly 50,000 Bushmen in Botswana (and a similar number in Namibia). Most have now been resettled into camps but about 3000 still live a semi-nomadic lifestyle in the Central Kalahari Reserve – although the Botswana government is trying to resettle them as well. Bushman culture is one of the oldest on earth, with an intimate knowledge of the harsh desert environment.

Kalahari Sunset Safaris   TOUR

Customized tours of three to six days with San Kalahari Bushmen, for groups of four to eight. The programmes can include food gathering walks, tracking and a (simulated) hunt, food preparation, traditional herbal medicines, dances, music (such as mouth bows and thumb pianos), jewellery-making and tool-making, myths and story-telling. If appropriate, there may be a trance dance – an important healing ritual. $250 per day fully-catered or $156 self-catering (under 12s, half price). Kalahari Sunset Safaris has links with **First Peoples of the Kalahari**, a Bushman pressure group.

■ PO Box 651, Ghanzi

❶ + ❶ 596-959

❷ permaculture@info.bw

Nata Sanctuary/Kalahari Conservation Society
SAFARI

A 31,000-hectare wilderness reserve, 170 kilometres north of Francistown. It was set up by the local Nata community and the Kalahari Conservation Society and includes part of the Makgadikgadi salt plains. Campsites, guided walks, birdwatching, wildlife viewing. British Airways Tourism for Tomorrow Awards, Southern region winner 1993.

■ Kalahari Conservation Society: PO Box 859, Gabarone

✆ + ✆ 374 557

Uncharted Africa Safari Co
SAFARI+

Uncharted Africa owns **Jack's Camp** and **San Camp**, two luxury safari camps in the Kalahari. While not community ventures, they offer guided walks led by Xai Xai Bushmen. $475 per day.

■ In the UK: Sunvil Discovery (see Responsible tour operators)

BRAZIL

International dialling code +55.

Brazil is a vast country but community-based tourism does not seem to be particularly well-developed – or maybe we just haven't heard about it yet. Brazil also has one of the most unequal distributions of land ownership, wealth and income of any country in the world, with extremes of both wealth and poverty. Such inequality has had a devastating environmental impact, too, as poverty-stricken settlers, denied access to land elsewhere, move into and cut down vast swathes of the Amazon rainforest.

The North-east is one of Brazil's most enticing regions, with strong black music and cultural traditions, historic cities such as Salvador and Recife and superb beaches. This coast is ripe for major tourism development but, again, the inequality of Brazilian society means that the benefits from tourism are unlikely to be shared by all.

ASPEC/Aldeia dos Lagos lodge/Silves Island
RAINFOREST

Silves Island is an island at the junction of the Urubu River and Canacari Lake in the Amazon rainforest, 300 kilometres downriver from Manaus. The area has many lakes and islands and rich aquatic wildlife. With the support of WWF Brazil, local people have formed an environmental organization, **ASPEC** (Silves Association for Environmental and Cultural Preservation) and opened the **Aldeia dos Lagos** jungle lodge. A Manaus tour agency runs four- and five-day packages to the lodge from $300 including transport. Rainforest walks, canoe trips, visits to local communities.

■ Canacari Turismo, PO Box NR 801, Manaus 69011-970

✆ + ✆ 92-651 2127; 92-656 3130

✉ silves@netium.com.br

Prainha do Canto Verde   ACCOM+

A fishing village 120 kilometres south of Fortaleza in north-east Brazil. The village has an excellent clean beach, guesthouses and restaurants serving fresh seafood. Residents are fighting to resist big-business tourist development and to develop sustainable small-scale, locally-controlled tourism, with a fund to ensure that the whole community benefits. There are also boat trips and guided nature walks to the sand dunes, mangroves and lagoons near the village.

■ René Sharer, Amigos da Prainha do Canto Verde: Caixa Postal 52722, 60151-000, Fortaleza, Ceará

❶ + ❶ 88-413 1426

📧 terramar@fortalnet.com.br

CANADA – FIRST NATIONS TOURISM

International dialling code +1. Prices are in Canadian dollars.
There are said to be roughly 1000 First Nations/Aboriginal-owned tourism businesses in Canada, employing about 15,000 people and generating around CDN$200 million in revenue. These businesses range from souvenir shops to lodges and tour companies. Clearly, we can't list every one and the listings below are only a small selection.

While nine out of ten Canadians live within 100 or so kilometres of the US border, there are First Nations communities far to the north (including the Inuit territory of Nunavut, which became self-governing on 1 April 1999). Tours to these northern reaches allow visitors to dog-sled across the ice, to see wildlife such as caribou, or to see the midnight sun or the aurora borealis.

Other regions with significant First Nations tourism include Ontario, with a number of tipi camps amidst the state's many forests and lakes, and the West Coast of British Columbia and Vancouver Island. The West Coast has whale-watching, mountains, wild coastline and beautiful temperate rainforest. Since white settlers arrived just over a century ago, huge tracts of this forest have been logged: tourism may provide an economic alternative to logging.

Anishinabe Experience   ACCOM+

A First Nations tourism project run by six Anishinabe/Ojibay communities living between Ottawa and the Algonquin Park wilderness area. Visitors stay in a tipi village and can participate in drumming, story-telling, craft-making workshops, explore traditional plant medicine trails etc. Annual events include a pow-wow in August and the Makwa Sno-Fest in February.

■ 1528 Mishomis Inamo, (Postal: PO Box 138), Golden Lake, Ontario K0J 1X0

❶ 613-625 2519 ❶ 613-625 2857

🌐 www.anishexp.com 📧 anishexp@renc.igs.net

Cowichan Native Village, Duncan   DAY

A tourist village in south-east Vancouver Island, owned by the local Hul'qumi'num community. The village includes a cafe, crafts shop, art gallery, carving demonstrations and videos about Cowichan history.

■ Cowichan Native Village, 200 Cowichan Way, Duncan, British Columbia BC V9L 4T8

☏ 250-746 8119 ✆ 250-746 4143

ⓦ www.cowichannativevillage.com

First Nations Travel   TOUR

First Nations-owned tour agency that can book First Nations tours.

■ Robert Obomsawin: 222 Rideau Street, Ottawa, Ontario K1N 5Y1

☏ 613-562 3970 (1800-265 6713) ✆ 819-562 3974

Kanio Kashee Lodge   ACCOM+

A lodge in a Cree community in northern Quebec, on the banks of the Rupert River. Kanio Kashee can arrange tours of the community and overnight stays with local people, accompanying them when fishing or hunting, etc, plus hiking and other backcountry activities.

■ PO Box 360, Waskaganish, James Bay, Quebec J0M 1R0

☏ 819-895 2005 ✆ 819-895 2008

Nuuhchimi Wiinuu Cultural Tours/Ouje-Bougoumou Cree Nation
TOUR

A Cree community 960 kilometres north of Montreal. As well as a far-north wilderness experience (cross-country skiing, snowshoe hiking, forest, lakes, snowmobiles, fishing, hiking, canoeing, etc), the settlement is a fascinating mix of traditional life and hi-tech facilities, and was included in a United Nations' list of 'the world's 50 most outstanding communities'. Five- or eight-day packages, plus customized itineraries. Tours run in both winter and summer. Prices from CDN$850 to CDN$1200, excluding travel.

■ David/Anna Bosum, Nuuhchimi Wiinuu Tours: 74 Opataca Meskino, Ouje-Bougoumou, Quebec G0W 3C0

☏ 418-745 3212 ✆ 418-745 3500

■ Ouje-Bougoumou Tourism: 203 Opemiska St, Ouje-Bougoumou, Quebec G0W 3C0

☏ 418-745 3905 ✆ 418-745 3544

ⓦ www.ouje.ca ⓔ tourism@ouje.ca

Quaaout Lodge Resort   ACCOM

A lodge on the shores of Little Shuswap Lake near Salmon Arm in the Okanagan region of British Columbia, owned and run by the Little Shuswap Indian Band. Horseriding, walks, fishing. Double room: CDN$150 per night.

■ PO Box 1215, Chase, British Columbia V0E 1M0

☎ 250-679 3090 (1-800-663 4303) 📠 250-679 3039

Shawenequanape Kipichewin (Anishinabe Village)   ACCOM+

ToDo! Award winner

A First Nations-run camp (campsites plus tipis for hire) on the shore of Lake Katherine in Riding Mountain National Park, Manitoba, a wilderness region of forests and lakes. The camp includes a restaurant and Anishinabe cultural centre/museum. There are also tour packages plus customized programmes based on traditional culture, such as herbal medicine, beadwork, spiritual practices, etc. Also horseriding and boat tours. Open May to September. The camp is owned by seven local Anishinabe communities.

■ Harold Flett, camp manager: 36 Roslyn Rd, Winnipeg, Manitoba R3L 0G6

☎ 204-925 2030; 204-848 2815 📠 204-925 2027

🌐 www.wredco.com ✉ wredco@mb.sympatico.ca

Six Nations   ACCOM/TOUR

The Iroquois Six Nations reserve, on the Grand River near Brantford in Ontario, is the largest First Nations community in Canada. Iroquois Pathways is an Iroquois-owned company running day and half-day tours of the reserve. There are also lodgings and a cultural centre.

■ Six Nations Tourism: PO Box 480, Ohsweken, Ontario N0A 1M0

🌐 www.sixnationstourism.com

Temagami Anishnabai Tipi Camp   ACCOM+/TOUR

An Anishnabai-owned tipi camp on Bear Island in Lake Temagami, northern Ontario. It offers weekend and five-day tour packages. Canoeing, walking, old-growth pine forest, healing and spiritual retreats. Weekend tours: $250.

■ Virginia Mckenzie: Bear Island, Lake Temagami, Ontario P0H 1C0

☎ 705-237 8876

🌐 www.venturenorth.com/temagtipi/ ✉ tipi@onlink.net

Tin Wis Resort Lodge/Sea Serpent Adventures   ACCOM/TOUR

Tin Wis is a hotel near Tofino on Vancouver Island's west coast. It is part of the Best Western chain but owned by the Tla-o-qui-aht First Nation. **Sea Serpent Adventures**, a Tla-o-qui-aht tour company (with the same website), offers whalewatching, boat trips, hot springs, fishing, hiking and camping trips around Tofino and the majestic Clayoquot Sound, which is one of the most intact areas of temperate rainforests in the world. CDN$75 per day.

■ Tin Wis: PO Box 389, 1119 Pacific Rim Highway, Tofino, BC, V0R 2Z0

☏ 250-725 4445 (1-800-661 9995) ☏ 250-725 4447

🌐 www.tinwis.com

■ Sea Serpent Adventures: PO Box 557, Tofino, British Columbia V0R 2Z0

☏ 250-725 2552 (1-888-249 8622)

🌐 www.tinwis.com ✉ cmoss@island.net

Tours Innu   TOUR

A First Nations-owned tour agency running trips to a number of First Nations communities in Quebec. Tours of one to eight days featuring cultural stays, wildlife, whalewatching, dog-sledging, hiking, canoe-trips, etc.

■ 50 Boulevard Bastien, Bureau 110, Wendake, Quebec G0A 4V0

☏ 418-843 5151 ☏ 418-843 7164

✉ stinnu@oricom.ca

Walk the Wild Side   DAY/TOUR

Guided day walks on Flores Island in Clayoquot Sound, near Tofino on Vancouver Island's west coast. Run by the local Ahousaht community. From CDN$30 per day. Rugged coastal scenery, temperate rainforest.

■ Walk the Wild Side, Ahousaht, Flores Island, British Columbia

☏ 250-670 9586 or book at Storm Light Marine, Main Street, Tofino, British Columbia

☏ 250-725 3342

COSTA RICA

International dialling code +506.

Costa Rica, along with Guatemala, is one of the most visited countries in Central America. But whereas Guatemala's big attraction is a large indigenous population, most *Ticos* (as Costa Ricans call themselves) are of mixed or Spanish descent – the indigenous population has been almost entirely wiped out. Nor does Costa Rica have Guatemala's great archaeological sites. Instead, the country enjoys a reputation as a nature-lover's paradise, with ten per cent of the country designated as national park. These parks protect tropical beaches, coral reefs, active volcanoes and tropical forest and contain more birds, animals and plant species than the whole of North America. The Pacific coast, in particular, has some of the best beaches in Latin America.

Costa Rica is the 'Switzerland of Central America': a stable and peaceful country in a region not known for these qualities. It abolished its army in 1948 and has been governed democratically for most of its history. Away from the national parks, Costa Rica is a predominantly rural, agricultural land whose main income comes from coffee and bananas. A couple of the projects below let you experience rural *Tico* life.

ATEC (Asociación Talamanqueña de Ecoturismo y Conservación)
ORG

A community-run tourism association based in Puerto Viejo on the Caribbean coast. The area includes a mix of Latin, Afro-Caribbean and indigenous BriBri people, and has wonderful beaches and tropical forest. Just south of Puerto Viejo, on the Panamanian border, the Gandoca-Manzanillo National Park protects coral reefs, beaches and rainforest. ATEC can arrange stays in nature lodges or on organic farms plus diving, kayaking, hiking and rainforest tours.

■ ATEC, Puerto Viejo de Talamanca Limon

❶ + ❶ 750 0191; 798 4244

❿ www.greencoast.com/atec.htm ❸ atecmail@sol.racsa.co.cr

COOPRENA (National Eco-Agricultural Cooperative Network of Costa Rica)
AGRI/ORG/VOL

COOPRENA comprises 11 small rural cooperatives and offers stays in a rural *Tico* community, plus opportunities for conservation and organic farming volunteer work. The region includes rainforest, beaches, mangrove swamps and dairy farms.

■ Apartado Postal 6939-1000, Costa Rica

❶ 259 3605 ❶ 259 3605

❿ www.agroecoturismo.net ❸ cooprena@sol.racsa.co.cr

Lapa Rios
ACCOM+/LUXURY

Considered one of the top ecolodges in Central America, this small resort is set in rainforest on the Osa Peninsula. Fine birdwatching, plus horseriding, hiking, kayaking, surfing and boat trips. The lodge is run by an American couple but supports a local school and conservation measures. British Airways Tourism for Tomorrow Awards, Americas winner 1995. From $135 per day.

■ Puerto Jiminez, Peninsula de Osa (Postal: PO Box 025216, SJO 706, Miami, Florida Fl 33102-5216, US)

❶ (Costa Rica) 735-5130; 735-5281 ❶ 735-5179

❿ www.laparios.com ❸ laparios@sol.racsa.co.cr

CUBA

International dialling code +53.
Cuba bursts with complexities and contradictions, from Fidel to salsa and
Santeria. It's a poverty-stricken nation with one of the best health and education services in the world. The largest island in the Caribbean, it has beautiful
beaches and scenery, as well as the exuberant nightlife and faded charm of the
capital Havana. It is also a powerhouse of Afro-Caribbean culture and music,
the home of *son* and *salsa*.

The collapse of its trading partners in the Soviet bloc threw Cuba into
chaos and made the US embargo even more keenly felt. In response, the
government has turned to tourism as a foreign currency earner. Unfortunately,
tourism has also reintroduced some problems that were wiped out by the
revolution, such as economic inequality and prostitution.

The beach resort of Varadero has been the main focus of tourist development. While the beaches are beautiful, development here is 'international' in
style and gives little feel for everyday life in the rest of the country. The two
tours we list here take you to different parts of the country and use music –
the heartbeat of Cuban culture – as a 'way in' to the island's idiosyncratic
magic.

Cubans are allowed to let two rooms in private homes, although often the
only way to arrange these homestays is when approached by people on the
streets. Hustlers usually ask a commission for finding you a homestay but it is
still a cheap option and a good way to get to meet Cubans.

Caledonia Languages Abroad   TOUR

Two-week holidays in Santiago de Cuba in the south of Cuba that combine
Spanish lessons and dance (son, rumba and salsa) classes. The holiday is run
with the Conjunto Folklorico Cutumba, one of the country's best-known dance
and music companies. Accommodation is with local families. The trip includes
tours in Santiago and the surrounding countryside and evening outings to dance
and music events. £485, excluding flight. Spanish language courses (all levels)
with homestays are also available.

■ The Clockhouse, Bonnington Mill, 72 Newhaven Road, Edinburgh EH6 5QG, UK

🕿 0131-621 7721/2 📠 0131-621 7723

🌐 www.caledonialanguages.co.uk 📧 info@caledonialanguages.co.uk

Casa del Caribe, Santiago de Cuba   ACCOM/ORG

The Promotor Cultural in the Casa del Caribe can arrange homestays. Santiago
is Cuba's second city and one of the cultural and musical centres of the country.

■ 154 Calle 13 y Calle 5, Visa Alegre

🕿 04-2285 📠 04-2387

Karamba Ltd   TOUR

Two-week music and dance holidays in Guantanamo, a little-visited town in the south-east of Cuba. Run with UNEAC (National Union of Cuban Artists and Writers) and Danza Libre, a group of musicians and dancers who mix traditional and modern styles. Holidays include percussion and/or dance lessons plus local culture, nightlife and countryside. £745 for two weeks, excluding flights.

■ Gary Newland: Ollands Lodge, Heydon, Norwich, Norfolk NR11 6RB, UK

❶ + ❶ 01603-872402

Ⓦ www.karamba.co.uk ❸ karamba@gn.apc.org

Las Terrazas/Moka Ecolodge   ACCOM+

Las Terrazas, about 70 kilometres west of Havana, is a village built as part of a successful government reforestation project in the 1960s. The comfortable Moka Ecolodge has been developed to create employment in the village. Pine forests, horseriding, hiking trails, crafts workshops, fishing. $72 a double room.

■ Moka Ecolodge, Las Terrazas, Pinar del Río

❶ 085-2996; 2921 ❶ 33-5516

ECUADOR

International dialling code +593.

Ecuador's most famous tourist attraction is the unique Galapagos Islands. The islands are undoubtedly special, but mainland Ecuador also packs an incredible variety of scenery, species and ecosystems into a relatively small area. In two or three weeks, you can see cloudforest, high moorland (called *paramo*) and snow-capped volcanoes in the Andean highlands, as well as the Pacific coast beaches and the Amazonian rainforest of the Oriente.

About half of Ecuadoreans are indigenous, with colourful Andean markets such as Otavalo. Ecuador's rugged topography is ideal for adventure tourism and agencies in the historic capital, Quito, offer whitewater rafting, kayaking, mountain-biking, horseriding, hiking, climbing and diving.

Ecuador has an unrivalled number of community tourism projects. These focus on two regions. The first is the Choco corridor, north-west of Quito. This loose, NGO-based project aims to link up a number of small reserves to protect a complete ecosystem that includes paramo, cloudforest and tropical coast and has unusually high numbers of endemic species. This area includes Maquipucuna, Bellavista, Golondrinas and Subir (all listed).

The other tours we list are in the Oriente – one of the most biodiverse places on earth. New roads have opened up this formerly inaccessible region.

Among other things, this has led to a tourism boom and many indigenous communities in the Oriente are now trying to develop their own tourism projects. These indigenous groups include Cofans, Siecoya, Siona, Huaorani, Shuar, Achuar and Quichua. Pressure on the forest's wildlife and resources from oil exploration, logging, tourism itself and a wave of colonists (landless peasants from the Ecuadorean coast or highlands) have made it hard for the Oriente's indigenous people to live traditionally (by hunting, etc), and tourism may be their most sustainable alternative.

The region around Tena is most affected by settlement, but it is still mainly forest and has great natural beauty. Covering the eastern slope of the Andes, this 'high forest' contains remote valleys, dramatic waterfalls and smoking volcanoes. To see much wildlife, however, you must travel away from the colonized region to places such as Cuyabeno National Park, Zabalo or Kapawi. These trips cost more because they require light aircraft or motorized canoe trips, but you'll see more wildlife.

Rainforest tours typically involve:

- guided walks in the forest to look at traditional use of plants for medicine, materials and food;
- canoe trips and walks to spot birds and wildlife, and probably fishing for piranhas;

- explanations of traditional customs, crafts etc.

Accommodation in most indigenous communities is in open-sided, thatched platforms on sleeping mats or in hammocks, with individual mosquito nets. Commercial lodges normally have enclosed, mosquito-netted rooms with more facilities, showers, etc. Mosquitoes are not a huge problem in the Oriente and the malaria risk is low. Prices listed are usually all-inclusive of transport, food, accommodation and guiding.

The lodges and commercial operators such as Tropic supply English-speaking guides but entirely community-run ventures are usually only in Spanish.

The political climate in Ecuador in 1999 was quite tense, with two general strikes. While Ecuador is known as a safe country, check the current situation before travelling.

Defending our Rainforest: A Guide to Community-Based Eco-tourism in the Ecuadorian Amazon by Wesche and Drumm (Accion Amazonia, 1999 – see Responsible tourism organizations and resources) gives more complete descriptions of many tours listed below, plus others not listed.

South American Explorers   ORG
The South American Explorers' Quito clubhouse is a great resource for visitors to Ecuador.

■ 311 Jorge Washington y Leonida Plaza (Postal: PO Box 17-21-431), Quito

🟢 02-225 228

🌐 www.samexplo.org 🅔 explorer@saec.org.ec

Amarongachi Jungle Trips   RAINFOREST
Trips (from one to five days) staying in cabins on the Jatun-Yacu river in rainforest near Tena. Run by Quichua families.

■ Ave 15 de Noviembre 438, (Postal: PO Box 154), Tena

🟢 + 🟢 06-886 372

■ you can also ask at the Restaurant Cositas Ricas or Hotel Travellers Lodging in Tena

ARVETUR/Pavacachi   RAINFOREST
Acangau Ruta Verde Tour (ARVETUR) is the community-based tour agency of the Quichua community of Pavacachi. The community is located on the Rio Curaray in the Yasuni National Park – a remote area of pristine primary rainforest with good bird and wildlife – one hour into the jungle by light aircraft from Shell. Quichua culture plus jungle walks and canoe trips. Extended jungle hikes can be arranged. Tours from four days upwards. Spanish-speaking (book through Tropic, below, for English-speaking guides). $92 per day, including flight.

■ ARVETUR, Raul Tapuy V, Calle Rio Amazonas, Shell, Pastaza

🟢 + 🟢 09-353 883

■ Tropic Ecological Adventures (see below)

ATACAPI Tours   RAINFOREST

Jungle tours run by an agency set up by OPIP, the regional indigenous organization. Most tours are in a settled area of the Oriente near **Puyo**. This easily
accessible region is high rainforest with valleys, waterfalls, good hiking and
birdwatching. Other tours (three to five days each) head east to a more remote
region where the wildlife and forest is less affected by settlement. These visit
Llanchamococha and **Jandiayacu** (the last two villages of the Zaparo people)
or **Curaray**, a Quichua village on the edge of the Yasuni National Park. $30–$60
per day. All these communities have basic but comfortable tourist cabins.

■ Programa de Ecoturismo de la OPIP: 9 de Octubre y Atahualpa, Antiguo Municipio,
Segundo Piso Puyo, Pastaza

☎ + ✆ 03-883 875

Bellavista Reserve   ACCOM+

A private cloudforest reserve near Mindo, north-west of Quito, which is developing community-based study tours and a research centre. Birdwatching.

■ Richard Parsons: Convivencia, Quito

☎ + ✆ 02-509 255

✉ aecie@aecie.org.ec

Capirona   RAINFOREST

Village stays and tours in a Quichua community in the high rainforest near
Tena. Capirona was one of Ecuador's first community-run projects, and is part
of **RICANCIE**. Quichua culture, plant medicines, rainforest ecology. $45 per
day. Spanish only.

■ Tarquino Tapuy, FOIN, Calle Augusto Rueda 242, Tena, Napo

☎ 06-886 288

■ RICANCIE (see below)

Casa Mojanda   ACCOM

A charming, comfortable hostel in the hills near Otavalo, with good vegetarian
food, horseriding, hiking. The owners support local community projects such
as a school.

■ Betti and Diego, Casilla 160, Otavalo

☎ 09-731 737 ✆ 06-922 969

🌐 www.casamojanda.com ✉ mojanda@uio.telconet.net

Cofan Dureno   BUDGET/RAINFOREST

A budget four-day jungle tour. This community, near the first oil well in the Oriente, has been hard hit by oil exploration, but the forest behind their village is still intact. I describe a visit to this community in my book *The Gringo Trail* (Summersdale, 1999). $35 per day.

■ No prebooking: simply turn up. Ask directions in Lago Agrio to Cofan Dureno. It's a two-hour bus ride: the driver drops you at a footpath to the river. Shout loudly enough and someone will row across to collect you! In the village, ask for Delfin or Laureano.

Fundación Golondrinas   TOUR/VOL

Four-day treks through a private cloudforest reserve, with income going towards community conservation projects. Starting at 4000 metres on the paramo, the trek heads downhill through changing climatic zones to the subtropical Mira Valley. It can be done using local guides or with a tour group. The Fundacion also has volunteer conservation opportunities. Golondrinas is part of the **Choco Corridor** plan.

■ La Casa de Eliza (hostel), Calle Isabel La Catolica 1559, La Floresta, Quito

🛈 02-226 602 🛈 02-222 390

🅦 www.ecuadorexplorer.com/golondrinas 🅔 manteca@uio.satnet.net

■ In the UK: Tribes Travel (see Responsible tour operators)

Huacamayos/Cabañas Llaucana Cocha   RAINFOREST

A tourism network of 11 Quichua communities in the Huacamayos Cordillera, an area of high rainforest near Tena. Rainforest walks, waterfalls, canyons, canoeing, pottery and local crafts. There are many petroglyphs (ancient rock carvings) in the area. The area is little known to tourists and reputedly very wild and beautiful.

■ In Tena: Benito Nantipa: Union Huacamayos, c/o FION, Calle Augusto Rueda 242, Tena, Napo

🛈 06-886 288

■ In Quito: Fundacion Sinchi Sacha

🛈 02-235 05 🛈 02-567 311

🅔 tianguez@uio.satnet.net

■ Tropic Ecological Adventures (see below)

Cuyacocha Ecological Reserve   RAINFOREST

A rainforest conservation project in the southern Oriente on the Rio Pindo Yacu, an area of primary forest, reached by a 40-minute light aircraft flight from Shell. Stay with families in the Quichua community of Cuyacocha.

■ Bartolomé Mashiant: Casilla 16-01-849, Shell, Pastaza

☎ 03-795 219

🌐 http://cuyacocha.iwarp.com ✉ cuyacocha@aol.com

Kapawi   LUXURY/RAINFOREST

A luxury lodge deep in the rainforest. It is run by a commercial agency which pays the local Achuar community $2000 per month plus seven per cent of its profit. In 15 years, the project will be entirely turned over to the Achuar. The lodge is at the top end of the market, competing with mainstream operators such as the Flotel. It is just about as far into the forest you can go in Ecuador and the wildlife viewing may be the best in the country. $160-180 per day, pl$200 return flight from Quito. English-speaking guides. British Airways Tourism for Tomorrow Awards, highly commended 1998.

■ Canodros SA, Luis Urdaneta, 1418 y Av de Ejercito, Guayaquil

☎ 04-285 711 📠 04-287 651

🌐 www.canodros.com ✉ eco-tourism@canodros.com.ec

■ In the UK: Penelope Kellie

☎ 01962-779 317

✉ pkellie@yachtors.u-net.com

Limoncocha   RAINFOREST

A Quichua community near Coca which has built tourist cabins in the forest about one hour from their village. Rainforest walks, canoe trips, birdwatching and wildlife. The village is accessible by bus from Quito (Putomayos bus company). $30 per day.

■ Tomas Creta Cerda, Parroquia Limoncocha, Canton Shushufindi, Sucumbios

☎ (c/o FOIN): 02-220326 📠 02-543 973

Maquipucuna   ACCOM+

A private cloudforest reserve two hours north-west of Quito, run by Fundación Maquipucuna, a conservation NGO. It involves local communities through ecotourism and sustainable farming. Maquipucuna is part of the Choco corridor (see introduction). The lodge is comfortable and attractive. Superb birdwatching. A British NGO, Rainforest Concern, helps fund the reserve.

■ Fundación Maquipucuna: Baquerizo 238 y Tamayo, Casilla 17-12-167, Quito

☎ 02-507 200/202 📠 02-507 201

✉ root@maqui.ecx.ec

■ Rainforest Concern: 27 Lansdowne Crescent, London W11 2NS, UK

☎ 020-7229 2093

Oyacachi   ACCOM+

A highland Quichua community in the Cayambe-Coca Ecological Reserve, accessible by road from Cayambe. Fine hiking (single or multiday hikes) with local guides in rugged mountain, paramo and cloudforest, with lakes, waterfalls, hot springs, horseriding. No accommodation yet – bring your own tent.

■ Ecocienca, Isla San Cristobal 1523 y Seymour, Casilla 17-12-257, Quito

❶ + ❶ 02-451 338

Pirana Tour (Siecoya)   RAINFOREST

This is the same Siecoya community, but different guides, described in the 'Being There' chapter. They offer two itineraries. The first, a four-day visit, involves staying in the community's guest cabin and learning about Siecoya culture, traditional uses of the rainforest, etc. A more intrepid eight-day canoeing and hiking trip visits the remote Rio Lagartococha on the Peruvian border. The Siecoya regard this as their ancestral home, and the wildlife and forest are reputedly superb. $40–$65 per day, including transport from Lago Agrio. Add $10 per day for an English-speaking guide, booked through Tropic. Guides: Cesar and Gilberto Piaguaje.

■ Manuel Silva, Pirana Tour: Casa de la Cultura, Colombia y 18 de Noviembre, Lago Agrio, Sucumbios

❶ 06-830 624 ❶ 06-830 115

■ Tropic Ecological Adventures (see below)

RICANCIE (Red Indigena Comunidades del Alto Napo para la Convivencia Intercultural y Ecoturismo)   ORG/RAINFOREST

A Quichua organization developing tourism in the Upper Napo region. RICANCIE markets ten Quichua communities, including **Capirona** (see above), **Chuva Urcu**, **Cuya Loma**, **Huasila Talag**, **Las Galeras**, **Machacuyacu**, **Rio Blanco**, **Runa Huasi**, **Salazar Aitaca** and **Union Venecia**. See *Defending Our Rainforest* (see the Books section of Responsible tourism organizations and resources) for more details. The communities all have lodges or cabins and RICANCIE runs five five-day tours, each of which visits two communities. Rainforest, waterfalls and caves, plus cultural attractions including crafts, medicinal plants, participation in communal 'minga' work, farming techniques, etc. Because they are close to Tena and the road network, RICANCIE's communities are among the most accessible and affordable jungle tours in Ecuador. $45 per day, including transport to/from Tena. Transport to/from Quito can be arranged on request.

■ Taquino Tapuy: Av. 15 de Noviembre 744, Tena

❶ + ❶ 06-887 072

■ Gregorio Munga 331 y Gaspar de Villarroel, Quito

❶ 02-453 914 ❶ 02-449 133 ricancie@interactive.net.ec

ECUADOR'S LEADING ECOTOURISM OPERATOR

Nature Lodges · Community Programs·
Birdwatching · Diving

AMAZON · GALAPAGOS · ANDES

tropic@uio.satnet.net
www.tropiceco.com

Winner of the 1997
ToDo! Award for Socially
Responsible Tourism

SionaTour   RAINFOREST

The tour agency of the Siona organization ONISE. It is developing tours to the
three Siona communities of **Orahueaya, Biana** and **Puerto Bolivar**. The latter is
close to the Lagunas Grande in the Cuyabeno reserve, one of the prime wildlife
destinations in the Oriente. Many other commercial trips to Cuyabeno involve
individual Siona but, to support community tourism, you should arrange travel
via SionaTour.

■ SionaTour (FEPP), 12 de Febrero 267 y 10 de Agosto, Lago Agrio, Sucumbios
(Postal: SionaTour (FEPP), Lago Agrio, Casilla 17-110-5202, Quito)

☏ 06-831 875 ☏ 06-830 232

SUBIR (Sustainable Uses of Biological Resources)   ORG

An NGO developing ecotourism in San Miquel and Playa de Oro on the edge
of the Cotacachi-Cayapas Reserve, on the Pacific coast near Esmeraldas.

■ Eloy Alfaro 333 y Plaza Doral, Quito

☏ 02-528 696/7 ☏ 02-565 990

✉ subir@care.org.ec

Tropic Ecological Adventures   RAINFOREST/TOUR

ToDo! Award winner

A travel company (run by Welsh naturalist Andy Drumm) with a special
commitment to community tourism. Tropic are the agents for two of Ecuador's
finest jungle tours. One is the five-day Huaorani trip to **Quehuiere'Ono**, which
won a 1998 ToDo! Award. The Huaorani are the least acculturated of the
Oriente's tribes and this is a fascinating trip. The community and guide Moi
Enomenga feature in Joe Kane's brilliant book, *Savages* (Pan, 1997). The second
tour is to **Zabalo**, a Cofan community on the Aguarico River in the Cuyabeno
reserve. Randy Borman, an American who grew up with the Cofan, lives in
Zabalo, and his unique 'double perspective' makes him one of the world's best
rainforest guides. Zabalo has some of Ecuador's best wildlife and rainforest

plus excellent accommodation. Trips of four to ten days. $50–$100 per day. Tropic also arranges shorter trips to Siecoya and Quichua communities, plus Galapagos cruises and customized itineraries in the highlands, and is the booking agent for **Maquipucuna**, **Kapawi**, the **Huacamayos** and the communities in **RICANCIE**. (See separate entries.)

■ Apartado 1a, Edificio Taurus, Av Republica 307 y Diego de Almagro, Quito

❶ 02-234 594; 02-225 907 ❶ 02-560 756

Ⓦ www.tropiceco.com Ⓔ tropic@uio.satnet.net

■ In the UK: Tribes Travel and Discovery Initiatives (see Responsible tour operators)

Tsanta Tours   RAINFOREST
Jungle trips run by an English-speaking Shuar guide, Sebastian Moya. $50 per day. Profits from tours contribute to an indigenous cultural foundation – Yawa Lee – which trains young Shuar to be shamans.

■ Tsanta Tours, Oriente y Eloy Alfaro, Banos or c/o Pension Patty, Banos

❶ 03-740 957

Yachana Lodge   RAINFOREST
A rainforest lodge near Coca on the Rio Napo. Run by an NGO called FUNEDESIN; profits go to local community projects. Guests can visit these projects, which include schools, health clinics and organic/permaculture farms, as well as the local Quichua community of **Mondana** and a traditional healer (shaman). Four-day package: $320, including transport from Quito.

■ FUNEDESIN: Francisco Andrade Marin 188 y Almagro (Postal: PO Box 17-17-92), Quito

❶ 02-237 278; 02-237 133

Ⓦ www.yachana.com Ⓔ info@yachana.com

EGYPT

International dialling code +20.

Egypt is one of the birthplaces of world civilization. Cairo is a historic and fascinating city (as well as an overcrowded modern one), with an atmospheric mediaeval market, one of the world's great museums and, of course, the Pyramids. The Valley of the Kings near Luxor is one of the world's great archaeological sites.

Few river trips can match the romance of the Nile. If you don't mind roughing it a bit and want your money to go into the local economy, then go to Aswan or Luxor and book locally on a *felucca*. These traditional sailing boats

wind

sand

stars

Sinai Summer Expeditions
Would you like to spend some time
EXPLORING, TRAVELLING, WORKING, LEARNING
in a place still well off the beaten track?

Wind, Sand & Stars
2 Arkwright Road, London NW3 6AD
Tel: 0207-433 3684 Fax: 0207-431 3247
office@windsandstars.co.uk / www.windsandstars.co.uk

are cheap and evocative, and you'll probably get to meet the captain's family too.

The Sinai peninsula features spectacular mountainous desert and coral reefs. The diving in Red Sea resorts such as Sharm el Sheikh is breathtaking, although perhaps overcrowded. Many Bedouin in the Sinai are involved informally in tourism (running cafés, guesthouses, selling clothes and handicrafts) especially in Dahab, which has become a backpacker hangout. Whether tourism in either Dahab or Sharm is sustainable and beneficial is debatable.

Basata   ACCOM
Small, environmentally-friendly resort on the Red Sea coast north of Dahab.

■ Sherif El-Ghamrawy: Basata, Ras El-Burga, Nuweiba-Taba Road, Sinai

☏ 062-500 481

✉ basata@mst1.mist.com.eg

Wind, Sand & Stars   TOUR
A UK-based company which run tours to the Sinai with local Bedouin communities. Trips include camel treks and desert hiking in the Sinai's mountainous interior. Customized itineraries are also available, plus trips for schools, a student Summer Expedition and special interest tours (eg biblical, wildlife). Helps fund local educational and health projects. British Airways Tourism for Tomorrow Awards, highly commended 1996.

■ Emma Loveridge/Janina Macdonald: 2 Arkwright Road, London NW3 6AD, UK

☏ 020-7433 3684 🖷 020-7431 3247

🌐 www.windsandstars.co.uk ✉ office@windsandstars.co.uk

ETHIOPIA

International dialling code +251.
Although Ethiopia is still 'off the beaten track', tourism expanded rapidly during the 1990s and is now the country's second-largest foreign income earner after coffee.

With much of the country consisting of highlands over 2000m, the climate is pleasant rather than searingly hot. The Rift Valley, Bale Mountains and Simien Mountains offer superb scenery and excellent hiking and birdlife.

The only African country not to have been colonised, Ethiopia has a longer history than other African nations and a distinctive Christian heritage. Almost half the population is Christian, and the unique rock churches of Lalibela and the holy city of Axium are two fascinating cultural sites.

Experience Ethiopia Travel   TOUR
A responsible tour operator that offers various tours around the country.

■ Churchill Road, next to Ras Hotel (Postal: PO Box 9354), Addis Ababa

❶ 1-152 336 ❶ 1-519 982

Ⓦ www.telecom.net.et/eet Ⓔ eet@telecom.net.et

FIJI

Fiji is a popular South Pacific destination, partly because it is on the air route to Australia or New Zealand and partly because it has fine beaches and coral reefs. Most tourists stay on the main island, Vitu Levu, in all-inclusive resorts along the coast (or on small off-shore islands) and see little of what lies outside these resorts. With their palm-fringed, white-sand beaches and thatched bars serving tropical cocktails, the resorts conform to many people's idea of a South Pacific paradise, but it would be a shame not to explore the island a little: Fijians are friendly and the scenery is attractive, with a volcanic, hilly interior – although much of the original forest cover has been replaced by sugar planta-tions. An unusually enlightened British colonial regime took measures to protect traditional Fijian culture, with the result that Fiji has a more intact indigenous culture than most other South Pacific nations. The British also imported Indian labourers to work the sugar plantations; today Indians make up half of Fiji's population – leading to occasional tension between indigenous Fijians and Indians.

Fiji's many outlying islands see far fewer visitors than Vitu Levu, are more 'traditional' and have better, less crowded coral for divers and snorkellers. Many of these islands are only connected to Vitu Levu by flights or ferries once or twice a week (which is why they see less tourists), but if you have time they are well worth the effort.

Navala   ACCOM

Accommodation in traditional thatched houses – called *bures* – in a village in the hilly interior of Vitu Levu, Fiji's main island. The village is one of the most traditional in the country and one of the few to still consist almost entirely of *bures*, and this is a chance to see Fijian life away from the coastal resorts. There is no formal tour, but you are free to wander around the village and its attractive surroundings. It's hard to arrange a visit in advance – simply turn up. Access by bus from the town of Ba on the north coast of Vitu Levu. $20 per night, including food.

THE GAMBIA

International dialling code +220.

English-speaking Gambia is a tiny finger of a country poking into Francophone Senegal in West Africa. It consists of little more than a narrow strip of land on either side of The Gambia River. In recent years, the short Gambian coastline has become a popular package tour destination, with cheap charter flights and winter sun. Inland, however, the country is little affected by tourism. Visitors who do make the effort will find ordinary rural African life, as well as interesting animal and birdlife along the banks of The Gambia river.

In 1999 The Gambian government banned all-inclusive resorts in an effort to spread income from tourism a little more widely.

The dry season in The Gambia is November to May.

Gambia Tourism Concern   ORG

This organization produces a magazine that is sold by 'bumsters' – young beach hustlers – on Gambia's beaches. It also campaigns on tourist issues and collaborated with Tourism Concern on an in-flight video designed to introduce incoming tourists to Gambian life and sensitivities.

■ Adama Bah: Bakadaji Hotel, PO Box 2066, Serrekunda

🕔 462 057 🕤 462 307

🅔 concern@qanet.gm

Tumani Tenda Ecotourism Camp   ACCOM+

Community-owned and run riverside accommodation in local-style houses in a Jola village south of Banjul. Boat trips, forest walks, workshops in batik making and other local crafts, dance and music performances. Nearby Brikama is known for its kora musicians. £10 per day, including meals. Excursions: £2–£5 per group per hour.

■ Bookings: Gambia Tourism Concern (see above)

■ In the UK: Tribes Travel (see Responsible tour operators)

GUATEMALA

International dialling code +502.

Guatemala has the most indigenous population in Central America and is one of the most scenically diverse and cheap countries in the region. This makes it a popular and rewarding destination, now that the violence of the 1980s seems to be over. Most tourists visit the rugged, Mayan-populated highlands. Attractions here include the old colonial capital of Antigua (famous for its Easter Week parades when locals cover the cobbled streets in huge tableaux of flowers), beautiful Lake Atitlan and the colourful, if touristy, market at Chichicastenango. Anyone interested in a more 'authentic' market should visit the Friday market at San Francisco el Alto, a small town near Quetzaltenango – it's said to be the biggest market in Central America.

Antigua is a popular place to learn Spanish. Twenty hours of one-to-one tuition, plus full board and lodging with a local family can cost as little as $100. There are dozens of Spanish schools in Antigua, and a course is easy to arrange once you are in town. Staying with a local family is a great way to practise your Spanish, to get to know local people and to put money into the local economy (although few Mayan families are involved in homestays in Antigua). The other centre for learning Spanish is Quetzaltenango, less picturesque but also less touristy. Schools here tend to have more of a 'social conscience', donating profits to community projects and giving students a chance to visit these projects.

Most visitors to Guatemala also take the one-hour flight (or 12-hour bus ride) north to Flores, the base for visiting the spectacular ancient Mayan city of Tikal. Tikal is set in the lowland rainforests of the Petén, which also offers jungle adventure opportunities. The Petén forest is threatened by logging and farming: community-based ecotourism may be one less destructive alternative.

Guatemala's tiny strip of Caribbean coastline, around the town of Livingston, is culturally distinct from the rest of the country, with a mainly black, English-speaking population that has more in common with neighbouring Belize.

Guatemala is the heart of the Mundo Maya, a huge tourism promotion involving the governments of Guatemala, Mexico, Belize and Honduras. This multi-million dollar enterprise uses the culture, history and imagery of the Maya to attract tourists to mega-resorts such as Cancún in Mexico, which in reality have little to do with the Maya and bring them little benefit. In this respect, it is typical of the way in which many governments exploit images of indigenous cultures for tourist marketing. Few Mayans are involved in tourism in Guatemala, except as souvenir sellers and porters, etc, while most hotels and tour companies are owned and run by Latinos.

Eco-Escuela/Bio-Itza School   SCHOOL

Two language schools in the rainforested Petén lowlands, supported by the US-based NGO Conservation International. The **Eco-Escuela** is on the shore of Lago de Petén Itzá, in the village of San Andres near Flores. It offers Spanish language tuition plus ecological field trips to the Petén rainforest and archaeological sites such as Tikal. Students stay with families and teachers are local. Profits go to community projects. One week (20 hours of one-to-one teaching and full board) costs approximately $200. The **Bio-Itza School**, in the nearby village of San José, also offers Spanish tuition and homestays, plus classes in the Maya Itza language and in traditional uses of rainforest resources and medicinal plants.

■ Book through EcoMaya (see below)

■ In the US: Conservation International (see Responsible tour operators)

① 800-429 5660 extension 264 ① 202-331 9328

ⓔ ecoescuela@conservation.org

EcoMaya/Pro-Petén/Caminos Maya   TOUR

Pro-Petén is a local development NGO, supported by US-based Conservation International, that works in the lowland Petén region of Guatemala. It has set up a travel agency in Flores called **EcoMaya** to market the **Eco-Escuela** and **Bio-Itza School** (above) and a range of community-based tours called the **Caminos Maya**. At present, there are three main tours. One is a rainforest hike to Tikal, visiting the little-known ruin of **El Zotz** on the way. Another is the **Scarlet Macaw Trail**, a four/five-day jungle tour with wildlife, river trips and more Maya ruins. The third visits the remote archaeological site of **El Mirador**, north of Tikal and thought by many scholars to have been the largest and most powerful of all the ancient Mayan cities.

■ Armando Castellanos, EcoMaya: Calle 30 de Junio, Ciudad Flores, Petén

① 926-1363 ① 926-3322

ⓔ ecomaya@guate.net

Hotel Backpackers   ACCOM/BUDGET

A backpackers' hostel in Rio Dulce that was set up by the **Casa Guatemala** orphanage to create jobs for teenagers from the orphanage. Rio Dulce is on the way to Livingston on the Caribbean coast. (The hostel is directly underneath the bridge on the south side.)

① 208 1779 ① 331 9408

ⓔ casa_guatamal@guate.net

PRODEFOR/Bosque Huito/Mirador Piedra Cuache   ACCOM+/AGRI

PRODEFOR (Proyecto de Desarrollo Forestal de la Sierra) is a Guatemalan environmental NGO that has helped two communities in the Cuchumatanes highlands (between Huehuetenango and Todos Santos) to set up tourist facilities. The **Proyecto Ecoturistico de Bosque Huito** in the village of El Rosario has lodgings, camping and guides. The Bosque Huito is a forest area – the Huito is a tree endemic to Guatemala. In the nearby village of Chiabal, the **Proyecto**

Ecoturistico Mirador Piedra Cuache also has lodgings, homestays and camping. There are local crafts for sale, archaeological sites, walking paths in the forested hills and a chance to learn about local Mam culture and farming methods.

■ PRODEFOR: Huehuetenango

❶ + ❶ 764 2832; 769 0683

❺ prodefor@guate.net

■ Piedra Cuache: Chiabal, Todos Santos, Huehuetenango

❶ 702 8004

Proyecto Linguistico Quetzalteco de Espanol, Todos Santos   SCHOOL

A language school in the village of Todos Santos where you can study either Spanish or Mam (the local Mayan language). A percentage of profits goes to local development projects. Todos Santos is set in the most rugged and scenic part of the Guatemalan highlands, among the Cuchumatanes mountains, and the village itself is one of the country's most interesting and traditional. Its fiesta (on 1 November) is one of Guatemala's most colourful, with a famously wild horserace.

■ 5C 2-40, Zona 1 (Postal: Apartado Postal 114), Quetzaltenango

❶ + ❶ 761 2620

Totonicapán   DAY/TOUR

Totonicapán is a small Kiche Maya town in the highlands, surrounded by hills and pine forest, 20 kilometres east of the Quatro Caminos road junction near Quetzaltenango. The town is not on the tourist circuit but known for its artisans and craftsmen and busy Tuesday and Saturday markets. The local Casa de la Cultura organizes one- or two-day tours which visit workshops (pottery, masks, musical instruments, costumes, etc) and traditional dance presentations, plus meals in family homes and overnight homestays.

■ Carlos Humberto Molina Gutierrez, Casa de la Cultura, 8a Avenida 2-17 Zona 1, Totonicapan

❶ 766 1309 ❶ 766 1575

Ⓦ www.larutamayaonline.com/aventura.html ❺ kiche78@hotmail.com

❺ larutamaya@hotmail.com

HONDURAS

International dialling code +504.

In tourist terms, Honduras is often overshadowed by neighbouring Guatemala. But the country has its own attractions, such as the magnificent Mayan ruins of

Copan, or the coral-fringed Bay Islands on the north coast which reputedly offer the world's cheapest scuba diving. The north (Caribbean) coast between Tela and Trujillo is an almost continuous stretch of sandy beach. This is the home of the Garifuna people, descendants of escaped slaves and indigenous Caribs, whose culture combines African, indigenous American, English, French and Spanish influences. There are houses to rent in many Garifuna villages. East of Trujillo, the roadless rainforests, savannah and coastal wetlands of the Moskito Coast constitute one of Central America's wildest regions. In 1998, Honduras was devastated by Hurricane Mitch but transport services, at least, are now almost back to normal.

El Carbon   ACCOM+/BUDGET/TOUR
A Pech village in forested hills three hours by bus south of Trujillo. The community is developing a tourism project with an NGO called WUATAH. It comprises two guesthouses, a visitor centre and guided hikes in the cloudforest. The surrounding forest contains over 200 bird species as well as spider monkeys, puma and jaguar and lovely waterfalls. Also Pech culture, medicinal plants.

■ See the Honduras section of the www.planeta.com website

Rio Platano Biosphere Reserve   BUDGET/TOUR
A World Heritage-listed reserve of primary rainforest and rich bird and wildlife on the Moskito Coast. Community tourism is being developed by the **Partnership for Biodiversity**. Funded by the US Agency for International Development, this involves **MOPAWI**, a local indigenous organization. There are lodgings in the Garifuna villages on the coast – eg Raista, Belén, Barra Plátano, Plaplaya – from where you can hire a boat to the Miskito/Pech village of **Las Marias**. In Las Marias, there are two basic hotels and the community organizes tours in the reserve, ranging from day walks and canoe trips to tough three-day hikes. Guides in Las Marias: $6–$8 per day per guide (one group needs two or three guides). Dry season: April to September. Access to the region is by light aircraft to Palacio from Tegucigalpa ($160 return) or La Ceiba ($50), or by boat from La Cieba, Trujillo or Limon.

■ Jorge Salaverre, La Mosquitia Ecoaventuras: PO Box 890, La Ceiba

☉ 0442 0104

ⓔ moskitia@tropicohn.com

■ MOPAWI: Puerto Lempiro

☉ 0598 7460

■ Arden Anderson (US Bureau of Land Management)

ⓔ a2anders@co.blm.gov

INDIA

International dialling code +91.

Love it or hate it – and many visitors seem to do both in equal measure – India is sure to leave a lasting impression. On its way to becoming the most populous nation on earth (its population broke the one billion barrier in 1999), it is one of the great historic centres of world civilization, shaped and reshaped over thousands of years by numerous invasions and empires. It is the birthplace of Hinduism and Buddhism, a country of *sadhus* and holy men, and esoteric and spiritual traditions such as yoga. It is also a modern, materialistic society with a growing middle class. It boasts the world's largest film industry and one of the world's most sophisticated classical musical traditions.

India's towns and cities assault the senses with their chaotic crowds, noise, traffic, pungent smells and vibrant colours. Yet there are also wild expanses, such as the Rajasthan desert or the Himalayan regions of the north – from lush, green Darjeeling to austere, Tibet-influenced Ladakh. (And it's worth noting that India still has a lower population density than England.) Throughout the country there are ancient cities, temples, shrines, palaces and monuments: Jodhpur, Jaipur, Jaisalmer, Varanasi, Agra and the Taj Mahal, the Hindu temple of Khajuraho, the ruins of Vijayanagar, the 900 Jain temples on Shatrunjay Hill in Gujarat. There are hundreds of festivals, such as the Pushkar Camel Fair or Puri's Rath Yatra chariot festival. But what makes the greatest impression on most visitors is simply the sheer bustle and exuberance of every-day life, both in city streets and rural villages.

Parts of the Indian coast – notably Goa and Kerala – are undergoing major tourist development, and this isn't always in the interests of local people. So-called 'rave tourism' in Goa has brought attitudes to drugs and sex that local people may find troubling: sensitivity and respect for local values is important here.

Alternative Travels   ACCOM+/TOUR

Tours in Rajasthan, including homestays. Also stays on their organic farm, called **Apani Dhani**. The Shekhawati region, between Delhi and Jaipur, offers hiking in the Arawalis hills, horseriding, cycling, etc, as well as a chance to sample rural Indian life. Minimum four people. They can also organize yoga, meditation and fasting courses.

■ Ramesh C Jangid, Nawalgarh-333042, Shekhawati, Rajasthan

❶ 01594-22239 ❶ 01594-24061

Ⓦ www.galilee.fr/apani-dhani ❷ rcjangid@jp1.dot.net.in

Dhami Dham Tours   TOUR
Customized low-impact hiking in the Himalayan region of Uttarkhand.

■ Paul Gonsalves: Kamaan Singh Dhami C-4/70, SDA, New Delhi 110016. Or 592 Dhami Dham, Egipuram, PO Viveknagar, Bangalore 560 047

☏ 080-571 3016

🌐 www.mahiti.org/dhamidham 📧 dhamidham@yahoo.com

Equations   ORG
An NGO which campaigns for fair and responsible tourism in India.

■ 198 2nd Cross, Church Road, New Thippasandra, Bangalore 560 075

☏ 080-529 2905 📠 080-528 2313; 529 2905

🌐 www.equitabletourism.org 📧 admin@equation.ilban.ernet.in

Green Hotel, Mysore   ACCOM
A former palace in Mysore (south of Bangalore in southern India), beautifully restored and converted into a small, environmentally friendly hotel (solar power, traditional materials, etc). The hotel was set up with the aid of the British Charities Advisory Trust to generate income for local charities and as a model of sustainable tourism, with good pay, training, conditions for staff, etc. Lovely one-hectare garden, good library about Indian history and culture.

■ The Green Hotel, The Chittaranjan Palace, 2270 Vinoba Road, Mysore 570 012

☏ 821-512 536 📠 821-516 139

🌐 http://web.ukonline.co.uk/charities.advisory.trust/

📧 grenhotl@giasbg01.vsnl.net.in

Insight India   TOUR
Arranges tours to the scenic Kulu Valley near Manali in Himachal Pradesh, and Haryana in the Himalayan foothills. Tours include visits to villages, development projects.

■ Kishore Shah/Vasanti Gupta: 33 Headley Way, Headington, Oxford OX3 0LR, UK

☏ 01865-764 639

📧 Kishorevasanti@msn.com

Kolam Responsible Tours and Soft Travel   TOUR
Small-group tours of India that aim to give an insight into the realities of contemporary life in India. Tours use local hotels and include meals with families, homestays, visits to development projects, etc. Most focus on southern India, in particular Tamilnadu, although tailor-made itineraries are available. Kolam also runs trips on behalf of Oxfam and Traidcraft.

■ Ranjith Henry, B-22, Bay View Apartments, Parvathy Street, Kalakshetra Colony, Besant Nagar, Chennai 600 090, South India

☎ 044-491 3404; 044-491 9872 📠 044-490 0939; 044-491 5767

🌐 http://ourworld.compuserve.com/homepages/kolam

■ In the UK: Tribes Travel (see Responsible tour operators)

Project India/Cross-Cultural Solutions   VOL

Three-week volunteer placements in partnership with Indian NGOs, run by a US-based non-profit organization called Cross-Cultural Solutions. Volunteer opportunities include English teaching, healthcare, arts, computing, etc. Cross-Cultural Solutions also run an annual tour of India focusing on women's issues.

■ Cross-Cultural Solutions: 47 Potter Avenue, New Rochelle, NY 10801, US

☎ 914-632 0022 (1-800-380 4777) 📠 914-632 8494

🌐 www.crossculturalsolutions.org ✉ info@crossculturalsolutions.org

ROSE (Rural Organization for Social Elevation)   ACCOM+/VOL

A small non-profit group that organizes village stays in Kanda, in the Himalayan foothills of Uttar Pradesh. Also organizes volunteer organic farming, English teaching, hiking (to glaciers) and joining in village life. Profits to community projects.

■ Mr Jeevan Lal Verma, ROSE, Village Sonargaon, Kanda, Bageshwar, UP263631

■ In the UK: HANSI co-operative

☎ 01273-821 274

Save Goa Campaign   ORG

An organization campaigning against the harmful effects of tourism in Goa.

■ Frederick Noranha: near Lourdes Convent, Saligao 403511, Goa

Tashila Tours and Travel   TOUR

Trekking trips in partnership with local communities in Sikkim.

■ 31/A National Highway (Postal: PO Box 70), Gangtok 737101, Sikkim

☎ 3592-22979 📠 3592-22155

🌐 www.sikkiminfo.com/tashila ✉ tashila@sikkim.org

INDONESIA

International dialling code +62.

Indonesia is the world's fourth most populous country and consists of thousands of islands. It has orang-utans and Komodo dragons, superb beaches, coral reefs, rainforest and volcanoes, colourful rural life, delicious food and a rich cultural heritage. Yogyakarta in Java, with its magnificent temples, and the island of Bali are the two most famous historical and cultural destinations but, as you would expect with a country of this size, there is tremendous cultural diversity, from the devoutly Muslim Aceh province in northern Sumatra to the animist Dayak culture in Kalimantan (the Indonesian part of Borneo).

The southern coast of Bali is now a popular package tour destination but much of the rest of the island is relatively untouched by tourism. East of Bali, there are hundreds of islands, including Sulawesi and the Moluccas, which see far fewer tourists. West of Java, Sumatra is one of Indonesia's wild frontiers, with expanses of rainforest.

Indonesia has a dubious human rights record: for instance, in relation to its brutal and illegal occupation of East Timor. There is also some opposition to Indonesian rule in Iran Jaya from the (mainly non-Indonesian) local population. Environmentally, too, an alarming proportion of Kalimantan's and Sumatra's rainforests have been destroyed in the last few decades, with many of the most harmful logging concessions having associations with the old Suharto dictatorship. In 1998, forest fires in Kalimantan were so bad that the smoke blotted out the sun for months.

The dry season in most of Indonesia is May–September, with some local variations.

Bina Swadaya Tours ORG/TOUR

Cultural and nature-tour operator set up in 1987. Tours combine conventional tourist highlights with visits to community projects and rural villages. They range from day trips to 26-day tours and offer a wide range of options, from artisan workshops to trekking in the rainforest and whitewater bamboo rafting. Destinations include the World Heritage-listed Ujung Kulon National Park in Java, the ancient temples of Yogyakarta, climbing active volcanoes, seeing orang-utans in Kalimantan and Sumatra, visiting Dayak villages in Kalimantan and much more. Bina Swadaya Tours is owned by the non-profit Bina Swadaya Foundation and its tours help to fund the foundation's community development projects. English-language brochure.

■ Jln. Gunung Sahari III/7, Jakarta Pusat, 10610, (Postal: PO Box 1456), Jakarta 10014

☎ 021-420 4422 ☎ 021-425 6540

✉ bst@cbn.net.id

Ciptarasa ACCOM+

A Sundanese mountain village on the edge of the Gunung-Halimun National Park in West Java, roughly 150 kilometres from Jakarta. Visitors stay with local families who will show them around the village. Also guided trips into the mountainous tropical forests of the national park.

■ Ekindo (Tours) JL. A Yani No 221–223, Ruko Segitiga Emas Kosambi Blok G, No 7, Bandung

☎ 022-727 9563 **✆** 022-727 6845

✉ ekindo@ibm.net

■ In the UK: Symbiosis Expedition Planning (see Responsible tour operators)

INDECON (Indonesian Ecotourism Network)   ORG

A network set up by the Institute for Indonesian Tourism Studies, Bina Swadaya Foundation and Conservation International to promote responsible ecotourism in Indonesia.

■ Ary Suhandi: Institute for Indonesian Tourism Studies, Jl Taman Margasatwa 61, Pasar Minggu, Jakarta 12540

☎ 021-7883 8624; 021-7883 8626 **✆** 021-780 0265; 021-794 7731

ⓦ http://indecon.i-2.co.id **✉** indecon@cbn.net.id **✉** indecon@indosat@net.id

Mitra Bali Foundation   AGRI/ORG/TOUR

A charity that can arrange transport, hotels and village stays on Bali. They also organize visits to community and development projects including organic farms, the famous irrigation systems in the centre of the island, crafts workshops, etc. This is a good way to see Bali beyond the resorts. Mitra Bali supplies 'fair-trade' handicrafts to Oxfam.

■ Agung Alit, Jln Sulari 1, No. 6 Denpasar 80237, Bali

☎ 0361-463 245; 0361-229 304

✉ mitrabali@denpasar.wasantara.net.id

■ In the UK: Emily Readett-Bayley

☎ 020-7231 3939

■ In the UK: Travel Friends International (see Responsible tour operators)

Sua Bali   ACCOM+

ToDo! Award winner

A 'mini-resort' of seven traditional guesthouses in a rural setting south of Ubud. A good base for exploring the island on day trips (tours or car hire can be arranged) or simply to relax. The resort also offers classes in local culture/crafts, including language, cookery, batik, woodcarving and herbal medicine. The owner works with the local village: staff, guides, instructors and most of the handicrafts on sale come from the village and guests pay $1 per night to a village fund. From $35 per night, full board. Also tours to Lombok and Sulawesi.

■ Mrs Ida Ayu Agung Mas: PO Box 155, Gianyar 80500, Bali

☎ 0361-941 050 **✆** 0361-941 035

ⓦ www.suabali.co.id **✉** suabali@indosat.net.id

Togean Ecotourism Network   ORG

The Togean islands are a small archipelago off the coast of Sulawesi, renowned for their excellent diving and snorkelling. Local communities have set up eco-sensitive tourism facilities, including boardwalks, and offer guided tours. Visitors can stay in a research centre on Malenge Island. The islands also have attractive rainforest and good birdwatching. Supported by Conservation International (see Responsible tour operators). British Airways Tourism for Tomorrow Awards, highly commended 1998.

■ Togean Ecotourism Network: Jl. Sisingamangaraja No. 10C, Palu

❶ + ❶ 0451-424 205

❷ togean@palu.wasantara.net.id

■ Ary Suhandi: Institute for Indonesian Tourism Studies, Jl Taman Margasatwa 61, Pasar Minggu, Jakarta 12540

❶ 021-7883 8624; 021-7883 8626 ❶ 021-780 0265

Ⓦ http://indecon.i-2.co.id ❷ indecon@cbn.net.id ❷ indecon@indosat@net.id

■ In the UK: Symbiosis Expedition Planning (see Responsible tour operators)

KENYA

International dialling code +254.

Kenya is the top African destination for British tourists. What attracts most of them, of course, is the wildlife in parks such as Amboseli, Tsavo and Maasai Mara. The country also has fine Indian Ocean beaches near Mombasa and Malindi, and most tourists divide their holiday between sea and safari.

The atmospheric Swahili island of Lamu on the north coast is a backpacker favourite. North of Nairobi, there are lakes with rich birdlife, forested highlands around Mount Kenya and, beyond that, the rugged scenery of the Rift Valley.

The far north, around Lake Turkana, is a desert beyond the reach of most tourists but an adventurous target for hardy travellers with time. The fertile south-west, around Lake Victoria, is another little-visited area and the place to see rural Kenyan life away from the tourist zones.

Most of Kenya's parks were created in the 1940s, although Amboseli was set up by Kenya's independent government in 1974, taking land from the Maasai without compensation or a share of tourism revenues. The Maasai argue that, while the government profits from the parks, they get nothing. We list wildlife and safari tours that aim to involve and benefit local communities, including Maasai. As well as wildlife, these tours often allow visitors to meet Maasai people and learn about their life and culture. Many of these community schemes are outside the national parks. But three-quarters of Kenya's wildlife also live outside the parks: in fact, the parks do not protect complete ecosystems and many animals depend upon the surrounding areas for survival.

African Wildlife Foundation (Conservation Services Centre)   ORG
Business support to community tourism projects in Kenya and Tanzania.

■ Richard Young, WEBS: PO Box 48177, Nairobi

☏ 02-710 367 ☏ 02-710 372

✉ ryoung@awfke.org

Amboseli Community Wildlife Tourism Project   ORG
Assists Maasai communities around Amboseli develop tourism programmes to help them benefit from wildlife (and thus have an interest in conserving it). **Kimana** and **Eselenkei** (see below) are part of this project and there are plans to develop tourism in other communities.

■ In the UK: David Lovatt Smith

☏ 01323-833 660 ☏ 01323-833 608

✉ lovatsmith@mistral.co.uk

The Ecotourism Partnership   ORG
A tour agency set up by the Ecotourism Society of Kenya (ESOK) to develop community-based tourism. It has three wildlife tours to less well-known game reserves. These are **Joy Adamson's Camp** in Shaba National Reserve, near Samburu National Park; **Ol Choro** in the Northern Mara Conservation Area, and **Shompole** in the Magadi Conservation Area.

■ PO Box 24295, Nairobi

☏ 02-751 620 ☏ 02-751 677

Eselenkei Community Wildlife Sanctuary   SAFARI
A 8000 hectare wildlife reserve near Amboseli National Park. It has most of the famous African wildlife including lion, leopard, cheetah and occasional migrating elephants, plus rarer species such as lesser kudu and gerenuk. The reserve is owned by the local Maasai community with tours organized in Kenya by a company called Porini Ecotourism.

■ In the UK: Jake Grieves-Cook, Tropical Places: Freshfield House, Forest Row, Sussex RH18 5ES, UK

☏ 01342-825 123 ☏ 01342-826 916

⊛ www.tropical.co.uk ✉ sales@tropical.co.uk

■ In the UK: David Lovatt Smith

☏ 01323-833 660 ☏ 01323-833 608

✉ lovatsmith@mistral.co.uk

Il Ngwesi Lodge ACCOM+/SAFARI

A community-owned lodge on the edge of Samburu National Reserve in northern Kenya. The lodge looks out over wooded plains and hills with plentiful wildlife and consists of four comfortable 'bandas' – thatched rooms on raised platforms. It is available only as a single-party booking, for up to 12 people. 4WD and Samburu-led walking safaris. British Airways Tourism for Tomorrow Awards, finalist 1997.

■ Lewa Wildlife Conservancy: Private Bag ISIOLO

❶ 02-48314 ❶ 02-447310

■ In the UK: Discovery Initiatives (see Responsible tour operators)

IntoAfrica SAFARI/TOUR

'Fair-traded' tours and wildlife safaris in Kenya and northern Tanzania. The company is African with a UK partner. Tours aim to provide insight into local life, environment and culture as well as visiting the wildlife and national parks. The company uses local guides, pays a negotiated fee per visitor to local communities and makes donations to health and education projects. Two-week tours from £1400 per person. Also mountain trekking to Mount Kilimanjaro, Mount Meru and Mount Kenya.

■ IntoAfrica Eco-Travel: PO Box 50484, Nairobi, Kenya

Ⓦ www.intoafrica.co.uk Ⓔ enquiry@intoafrica.co.uk

■ In the UK: Chris Morris: 59 Langdon Street, Sheffield S11 8BH, UK

❶ 0114-255 5610

Kimana Community Wildlife Sanctuary SAFARI

A 4000 hectare Maasai-owned wildlife sanctuary between Amboseli and Tsavo. All the big African wildlife can be seen. Maasai culture plus wildlife viewing on foot led by Maasai guides. Profits to community projects.

■ Kimana Lodge: PO Box 30139, Nairobi

❶ 02-332 334

■ In the UK: David Lovatt Smith

❶ 01323-833 660 ❶ 01323-833 608

Ⓔ lovatsmith@mistral.co.uk

Tawasal Institute ORG/TOUR

Tawasal's main focus is academic trips and placements, but they also organize travel for tourist groups who want grassroots insight into Kenyan life. They can arrange visits to Maasai villages, *dhow* trips and safaris, plus opportunities to learn Swahili and traditional crafts such as beadwork and carving, stays with Kenyan families and visits to development projects.

■ PO Box 248, Lamu

❶ 0121-33584

❷ tawasal@africaonline.co.ke

■ In the US:

❶ 516-733 0153

■ In the UK: Tribes Travel (see Responsible tour operators)

Tortilis Camp SAFARI

A safari camp in Amboseli. A share of income is paid to the local Maasai community. British Airways Tourism for Tomorrow Awards, Southern region winner 1995.

■ Cheli and Peacock, PO Box 39806, Nairobi

❶ 02-748 307; 02-750 485 ❶ 02-750 225

❷ chelipeacock@attmail.com

KYRGYZSTAN

Kyrgyzstan is a mountainous former Soviet republic in Central Asia. Many people still live traditional nomadic lives, herding sheep on high pastures during the summer and living in yurts. There are historic silk-route towns such as Osh, Uzgen and Dzhalalabad, but the country's main attraction is hiking in the mighty Tian Shan and Pamir Alai mountains. Kyrgyzstan is one of the world's great 'undiscovered' trekking destinations, offering big mountain trekking comparable to the Himalaya or the Andes with traditional local cultures and few tourists. The trekking season is June to August.

Karakol Intercultural Programme VOL

Organizes English-teaching volunteer placements (12 hours a week) in return for homestays with local families in Karakol, on the central Asian steppes near the Tian Shan mountains and on the silk route. Programmes run June-September. The aim is to establish continuing friendships that may last beyond the initial holiday.

■ Brian Goddard: brian@kkoluniv.freenet.bishtek.su

Ⓦ www.geocities.com/TheTropics/Cabana/2715/kipintro.html

MALAYSIA

International dialling code +60.

Malaysia has two distinct parts: the Malaysian peninsula between Thailand and Singapore, and Sarawak and Sabah on the island of Borneo. (Most of the rest of Borneo belongs to Indonesia.)

The Iban are the largest ethnic group on Sarawak. Living in a rich region of rainforest and maintaining fairly traditional lifestyles and animist beliefs, the Iban are a popular draw for 'adventure tourists' and backpackers, and many Iban villages host visitors in traditional longhouses – communal buildings in which the whole village lives under one roof.

Ulu Ai   ACCOM+

An Iban village in the rainforest of Sabah on Borneo that hosts visitors in a longhouse in partnership with a private tour operator. Stays offer a glimpse of Iban life, plus guided walks in the forest to spot wildlife, including orang-utan. British Airways Tourism for Tomorrow Awards, highly commended 1994.

■ Borneo Adventures: 55 Main Bazaar, 93000 Kuching (Postal: PO Box 2112, 93741 Kuching), Sarawak

☎ 82-245 175 ☏ 82-422 626

■ In the UK: Symbiosis (see Responsible tour operators), Magic of the Orient: 01293-537 700

MEXICO

International dialling code +52.
Despite the overbearing presence of its powerful northern neighbour, Mexico is a country with a strong identity and culture that expresses itself in distinctive architecture, art, films, music, cooking, religion, pottery and weaving. This culture clearly reflects the *mestizo* ethnicity of most Mexicans, who combine Spanish and indigenous ancestry. This blending is easily seen, for instance, in the colourful imagery of the 'Day of the Dead' on 1 November.

Mexico was another of the great centres of early world civilization – from the Olmecs, Toltecs and Mayans to the Aztecs. When the *conquistadores* arrived, they marvelled at Tenochtitlán, the Aztec predecessor to Mexico City – a beautiful stone city of 300,000 people built in the middle of a lake and as magnificent as any city in Europe. The *conquistadores* destroyed most of this mighty city but there are other superb archaeological sites: the Mayan ruins of the Yucatan peninsula (such as Chichén Itzá), the hilltop city of Monte Alban near Oaxaca and the massive pyramids and ceremonial avenues of Teotihuacán on the outskirts of Mexico City.

Many tourists fly in and out of the package holiday destinations of Acapulco on the Pacific coast or Cancún on the Yucatan. But Mexico is a large country with much more to see and do. Ecotourists head for the wild (although shrinking) rainforest of the southern Yucatan or Chiapas, or the finger-like Baja California peninsula in the north, with its great beaches, sea-kayaking and whalewatching, or the mighty Copper Canyon – twice the size of the Grand Canyon – in the dry northern Sierras.

Indigenous culture is strongest in the south, in Oaxaca, Chiapas and the Yucatan. Oaxaca and San Cristóbal de la Casas, the capital of Chiapas, are especially famous for their handicrafts.

The Zapatista uprising, which began in 1994, draws its support largely from the indigenous population in Chiapas. Foreigners suspected of sympathizing with the rebels have been deported and parts of Chiapas may not be safe. The website of SIPAZ, the International Service for Peace – www.nonviolence.org/sipaz – provides updates on the security situation, while those interested in the conflict should see the EZLN (Zapatistas) supporters' website on www.ezln.org.

Many rural communities in Mexico are officially organized as *ejidos* with elected village councils; many of the facilities listed below are managed by these *ejidos* (although they may be part of wider government schemes such as the Tourist Yu'u or FONAES).

A good guidebook with more information on ecotourism and community tourism in Mexico, including many projects listed here, is *Mexico: Adventures in Nature* by Ron Mader (Santa Fe: John Muir Publications, 1998). You can order the book from Ron's excellent www.planeta.com website on Mexico and Latin America.

Agua Clara/Misol-Ha ACCOM+

Two attractive community-owned hotels near the spectacular cascades of Agua Azul in Chiapas. The Hotel Sna Ajaw is 50 kilometres from Palenque on the banks of the Rio Shumulhá in the *ejido* of **Agua Clara**. Canoes/kayaks for rent. $30 per night. **Misol-Ha** has cabins and a restaurant beside a lovely waterfall, 20 kilometres south of Palenque. A great swimming spot.

■ Agua Clara: Andrés Cruz López

🟠 01-934 50 356; 01-934 51 210. Or c/o STAACH: Tuxtla Gutiérra

🟠 961-11410 🟠 + 🟠 934-51130

🟢 jkinalti@chisnet.com.mx 🟢 staach@laneta.apc.org

■ Misol Ha: Estaban Pérez López

🟠 + 🟠 934-51210

Agua Selva Ecotourism Project ACCOM+

A scheme to develop community-based guesthouses in the villages of the **Sierra Huimanguillo** south of Villahermosa. The Sierra has great hiking, caves, canyons, waterfalls, wildlife and pre-Colombian ruins. There are two guesthouses in **Malpasito** (the budget Albergue Ecológico and the comfortable, secluded Albergue La Pava just outside town) and another, Cabana Raizes Zoque, in **Mujica**, where there are also local guides. In **Huimanguillo**, the Cafeteria Orquidias (or the pleasant Hotel del Carmen upstairs) has information on the project.

■ George Pagole del Valle: Hotel del Carmen, Morelos 39, Huimanguillo, Tabasco

🟠 + 🟠 937-50915

Botadero San Pastor   ACCOM/BUDGET

A community-owned tourist centre with cabañas and camping in a peaceful
setting on the shores of Bacalar lagoon, 30 kilometres inland from Chetumal in
the Yucatan. Kayaks for hire.

■ Raúl Tirriza

❶ 01-983 29 610 **❶** 01-983 28 284

CICE (Centro Internacional para la Cultura y Ensenanza de la
Lengua)   TOUR/SCHOOL

Cuernavaca, one hour from Mexico City, is a lively city and a popular centre
for Spanish immersion courses. CICE offers tuition in Spanish and Náhuatl
plus homestays with local families. It also runs a twice-yearly programme of
workshops in traditional ancient medicine, including Aztec sweat lodge, plant
use, massage etc. Two week courses: $350. Lodging from $15 per night. Part of
the income from the programmes goes to local health clinics for low-income
families and other community projects. CICE also organizes tours with the
US-based Rethinking Tourism Project.

■ Estela Roman: Apartado Postal 1-166, Cuernavaca, Morelos, Mexico CP 62001

❶ 073-250 683 **❶** + **❶** 073-124 468

ℯ cice@laneta.apc.org

■ In the US: Rethinking Tourism Project (see Responsible tour operators)

FONAES   ORG

A section of the Mexican government's Department of Social Development
that supports rural development, including community-based tourism. Their
website features many of the projects listed here, plus additional projects.

❶ 05-273 2665; 05-515 6666

ⓦ www.fonaes.gob.mx **ℯ** fonmicro@fonaes.gob.mx

Grupo Ecologico Sierra Gorda   ORG/TOUR

A non-profit group promoting conservation and community development in a
biosphere reserve of rugged hills, canyons and forests near Querétaro, 300
kilometres north of Mexico City. Small-group ecotours and naturalist guides.
Good walking, biking, horseriding, birdwatching and wildlife (jaguar, black
bear, monarch butterfly, peregrine falcon, macaw).

■ Martha Isabel Ruiz Corzo: Grupo Ecological Sierra Gorda, Juarez 9, Col Centro,
Jalpan de Serra, Querétaro CP76340

❶ + **❶** 429-60242; 429-60222

ℯ sierrago@ciateq.mx **ℯ** sierrago@sparc.ciateq.conacyt.mx

Las Canadas
ACCOM+/TOUR

A private cloudforest reserve east of Puebla (between Mexico City and Veracruz) which works with local communities and provides training in sustainable agriculture to local farmers. Tourist facilities include cabins, organic meals, marked trails in the cloudforest, weekend guided tours, mountain biking, hiking, birdwatching, workshops in organic farming and medicinal plants. Three-day packages: $200.

■ Ricardo Romero: AP 24, Huatusco, Veracruz 94100

❶ + ❶ 273-41577

Ⓦ www.edg.net.mx/empresas/niebla Ⓔ niebla@edg.net.mx

Maruata 2000
ACCOM+/BUDGET

Fourteen communally-owned cabañas in the Náhuatl village of Maruata 2000, near Aquila on the Michoacán coast just south of Colima. A contrast to Acapulco and other big resorts, it offers a good beach in a quiet setting plus guided nature tours, a turtle/iguana conservation project, fishing, etc. From $5 per night. Horses, boats and bicycles for rent.

■ Ezequiel García Palacios: Caseta Maruata, Aquila, Michoacán

❶ 01-332 50368

Maya Ik/Yaxche, Arbol de la Vida
ORG

Two separate organizations that work, often together, to assist Mayan and other indigenous communities in southern Mexico, including community tourism projects. In the Yucatan, these include the **Nohoch-tunich cabañas** near Tulum and, further south, horseriding and guiding in **Felipe Carrillo Puerto** (Carlos Meade: tel: 983-40842) in the heart of the 'zona Maya'. Nearer Merida, the Mayan community of **Rio Lagartos** (Juan Velazco: tel: 992-60481) offers boat trips into the Rio Celestun Biosphere Reserve with good birdwatching (flamingos and ibis). Near Villahermosa in Tabasco, the Chontal community of **Nacajuc** runs an animal sanctuary with manatees, alligators, etc, and demonstrates traditional agricultural techniques and handicrafts. The Maya Ik office in San Cristobal de las Casas arranges tours to the surrounding villages and both organizations can recommend local guides.

■ Maya Ik: Margarito Ruiz: San Cristobal de las Casas, Chiapas

❶ + ❶ 967-86998

Ⓔ mayaik@sancristobal.podernet.com.mx

■ Victor Sumuhano, Yaxche Arbol de la Vida: Altos SM4, 77500 Cancun, Quintana Roo

❶ + ❶ 98-877 248/9

Ⓔ vikingo2@qroo1.telmex.net.mx

Monte Azules Biosphere Reserve/Selva Lacandona   RAINFOREST

The Lacandón rainforest south of Palenque merges with the Petén forest of Guatemala to form the largest area of rainforest north of the Amazon. Wildlife includes howler monkeys, jaguars, scarlet macaws, toucans and crocodiles. The area includes the Mayan ruins of Bonampak, Yaxchilán, Chan Kin and Lacantum and the Monte Azules Biosphere Reserve. Many of the inhabitants of the forest are indigenous Lacandón. There are various community-based cabañas and guides in the area, including **Las Guacamayas** in the *ejido* of Reforma Agraria (140 kilometres from Palenque on the road to Frontera Corozal), **Escudo Jaguar** on the Usumacinta river in Frontera Corozal (supported by Conservation International and FONAES), **Ara Macao** (near Frontera Corozal), **Lacanja Chansayab** (also near Frontera Corozal: guided tours to Bonampak) and **Emiliano Zapata**. This last community is near a large lake, Lake Miramar, where they have built a simple lodge. In all these places, accommodation costs approximately $30 per night with guided tours from $5–$10 per day. Near the reserve, **Ixcan Lodge and campsite** is another community-run project aided by Conservation International.

■ Ara Macao

❶ 01-5201 5979; 01-5201 5928

■ Maya Ik (see above)

❶ 961-53476; 961-13624; 961-13228

■ Escudo Jaguar: Luis Arcos-Pérez, domicilio conocido, Frontera Corozal, Chiapas

❶ 934-50356; 01-5201 6441 ❶ 01-5201 6440

■ Las Guacamayas: STAACH, Tuxtla Gutiérrez

❶ 961-11410

✉ jkinalti@chisnet.com.mx ✉ staach@laneta.apc.org

■ Emiliano Zapata/Lake Miramar: Dana Foundation, La Casa de Pan, Dr Navarro 10, Barrio El Cerrillo, San Cristobal de las Casas

❶ 967-80468 ❶ 967-84307

✉ danamex@mail.internet.com.mz

■ Ixcan Lodge/campsite: Conservation International Mexico

❶ + ❶ 56-31 3032

✉ ci-mexico@conservation.org

San José el Hueyate   ACCOM+

Community-run cabañas and a restaurant in a village on the south Chiapas coast, close to the Guatemalan border. Beaches, surfing, good wetlands birding, boat trips, watersports. Supported by FONAES.

■ Samuel Hidalgo de la Cruz/Daniel Eslava Ibarra

❶ 01-962 53 940

Sian Ka'an Biosphere Reserve   DAY

A 528,000-hectare biosphere reserve on the Yucatan coast that includes tropical forest, mangroves, beaches and coral reef. Good bird and wildlife includes jaguar, puma, ocelot, howler monkey, tapir, manatee, turtles and crocodiles. The non-profit group **Amigos de Sian Ka'an** organizes trips to the reserve from Cancún and Tulum, run by **Lomas Travel** in Cancún. The organization works with local communities to help them benefit from conservation.

■ Amigos de Sian Ka'an: Piso 3, Plaza America, Av Cobá 5, Postal: Apartado Postal 770), Cancún 77500, Quintana Roo

☎ 98-84 9583 ☎ 98-87 3080

@ sian@cancun.rce.com.mx

■ Lomas Travel

☎ 98-87 1970/1

Sierra Tarahumara   ACCOM+

The rugged Sierra Tarahumara is one of Mexico's most scenic regions with vast canyons, bizarre rock formations, lakes, caves and waterfalls. The Sierra is great for hiking or mountain biking and biologically diverse: the high plateau has cool pine forest and snow, while in the canyons the climate is subtropical. Creel is a popular and pleasant base for exploring the Sierra. The *Chihuahua al Pacífico* railway is a one of the world's great train journeys, with 87 tunnels and 37 bridges in its spectacular 16-hour, 500-kilometre climb from the coast. The local Tarahumara are north America's second largest indigenous people (after the Navajo) and preserve many traditional beliefs and ceremonies. Many Tarahumara want little to do with outsiders, but a few communities are involved in tourism. **Arareko** is a community-run tourist complex in San Ignacio, a Tarahumara village. Facilities include a hotel, cabañas, a museum, café and souvenir shop. There are bicycles and horses for rent and guided tours in the canyons and Sierra. Accommodation: $6 or $25 per night. Guides: $10 for a half-day trek. 20 kilometres south of Creel, **Cusárare** is another Tarahumara community developing tourism facilities. Slightly further away, the **Hostal de Uruachi** is a community-run hostel near the Uruachi canyon. A six-bed cabin costs $60 per night. Guided horseback trips: $10. Nearby, the 453m Piedra Volada waterfall in Basaseachi Falls National Park is Mexico's highest. There are also rustic community-run cabins at **Cueva de los Leones**, just outside the village of Bocayna near Creel.

■ Arareko: Tomás Alvino Toribio

☎ + ☎ 01-145 60126 or FONAES Chihuahua ☎ 914-130627

■ Uruachi: Fernando Domíngez, Parque Nacional de Basaséachi, Chihuahua

☎ 01-1415 7951; 01-1415 9717

■ Cueva de los Leones: Rigoberto Rodríguez Yánez

❶ 01-1429 3421; 01-1456 0176

■ FONAES: (see below)

Taselotzin   ACCOM/BUDGET
Cabañas in wooded hills near the village of Cuetzalan, north of Puebla (to the south of Mexico City). The complex is run by a local women's craft organization called Maseualsiuame Mosenyolchikauani. Nearby attractions include the ancient pyramids of Yohualichan, plus walks, forest, caves and waterfalls.

■ Juana María Nicolasa Chepe: Barrio Zacatipan, Cuetzalan, Puebla

❶ 01-233 10 480

Tourist Yú'u, Oaxaca   ACCOM
A programme of small, locally-run guesthouses (with self-catering and camping facilities) in the villages in Oaxaca's Central Valley. The scheme was set up by SEDETUR (the state tourist agency) to generate income for the communities. There are Tourist Yú'u in nine villages: Teotitlán, Benito Juárez, Tlacolula de Matamoros, Quialana, Tlapazola, Santa Ana del Valle, Santa Cruz Papaluta, San Sebastian Abasolo and Hierve el Agua. Most of these villages also have community museums. (See **Union de Museos Comunitarios de Oaxaca**, below.) This is arguably the best region in Mexico for indigenous traditions, crafts and fiestas, while the amazing Zapotec ruins of Monte Alban are nearby. Most of the villages in the scheme are quiet and off the beaten track. The most visited is **Hierve el Agua**, where there is a remarkable petrified waterfall and hot springs. $5 per night.

■ SEDETUR: Independencia 607, Oaxaca

❶ 951-60123; 951-64828 ❶ 951-60984

Union de Museos Comunitarios de Oaxaca   CENTRE/ORG
The Union de Museos represents 18 villages around Oaxaca that have (or are setting up) small museums. It also organizes one- and two-day tours to the villages focusing on local rural life and crafts – cooking, weaving, pottery, etc – and may be able to arrange lessons in these crafts. There is also cycling, horseriding, hiking trips in the area's hills, caves, natural springs and archaeological sites. Villages with museums include San José el Mogote, Teotitlán, Santa Ana, Tlaxiaco, San Miguel el Progreso, Santa María Cuquila, San Martin Huamelulpan and Santiago Suchilquitongo. See also Tourist Yú'u, above.

■ Tinoco y Palacios 311-12, Col. Centro, Oaxaca OAX CP 68000

❶ + ❶ 951-65786

ⓦ http://antequera.com/muscoax ⓔ muscoax@antequera.com

MOROCCO

At its closest, Morocco is only a few kilometres from Europe. Yet its culture and landscapes can seem a world away. Morocco has a rich cultural heritage, isolated mountain villages, desert oasis communities and historic cities such as Fez and Marrakesh, with their fantastic architecture and enormous markets (*kasbahs*). It has mountains as well as desert: you can ride a camel through the Sahara and then hike or even ski in the Atlas Mountains. Moroccans are a mix of Arabic Muslims and indigenous tribal people, such as the Berbers. Small areas of the country, mainly the northern ports, have a reputation for hassling tourists, but once you travel south you'll find people are friendly and welcoming.

Tizi-Randonnées   TOUR
A Berber-owned company offering 'soft adventure' tours throughout Morocco, including trekking in the High Atlas mountains. They work with about 30 different communities around the country and money from their trips goes to community development projects.

■ In the UK: Tribes Travel (see Responsible tour operators)

NAMIBIA

International dialling code +264.
Namibia has no white sandy beaches, warm tropical waters or big hotels, so does not appeal to mass tourism. What it does have is fantastic scenery: huge tracts of pristine and virtually empty wilderness with stunning wildlife. In vast open areas such as the Namib-Naukluft National Park, you can drive for hours through endless deserts, plains, huge mountain massifs and spectacular canyons without seeing a soul. Namibia is four times the size of Britain with a population of 1.5 million, little industry and virtually no pollution, so you look up at the clearest stars you'll ever see. The Namib Desert has plants and animals found nowhere else on earth. The famous Skeleton Coast is the resting place of dozens of shipwrecks. And Namibia's wilderness is easy to explore independently – even in Etosha, one of Africa's top parks, driving around is easy – and prices are lower than elsewhere in southern Africa.

Namibia's tiny population includes a wide diversity of ethnic groups, such as the Himba, San (Bushmen) and Damara. A number of these communities are now becoming involved in tourism, usually by setting up basic campsites. Indeed, Namibia is one of the best African countries for community-based tourism projects, at least partly due to the efforts of organizations such as the **IRDNC** (see below). Some privately owned lodges have also set up cultural side projects involving local communities.

For more detailed information, contact either **NACOBTA** (see below) or see *Namibia: The Bradt Travel Guide* by Chris McIntyre (Bradt Publications). This is one of the first mainstream guidebooks to any country to include comprehensive information about community-based tourism and is therefore recommended.

Aba Huab Community Campsite ACCOM+

An attractive, well-managed community-run campsite in Damaraland, with shady camping spots or A-frame shelters. Guided walks or donkey rides can be arranged, including visits to the important rock-art site of Twyfelfontein. Camping: £2–£3 per night.

■ Elias Aro Xoagub: PO Box 131, Twyfelfontein via Khorixas

■ In the UK: Sunvil Holidays (see Responsible tour operators)

Damaraland Camp ACCOM+/SAFARI

This camp in northern Damaraland was developed by the South African company Wilderness Safaris in partnership with **IRDNC** (see below), WWF and the local Damara community. It features guided nature walks, birdwatching, wildlife and spectacular scenery. The local community are joint owners of the lodge and receive ten per cent of all income. In ten years, the lodge will become fully community owned. £120–£200 per day.

■ Namib Wilderness Safaris, PO Box 5048, Windhoek

❶ 061-225 178 ❶ 061-239 455

■ In the UK: Sunvil Holidays (see Responsible tour operators)

Etendeka Mountain Camp SAFARI

A comfortable tented safari camp on the Etendeka plains of northern Damaraland. The camp give a percentage of income to local communities. Guided nature walks, birdwatching, wildlife, spectacular scenery. £80–£110 per day including meals, drives and walks.

■ PO Box 21783, Windhoek

❶ 061-226 979 ❶ 061-226 999

Intu Afrika Kalahari Game Reserve SAFARI

A privately-owned wildlife lodge and game reserve near Mariental in the Kalahari Desert. Good wildlife including meerkats, zebra, springbok, giraffe and wildebeest. Guests can visit a community of about 40 !Xoo Bushmen, who lead guided walks to spot wildlife and demonstrate traditional cooking, gathering, crafts, etc. Lodge: £100 per night; some cheaper tents are also available. Bushman tours extra. (Note: there is some controversy over whether the lodge is paying the Bushman community a fair rate.)

■ PO Box 40047, Windhoek

❶ 061-248 741/2/4/5 ❶ 061-226 535

IRDNC (Integrated Rural Development and Nature Conservation)
ORG
A well-established organization that supports rural communities in Namibia. It has been involved in establishing community-tourism projects at **Damaraland**, **Etendeka** and **Lianshulu Lodges**, **Khowrib** Camp (all listed in this section) and **N//goavaca Camp** at **Popa Falls** in the Caprivi Strip.

■ Garth Owen-Smith/Margaret Jacobsohn: Palamway, Box 1715, Swakopmund

✆ 061-228 282

✉ irdnc@iafrica.com.na

Kaokohimba Safaris
TOUR
Tours to the remote, rugged desert of Kaokoland in northern Namibia, inland from the Skeleton Coast, featuring walking, wildlife, desert scenery. Kaokohimba also run adventurous donkey-treks of up to 12 days led by Himba guides, and are involved in a number of community development projects with local Himba communities. Two-day tours: £450; six days £800.

■ Koos Verwey, Kaokohimba Safaris, PO Box 11580, Windhoek

✆ + 📠 061-222 378

Khowarib Camp
ACCOM+
Community-owned accommodation near Warmquelle in northern Damaraland, consisting of seven traditionally built huts and camping space. Guided walks and camel rides. £3–£4 per night. Nearby, the **Anmire Traditional Village** is run by a Damara community and provides an insight into Damara life and culture.

Lianshulu Lodge Safari
SAFARI+
A private lodge on the banks of the Kwando River in Mudumu National Park, eastern Caprivi. Good birdwatching and wildlife (hippos, elephants, crocodiles, etc). A percentage of income goes to local communities and the lodge has supported various community-based conservation projects. A stay at the lodge can be combined with a day tour to nearby **Lizauli Traditional Village**, where local people demonstrate traditional crafts and you can learn about local life, music, medicine, etc. Lianshulu: £80 per night. Lizauli: £3 entry.

■ PO Box 142, Katima Mulilo

✆ (c/o Namibia Mirages): 061-214 744 📠 061-214 746

■ Wilderness Safaris (see South Africa)

■ In the UK: Sunvil Holidays (see Responsible tour operators)

NACOBTA (Namibian Community Based Tourism Association) ORG
NACOBTA represents and promotes 21 community camps, museums and

tours – including many listed here – and is helping 16 more communities set up tourism enterprises. NACOBTA is not a travel agency but can provide contacts for individual projects and is planning to set up a central booking system in Windhoek.

■ Andee Davidson/Maxi Louis: 18 Lilliencron St, (Postal: PO Box 86099), Windhoek

☎ 061-250 558 ✆ 061-222 647

✉ nacobta@iafrica.com.na

Nyae Nyae Conservancy/Development Foundation   ORG

The Nyae Nyae Conservancy is a game area in the Kalahari, near Tsumkwe, belonging to local Bushman communities. The Development Foundation – an NGO which helped set up the conservancy – is planning various community-based tourism projects, including camps and wildlife/cultural tours, and hopes to open a tourist office in Tsumkwe soon.

☎ 061-236 327 ✆ 061-225 997

✉ nndfn@iafrica.com.na.

Omatako Valley Rest Camp   ACCOM+

A campsite run by a !Kung San community in Bushmanland, on the road between Groofontein and Tsumkwe, plus some *rondavels* (huts). Tours and guided walks are available, including game viewing, birdwatching, horseriding, dance performances. There are also 'bush food' meals and crafts for sale. Camping: £2–£3 per night. Half-day tours: £10.

■ PO Box 1391, Grootfontein

■ John Arnold: Private Bag 2093, Omatako

Ongongo Camp   ACCOM+

A community-run campsite near Warmquelle in northern Damaraland, with the beautiful Blinkwater waterfall nearby. £2–£3 per night.

Purros (Ngatutunge Pamue) Campsite   ACCOM+

A community-run campsite in a Himba community in northern Damaraland, set up with help from the IRDNC (see above). Local guides lead walking safaris, walks to find medicinal plants and visits to Himba villages. Camping: £3–£4 per night. Guides: £5 per half-day.

■ 100 kilometres north of Sesfontein, near Purros village. (Post: c/o IRDNC: see above)

Salambala Campsite   ACCOM

Community-run campsite in the Caprivi Strip, 50 kilometres south of Katima Mulilo. £4–£5 per night.

Sunvil Discovery
SAFARI+/TOUR

A mainstream British tour operator which tries harder than most to practice responsible tourism and is a good choice for Namibia. They market a number of the lodges featured in this section, including **Tsumkwe Lodge, Damaraland Camp, Lianshulu Lodge** and **Etendeka Camp**. Brochure. ATOL-bonded.

■ Chris McIntyre: Sunvil Discovery, Sunvil House, Upper Square, Old Isleworth, TW7 7BJ, UK

☏ 020-8232 9777   ☏ 020-8568 8330

🌐 www.sunvil.co.uk   ✉ africa@sunvil.co.uk

Tsumkwe Lodge
SAFARI+

A safari lodge in Bushmanland in the Kalahari Desert, just outside the town of Tsumkwe. As well as wildlife, visitors can visit local !Kung Bushman villages, and take part in such daily activities as hunting, gathering and tracking. Although the lodge is privately owned, guests pay the community directly for these activities. Lodge: £30 per day. Local guides for community tours: £12 per hour.

■ Arno/Eselle Oosthuysen: PO Box 1899, Tsumeb

☏ + ☏ 067-220 060

WIMSA (Working Group of Indigenous Minorities in Southern Africa) ORG

An advocacy group for the San (Bushmen). Has helped San communities to negotiate with tourist lodges, tour operators, etc.

■ Linda Vanherck, tourism worker: PO Box 80733, Windhoek

☎ 61-244 909 **✆** 61-272 806

ⓔ wimsareg@iafrica.com.na

NEPAL

International dialling code +977.

The big draw in Nepal, of course, is trekking in the Himalaya. Most tourists come to trek, and the majority head for Everest Base Camp, the Langtang Valley or Annapurna.

Kathmandu is a vibrant, bustling capital that still manages to feel like an overgrown village, while the Kathmandu valley offers a gentler mix of rural life, plus historic temples and towns. Heading down towards the Indian border there are tropical forests, including the well-known Chitwan National Park.

Trails in the Nepalese Himalaya tend to follow existing local pathways through the valleys. Rather than remote wilderness, you are walking along well-used paths and constantly passing through villages, many of which provide food and lodgings for trekkers. This means you see a lot of local life and this can be one of the pleasures of trekking in Nepal. But it also means that tourists need to be aware of their impact on local people and on a fragile environment.

Our own Himalayan Code, drawn up with the **ACAP (Annapurna Conservation Area Project)**, offers guidelines concerning the environment and local culture. The **IPPG (International Porter Protection Group)** has also produced a code covering the employment of local porters. Not only are porters poorly paid, but every year porters die because trekkers and tour leaders fail to provide proper medical attention or adequate clothing in the mountains. Porters suffering from altitude sickness are often sent down unaccompanied. See 'Responsible tourism codes' in Section Three of this book. ACAP and IPPG are both listed below.

ACAP (Annapurna Conservation Area Project) ORG

An organization that uses trekking fees for protecting the environment and local culture, and to fund community development projects. Part of the King Mahendra Trust for Nature Conservation.

■ PO Box 183, Pokhara, Nepal

☎ 061-21102; 28202 **✆** 061-28203

ⓔ acap@mos.com.np

Explore Nepal TOUR

A trekking company committed to good employment and conservation practices. It also donates to community and environmental projects, such as reforestation schemes.

■ In the UK: Tribes Travel (see Responsible tour operators)

Himalayan Foundation for Integrated Mountain Development ORG

A non-profit organization helping local communities in the Sallery region of Solu Khumbu to develop tourism businesses. The region, near Everest, is expecting a large growth in trekkers in the next few years. The project includes training for local people and the development of a visitor centre to promote responsible tourism.

■ Himalayan Foundation for Integrated Mountain Development, Solu Khumbu Sallery, PO Box 4995, Kathmandu

Ⓦ www.nepal-connect.com/hf Ⓔ hf@sallery.wlink.com.np

IPPG (International Porter Protection Group) ORG

A campaign to improve conditions and safety for trekking porters in the Himalaya.

■ Prakash Adhikari: Himalayan Rescue Association, PO Box 4944, Thamel, Kathmandu (see 'Responsible tourism organizations and resources' for UK, US and Australian contacts)

Ⓔ hra@aidpost.mos.com.np

KEEP (Kathmandu Environmental Educational Project) ORG

KEEP is a non-profit organization that provides advice on low-impact trekking and tourism in Nepal to tourists and local communities. It has a visitor centre in the Thamel district of Kathmandu which it shares with the **Himalayan Explorers Club** (www.hec.org). This includes useful trekking information, a library and the Keep Green coffee shop.

■ Partemba Sherpa/PT Sherpa Kerung: KEEP, Jyatha Road, Thamel (Postal: PO Box 9178), Kathmandu

Ⓣ 01-259 567; 01-259 275 Ⓕ 01-411 533

Ⓦ www.nepal-connect.com/keep Ⓔ tour@keep.wlink.com.np

Muir's Tours TOUR

A non-profit tour operator run from the UK, but set up by the Nepal Kingdom Foundation. Tours are mainly trekking and mountain-based adventure travel. Also cultural tours. Profits go to charities and local development projects.

■ Maurice Adshead: 97a Swansea Road, Reading RG1 8HA, UK

Ⓣ 0118-950 2281 Ⓕ 0118-950 2301

Ⓦ www.nkf-mt.org.uk Ⓔ info@nkf-mt.org.uk

Trekking to make a difference **Specialist Trekking**
Nepal ● Tibet ● Bhutan

SPECIALIST TREKKING

Trekking ● Walking ● Culture ● Mountain biking ● Whitewater rafting ● Jungle safaris ●
Climbing ● Standard/tailor-made treks/holidays. ● Call today for a free colour brochure and
discover how your holiday can support your host country's economy.

Tel: 01228 562358. email: Trekstc@aol.com
Community Action Nepal... building firm foundations (reg charity no 1067772)

The Nepal Trust   ORG/TOUR

The Nepal Trust is a Scottish charity that works with local communities in Nepal to develop health, education and other community projects. It runs annual treks that combine trekking with work on a community project such as building a health clinic or restoring religious sites. The Trust is also helping the **Women's Welfare Service** – a local NGO in the Humla region of Nepal – to develop a women's trekking cooperative and a guesthouse/restaurant in Simikot. The Trust can arrange educational programmes in Humla, including study of local culture, herbal medicine, religion and environment, plus work on community projects.

■ In Nepal (office in Kathmandu)

t 01-429 112 **f** 01-436 224

e ntrust@chun.mos.com.np

■ In the UK: PO Box 5864, Forres, Moray IV36 3WB, Scotland, UK

t + **f** 01309-691 994

w www.thenepaltrust.demon.co.uk **e** admin@thenepaltrust.demon.co.uk

Specialist Trekking   TOUR

Trips to popular regions such as Everest Base Camp and Langtang Valley, plus off-the-beaten-track destinations such as Mustang, Dolpo and Kangchenjunga or Makalu base camps. Also climbing trips. From £1400 to £2000 for 17- to 31-day tours. Trips are led by Nepali guides and profits go to schools and health projects in rural Nepalese communities. Brochure available. Passenger Protection bonding.

■ Specialist Trekking: Chapel House, Low Cotehill, Carlisle, Cumbria CA4 0EL, UK

t 01228-562 358 **f** 01228-562 368

w www.specialisttrekking.com **e** trekstc@aol.com

NEW ZEALAND – MAORI TOURISM

International dialling code +64.
The Maoris of New Zealand have fared slightly better than many other First Nations peoples: Maoris don't suffer the extreme health problems and discrimination of, say, the Australian Aboriginals. In some areas, too (notably Rotorua and Kaikoura), Maori tourism is well integrated into the mainstream tourism industry. In Rotorua, in particular, Maori tourism is geared to coach parties and high turnover rather than in-depth cultural insight, with up to 200 people a night for cultural shows. It does, however, generate income for Maori communities and helps to preserve traditional crafts such as woodcarving.

Aotearoa Maori Tourism Federation   ORG
Established in 1988 to promote Maori Tourism.

■ PO Box 6104, Rotorua

❶ 21-963 083

Main Street Backpackers and Te Wero Nui Cultural Centre, Kaitaia
ACCOM+
Kaitaia is the northernmost town in New Zealand, with a large Maori population. Te Wero Nui is a Maori cultural centre that offers marae stays and cultural activities. Main Street Backpackers is New Zealand's first Maori-run hostel and also arranges cultural tours, plus trips to Cape Reinga and Ninety-Mile Beach.

■ Te Wero Nui

❶ + ❶ 09-408 4884

❷ tall-tale-tours@xtra.co.nz

■ Main Street Backpackers, Peter Kitchen: 235 Commerce Street, Kaitaia

❶ 09-408 1275 (0508-624 678) ❶ 09-408 1100

Ⓦ www.tall-tale.co.nz ❷ mainstreet@extra.co.nz

Maori Tourism Directory   ORG
A section of an excellent website produced by the Ministry of Maori Development (Te Puni Kokiri), this is about as complete a guide to Maori tourism as you could wish for.

Ⓦ www.tpk.govt.nz/tourcont.htm

Rotorua   DAY
There are a number of Maori tourist enterprises in this touristy town. They offer short (eg two-hour) cultural tours, a look inside a *marae, hangii* feasts and dance shows. They cater for a mass market and the cultural experience is superficial, but they are successful Maori-run community enterprises. They include **Whakarewarewa** (incorporating the **National Maori Arts and Crafts Institute**)

(tel: 07-348 9047); Magic of Maori concerts at Ohinemutu village (tel: 07-349 3949) and **Tamaki Tours** (tel: 07-346 2823).

Whale Watch Kaikoura   DAY

Whalewatching boat tours. No cultural element, but this company is a successful Maori-owned business that invests some profits into cultural education. Kaikoura is a largely Maori town two hours' north of Christchurch and is one of the best places on earth to see giant sperm-whales, plus dolphins, seals and other whale species. British Airways Tourism for Tomorrow Awards, winner 1994.

■ PO Box 89, Kaikoura, South Island

✆ 03-319 5045 ☏ 03-319 5160

Ⓦ www.whalewatch.co.nz Ⓔ admin@whalewatch.co.nz

NICARAGUA

International dialling code +505.

Nicaragua is the largest country in Central America and the least visited. There is little indigenous culture, most of the country is oppressively hot and humid and Managua is a less-than-attractive capital. In the 1980s, idealistic foreigners joined voluntary work brigades in support of the Sandinista regime. Today, a few tourists – mainly backpackers – come to Nicaragua for the crafts market of Masaya, surfing on the Pacific coast, hiking in the lush volcanic highlands near Matagalpa, and the islands in Lago de Nicaragua (see below). For anyone wanting to get off the 'tourist trail', however, Nicaragua can be a rewarding destination, with vibrant culture and arts, a complex, heroic recent history and exceptionally hospitable and articulate people.

The steamy Caribbean coast is virtually a separate country, cut off from western Nicaragua by a lack of roads. Its inhabitants are mostly indigenous Miskito, Rama or Suma or descendants of black slaves. Music and culture is Caribbean rather than Latin American and most people speak English rather than Spanish.

Fundación Entre Volcanes/Isla de Ometepe   ACCOM/DAY/ORG

Isla de Ometepe is one of Nicaragua's prime attractions: a distinctive 'double-island' rising out of the waters of Lago de Nicaragua, its two towering volcanoes linked by a narrow isthmus. The island's fertile lower slopes support rich tropical crops and patches of rainforest, while visitors come for the peaceful atmosphere and for horseriding, walking and climbing the volcanoes. The **Fundación Entre Volcanes** is a locally-run organization which acts as a tourist office and offers day tours and hikes. $5–$20 per day. There are small hotels on the island.

■ Fundación Entre Volcanes: Moyogalpa. Isla de Ometepe

✆ 459 4188

PAKISTAN

Pakistan is not well known as a tourist destination but for mountain lovers the far north, bordered by Ladakh, Kashmir and China, is an undiscovered jewel. The region contains the greatest concentrations of high peaks on earth, including sixty peaks over 7000 metres and four over 8000 metres. There are amazing trekking opportunities with none of the crowds of Nepal. These include K2 base camp and the Deosai plains, and wildlife includes the elusive snow leopards and Himalayan bears. Indigenous languages here are related to Tibetan and the region was predominantly Buddhist until the 15th century.

Full Moon Night Trekking   TOUR
Trekking holidays to the Karakoram and Himalayan mountains of Baltistan in northern Pakistan. Treks in prime snow-leopard habitat (with a chance to spot this endangered cat), plus other treks with different themes (conservation, nature, culture) and levels of difficulty. Also tailor-made treks. All treks involve staying with local people and using local guides, with a strong element of local management. Profits go to local community and conservation projects. Tours start from Skardu, one hour's flight from Islamabad. From £800 for a 10–12-day trek, excluding international flights.

◼ 9a Avonmore Mansions, Avonmore Road, London W14 8RN, UK

➊ 020-7603 9893

Ⓦ www.fmntrekking.com Ⓔ info@fmntrekking.com

PALESTINE

International dialling code +9722.
Bethlehem is just about the only place in the West Bank and Gaza that tourists ever see. An estimated one million tourists visit the city each year but most come on Israeli-run day trips that have little benefit for local people.

International Centre of Bethlehem   ACCOM+

An organization trying to help local people benefit from tourism. The centre
has opened a guesthouse and runs city tours and a crafts shop, and is training
local people for jobs in tourism.

■ Dr Mitri Raheb: Evangelical Lutheran Christmas Church, PO Box 162, Bethlehem,
West Bank, via Israel

t 647 0047 **f** 647 0048

e annadwa@planet.edu

PANAMA

International dialling code +507.

Panama is one of the least-visited Central American nations. It's also one of the
most expensive and certain parts – notably Colon – have a reputation for
robbery and muggings. Crossing the Darien Gap is one of Latin America's great
adventures, but may be unsafe due to smuggling activity. On the other hand,
most of the country away from these danger spots is pleasant and safe, with
good hiking near the Costa Rican border and the largest indigenous population
in Central America outside of Guatemala. The main region of interest for
community-based tourism is the beautiful San Blas Islands. This archipelago of
365 tropical islands (40 of which are inhabited) off Panama's Caribbean coast
is the semi-autonomous homeland of the Kuna. The *Rough Guide to Central
America* has good details on Kuna and Comarca Emberá tourism.

Puerto Indio/Comarca Emberá   BUDGET/RAINFOREST

Puerto Indio, on the edge of the Darién National Park, is the main settlement
of the indigenous Comarca Emberá. It is a day's boat ride from La Palma or
accessible by light aircraft from Panama City. Guides from Puerto Indio will
take you on canoe trips into the forests of the Comarca. For accommodation
with local families, ask the headman at Puerto Indio.

San Blas islands (Kuna Yala)   ACCOM+

The Kuna of the San Blas islands enjoy a degree of self-government that is
perhaps unique in Latin America. They also own (or at least co-own) and manage
all tourist facilities on the islands. The main attraction of the San Blas is their
tropical island setting: palm-fringed beaches, untamed forested coastline, sun,
coral reefs and colourful marine life. There are no cultural tours as such but you
will see daily Kuna life all around you. Kuna women are famous in the region for
their intricately woven blouses, known as *molas*. Some islands have become
popular stopovers for cruise ships and this has had some negative impacts.

The following hotels are Kuna-owned and run: Hotel San Blas (tel: 262
5410) on **Nalunega**; Hotel Kwadule (only partially Kuna-owned); Hotel

Kuanidup; Hotel Iskardup; Hotel Delfin near **Achutupo**; Hotels Anai (tel: 239 3025) and Kuna Niskua (tel: 227 5308) on **Wichubhuala**; Hotel Kuna Yala on **Isla Raton**; Hotel Ikasa (tel: 224 8492) on **Ailigandi** (has an interesting cultural centre which you can visit). There are also basic hotels on the islands of **Carti Suitupu** (which also has a small museum) and **Rio Sidra**.

Travel agencies in Panama City will book most of the larger hotels. Except at Christmas, Carnival and Easter it is cheaper to fly with Aerotaxi, Ansa, or Aviatur to one of the airstrips on the coast or the islands. For the hotels on Nalunega and Wichubhuala, fly to **Porvenir** ($54 return) where hotel representatives meet the planes. For the Hotels Kuna Yala and Kuanidup, fly to Rio Sidra. There are also airstrips on Carti (for Carti Suitupu) and Ailigandi. Manuel, a Kuna who works for Aerotaxi, can provide information about the islands: he owns the Hotel Kuna Yala.

To visit other islands on San Blas, you need permission from the local *sahila* (an elected village elder) in each community, who can often arrange accommodation with families and maybe a guide. The **Kuna General Congress** office in Panama City (tel: 263 3615) in Edificio Dominó on Via Espana publishes a pamphlet entitled *Tourism in Kuna Yala*.

In a stretch of Kuna territory on the mainland is the 1000 square kilometre **Nusagandi Nature Reserve**. Visiting the reserve, which is mountainous tropical forest, costs $15 a day, including accommodation in the research lodge. You need permission from **PEMASKY**, a Kuna organization that manages the reserve, before you visit. There is good wildlife and birdwatching, but bring your own food. (This lodge may close – check before visiting.)

■ Kuna General Congress: Edificio Dominó, Via Espana, El Cangrejo, Panama City

❶ 263 3615

■ PEMASKY: C37 (between Via Espana and Av Peru), Panama City

❶ 225 8084

PERU

International dialling code +51.
Following the demise of the Shining Path, Peru has rapidly regained its place as one of the most popular tourist destinations in South America. The country is a paradise for hikers and climbers, with some of the most accessible big-mountain peaks on earth in the Cordillera Blanca near Huaraz. There are many other superb hiking regions, too, including the Cuzco region and the Colca Canyon near Arequipa – often said to be the world's deepest canyon, although in fact that honour belongs to nearby Cotahuasi Canyon. The huge slopes of the Andes and many dramatic canyons also offer amazing whitewater rafting and kayaking – Cuzco is the best place to book whitewater trips.

Peru's monumental heritage rivals Egypt or Greece. Machu Picchu is just one of many Inca archaeological sites near Cuzco, while Cuzco itself is one of the most attractive and historic towns in the Americas, with fine colonial buildings. There are also impressive *pre*-Inca ruins throughout the country, such as the mysterious Nazca Lines on the south coast, or the massive Chimu and Moche pyramids and cities on the north coast near Trujillo and Chiclayo, or around Chachapoyas in the northern Andes, which includes the mighty city-fortress of Kuelap.

Peru's contemporary culture is extremely rich, too, with festivals, markets and colourful traditional dress. For culture and scenery, the central highlands around Huancayo and Ayacucho offer an interesting and less-visited alternative to Cuzco.

The coastal desert, cloaked in grey (but rainless) cloud for eight months every year, is less obviously appealing but contains a wealth of ancient sites, plus a few ecotourism destinations such as Paracas. Half-way up the coast, Lima is a more modern face of Latin America – a sprawling metropolis with shanty towns and leafy middle-class suburbs, a rich historic centre and at least one unmissable museum (the Museo de la Nacion).

In the southern Peruvian Amazon, Manu and Tambopata are rated among the world's top rainforest parks, reached by air from Cuzco. The other tourist area in Peru's Amazon is Iquitos in the far north. The central Amazon sees few tourists.

Agencies in Cuzco offer guided four-day hikes along the Inca Trail to Machu Picchu for as little as $60. To maintain this low price, however, porters are often underpaid and overloaded, not given return transport from Machu Picchu, etc. When booking the Inca Trail (or other trips in Peru) look for companies that are members of the **Peruvian Ecotourism Association (APTAE)** – they assure fair wages, plus good employment and environmental standards. Similarly, when visiting Manu National Park, look for members of Eco-tour Manu, a group of tour operators whose members guarantee good environmental practices and support for conservation projects.

■ The South American Explorer's Club (www.samexplo.org) has good information about travel in Peru. It has clubhouses in Lima at: Av Rep de Portugal 146 (Postal: PO Box 3714), Lima 100

❶ 14-250 142

ⓔ montague@amauta.rcp.net.pe and in Cuzco at: 930 Av del Sol, (Postal: PO Box 500), Cuzco

ⓔ saec@wayna.rcp.net.pe

Aracari   TOUR

An upmarket tour agency which works with communities on some trips.

■ Marisol Mosquera, Malecon Cisneros 1270, 1201 Miraflores, Lima 18

☎ 014-479 003 ☏ 014-471 861

🌐 www.aracari.com ✉ aracari@amauta.rcp.net.pe

Casa Machiguenga/Manu Expeditions   RAINFOREST

Manu, east of Cuzco in the high rainforest of Madre de Dios, is considered by
many people to be the best rainforest park in the world, with fantastic bird and
animal life in pristine forest. **Casa Machiguenga**, which opened in 1999, is a
jungle lodge built by an indigenous Machiguenga community with the help of
a German NGO. All profits go to Machiguenga communities and local
Machiguenga are being trained to run the lodge. **Manu Expeditions**, run by
Englishman Barry Walker (who owns the Cross Keys pub) are the Cuzco agents
for the lodge and also manage another lodge, **Manu Wildlife Center**, which is
co-owned by a local community.

■ Manu Expeditions (Expediciones Manu): Avenida Pardo 895, Cuzco

☎ 084-226 671 ☏ 084-236 706

🌐 www.manuexpeditions.com ✉ adventure@manuexpeditions.com

✉ manuexpe+@amauta.rcp.net.pe

■ In the UK: Tribes Travel (see Responsible tour operators)

Granja Porcon   AGRI

A farming cooperative (**Cooperativa Agraria Atahualpa-Jerusalen**) near
Cajamarca in the northern Andes that offers stays, including a three-day
programme. Visitors join in with day-to-day farming tasks, crafts, fiestas, etc, as
a way of learning about local life. Other activities include horseriding and
walking in the surrounding hills and pine forests. Supported by an NGO called
ADEFOR. This cooperative is one of the few surviving from the land reforms
of the 1960s.

■ Hector Quispe: Cooperativa Agraria de Trabajadores Atahualpa-Jerusalén, Jr
  Chanchamayo 1383, Cajamarca

☎ 044-825 631 ☏ 044-822 023

■ ADEFOR: Carretera al aeropuerto km3, Fundo Tartar, Cajamarca

☎ + ☏ 044-821 369; 044-823 097

✉ adeforc@mail.cosapidata.com.pe

InkaNatura Travel/Machiguenga Center for Tropical Studies
RAINFOREST/TOUR

InkaNatura Travel is a non-profit travel company set up by two Peruvian NGOs (Peru Verde and Selva Sur). It has helped the indigenous Machiguenga community of **Timpia** build a rainforest lodge in the rugged lower Urubamba Valley. The lodge is entirely community-owned and set amidst pristine high rainforest, close to the spectacular Pongo de Mainique gorge and a fabulous macaw salt lick. Access by plane or river from Cuzco – the river journey includes the Pongo. InkaNatura Travel arranges visits to three other jungle lodges that are 50 per cent owned by local indigenous communities. These are the **Manu Wildlife Center** in Manu National Park, **Pantiacolla Lodge** and **Sandoval Lake Lodge**. All are located in superb rainforest with rich wildlife. InkaNatura also organizes tours throughout Peru, with profits reinvested in conservation projects.

■ InkaNatura Travel: Manuel Banon 461, San Isidro, Lima

❶ 014-402 022; 014-228 114 ❶ 014-229 225

Ⓦ www.inkanatura.com ❸ postmaster@inkanatura.com.pe

■ In Cuzco: Avenida el Sol 821 (2 piso), Cuzco

❶ 084-243 408 ❶ 084-226 392

■ In the US: InkaNatura Travel: 17957 SW 111th St, Brooker, FL32622, US

❶ 352-485 2514 (1-888-287 7186) ❶ 352-485 1452

❸ kit@inkanatura.com

Llama Trek, Cordillera Blanca
TOUR

A moderate four-day hike on an ancient pre-Incan route from Olleros to the famous archaeological site of Chavin de Huantar, considered by many to be the centre of early Peruvian culture. The hike passes through spectacular mountain scenery in the Cordillera Blanca. The trek is organized by the Asociacion de Auxiliares de Montaña, whose members come from the communities of Olleros and Canrey Chico. Llamas are used as pack animals instead of donkeys. The trek also includes cultural elements, such as visits to artisans, local communities, music performances. Tour starts from Huaraz. $133–$285, depending on numbers. Dry season: May to September.

■ Jorge Martel Alvarado, Calle Agustin Loli 463, Plazuela de la Soledad, Huaraz

❶ + ❶ 044-721 266

Ollantaytambo Heritage Trails/DRIT
DAY

Cultural walking (or horseback) trails around Ollantaytambo in the Sacred Valley near Cuzco, connecting villages and archaeological sites. Local guides are available. The aim is to encourage tourists to learn more about local life and culture and to spend more time (and thus money) in the area rather than rushing through on their way to and from Machu Picchu. Trails visit villages, weaving workshops, etc. Similar projects are being set up in the nearby town of **Urubamba**. Superb scenery. These schemes are being developed by a government agency in Cuzco called **DRIT (Dirección Regional de Industria y Turismo** – there are DRITs in every department of Peru.)

◼ Asociación CATCCO, Museo de Sitio, Ollantaytambo

◑ 084-204 024

Ⓦ www.cbc.org.pe/rao Ⓔ rao@apu.cbc.org.pe

◼ DRIT: Avenida de la Cultura 734 (3er piso), Cuzco

◑ 084-223 701 ◐ 084-223 761

Ⓦ www.cbc.org.pe/rao Ⓔ dritcus@mail.interplace.com.pe

PromPeru (The Commission for the Promotion of Peru) ORG
A government agency set up in 1993 to promote Peru and Peruvian tourism. One of its programmes aims to develop community-based tourism, including some of the projects listed here. It may be worth contacting them for details of similar new projects.

Ⓦ www.peruonline.net Ⓔ sit@promperu.gob.pe

Taquile ACCOM+/BUDGET
This island community, towards the Puno end of Lake Titicaca, offers homestays. The location is beautiful and peaceful and this is a fine opportunity to sample rural Andean life. Families host tourists on a rota basis.

◼ Mision, Lago Titicaca, Casilla 312, Taquile, Puno

◑ 054-367 771 ◐ 054-351 574

Ⓦ www.incacorp.com/taquile Ⓔ taquile@incacorp.com

◼ The neighbouring island, Amananti, runs a similar scheme

Willoc: Living Inca Culture TOUR
Willoc is an Inca village in the Sacred Valley near Ollantaytambo. Visitors can stay in the village and join in daily life, including visiting the weaving workshop. Good walking and beautiful mountain scenery.

◼ Silvia Uscamaita Otarola, Personal Travel Service: Portal de Panes 123 oficina 109, Cuzco

◑ 084-244 036 fax: 084-233 912

Ⓦ www.cbc.org.pe/rao Ⓔ ititoss@mail.cosapidata.com.pe

Winaymarka/Anapia
ACCOM+/AGRI

Tours to **Anapia** island on Lake Winaymarka, which is part of Lake Titicaca. Tours are organized by All Ways Travel, a tour agency in Puno and include homestays, sailing on the lake, beautiful setting, insights into rural Andean life and Aymara culture. All Ways Travel can also organize tours to two lakeside communities, **Capachica** and **Llachon**. There are boats from Capachica to Taquile and Amantani (see above).

■ Eliana Pauca, All Ways Travel: Jr Tacna 234, Puno

☏ + ☏ 054-355 552 ☏ 054-367 246

@ awtperu@mail.cosapidata.com.pe

PHILIPPINES

International dialling code +63.

The Philippines consists of over 7000 islands, of which Luzon in the north and Mindanao in the south are the largest. (The capital, Manila, is on Luzon.) The country sees less tourists than other South-east Asian nations and is less traditionally 'Asian': four centuries of Spanish and American colonial rule have resulted in Asia's only Christian (Catholic) country, with a passion for fast food and basketball.

Still, there is much to attract the visitor, with plenty of scope for island-hopping plus thousands of great beaches, superb diving and snorkelling and some of the most diverse wildlife and birdlife in South-east Asia – especially on Palawan. Two famous attractions are the bizarre Chocolate Hills on Bohol and the vast Ifugao rice terraces near Banaue in northern Luzon. The tiny island of Boracay is an established backpackers' favourite.

Filipinos love to party: nightlife ranges from lively to wild with many fiestas. January's Ati-Atihan festival, in Kalibo on the island of Panay, is the most spectacular.

Most Filipinos are Malay but there are indigenous and tribal communities in northern Luzon, Palawan and Mindoro. The predominantly Muslim island of Mindanao has a separatist movement: check the current situation before visiting. As in Thailand, sex tourism is an issue in the Philippines.

The Philippines is hot and tropical. The dry season is January to June.

Aeta Jungle Environment Survival Tour
DAY/RAINFOREST/TOUR

The Aeta are an indigenous group who live near Subic Bay. During and after the Vietnam War, there was a large US military base at Subic Bay and the Aeta were employed to train American soldiers in jungle survival techniques in the surrounding rainforest. (The presence of the base also helped protect the rainforest from loggers.) Since the base closed, Aeta guides have been leading tourists into the forest instead. The main guide is Gary Duero. Best time to visit is between November and April.

■ Subic Tourism Department

☎ 047-252 4242

■ Freeport Service Corporation

☎ 047-252 21

Biyaheng Pinoy/Initiatives for International Dialogue (IID)   TOUR

Biyaheng Pinoy is a programme of four- to five-day tours with local communities in Samal Island, Mount Apo and Maragusan Valley in Mindanao in the southern Philippines. The programme is organised by **Initiatives for International Dialogue**, a Filipino NGO. Tours include a five-day trek to Mount Apo, the highest peak in the country; an urban tour in Iligan City which looks at self-help projects (and interfaith dialogues between Muslims and Christians); and a tour to Samal Island. With many caves, pristine beaches and coral, Samal Island has been targeted by the Filipino government for major tourism development. The tour meets the indigenous Dinagat people on the island and looks at how this development will affect their lives. Also homestays, handicrafts.

■ Mary Ann Arnado: 27d Rosario Townhouse, Galaxy Street, GSIS Heights, Matina, Davao City

☎ 082-299 2574 ☎ 082-299 2052

Ⓦ www.skyinet.net/~iiddvo ⓔ iid@skyinet.net

RUSSIA

Russia may not quite count as a developing country but many Russians are certainly struggling. For tourists, Moscow and St Petersburg are rich in culture. Siberia has vast ecotourism potential, with grand scenery and a large indigenous population – particularly around Lake Baikal (the world's deepest freshwater lake) and in the volcanic, rugged far east. Tourism is in its infancy here: the Trans-Siberian railway journey is an established classic but few tourists get off the train for long. Elsewhere, the Caucasus are Europe's highest mountains (higher than the Alps) and will surely become a major holiday destination one day.

Ecologia Trust   ORG

A Scottish charity that arranges student, group and independent travel to Russia (mainly St Petersburg and Moscow), including homestays. Profits go towards a children's home in Russia.

■ Liza Hollingshead: Eco-Travels/Ecologia Trust, 66 The Park, Forres, Morayshire IV36 3TZ, Scotland

❶ + ❶ 01309-690 995

Ⓦ www.rmplc.co.uk/eduweb/sites/ecoliza Ⓔ ecoliza@rmplc.co.uk

SAMOA

International dialling code +685.
Samoa is a collection of South Pacific islands divided into two: the US territory of American Samoa and an independent country that used to be called Western Samoa, but is now officially just plain Samoa. The tours below are in independent Samoa.

Samoa consists of two main islands, Savai'i and Upolu, both hilly and volcanic, with a few smaller offshore islets. The small capital, Apia, is on Upolu.

Unlike its American counterpart, independent Samoa has retained a distinctly traditional Polynesian culture – perhaps the most traditional in the South Pacific – with an intricate village-based traditional power system. Samoans are exceptionally friendly and visitors are often invited to stay in villages.

The islands' natural attractions are coral reefs, diving and snorkelling, beaches and areas of rainforest. Although the usual catalogue of environmental worries applies – overfishing, deforestation and damage to coral – much of the country is wild and undeveloped and tourism is smaller scale and less resort-based than, for instance, on Fiji.

Eco-Tour Samoa/Rainforest Ecolodge ACCOM/TOUR

The Rainforest Ecolodge is a converted colonial homestead near Apia. The owners organize tours, including a seven-day tour on their 'eco-bus' which includes five village stays ($140 per day). They also offer sea kayaking trips with the option of overnight stays in villages on the way, and can help arrange longer village stays. Winner of the 1997 South Pacific Ecotourism Award.

■ Funealii Lumaava Sooaemalelagi/Steve Brown: PO Box 4609, Matautu-uta

❶ + ❶ 22144; 25993

Ⓦ www.ecotoursamoa.com Ⓦ www.samoa.net/ecotourism_winners/Home.htm

Ⓔ enquiries@ecotoursamoa.com Ⓔ ecotour@samoa.net

Samoan Customized Tours ACCOM+/TOUR

Runs a Manono Island Homestay Programme, among other culturally based tours.

■ PO Box 4228, Apia

❶ 24204 ❶ 26905

Samoa Visitors Bureau ORG

Can arrange overnight stays to rural villages. Their website lists various ecotour operators.

■ Beach Road (Postal: PO Box 2272), Apia

🕿 20878 📠 20886

🅦 www.pi.se/~orbit/samoa/welcome.html 🅔 samoa@samoa.net.ws

SENEGAL

International dialling code +221.
Senegal is a Muslim, French-speaking West African country that surrounds The Gambia. The northern half of the country, above The Gambia, is predominantly Wolof. The capital, Dakar, is here, and inland the holy city of Touba is one of the great religious centres of West Africa.

The southern part of Senegal, south of The Gambia, is the Casamance. The village *campements* are all in this region, which is closer to Banjul in The Gambia than to Dakar. The lush and tropical Casamance is unlike dry northern Senegal, and consists of a blend of forests, rivers and rice fields. Inland, the Niokolo Koa National Park is one of West Africa's best national parks.

The people of the Casamance are largely non-Muslim Jola. Since 1990 there has been a separatist struggle in the region and the number of visitors has fallen greatly. It is usually safe to travel but check the current situation.

Senegal is renowned for its music and has produced such international stars as Youssou N'dour and Baaba Maal.

Campement Villageois ACCOM+

Community-run village guesthouses in the Lower Casamance in southern Senegal, run by the Association of the Development of Integrated Tourism. The scheme was set up in 1974 by French ethnologist Christian Saglio. It has since grown from two to 11 villages, all within reach of Ziguinchor, the regional capital. Attractions include village tours, hiking, birdwatching, canoeing trips, crafts and the chance to see everyday African village life. Most villages are inland on rivers and surrounded by mangroves, silk-cotton trees and rice fields. Two (Kafountine and Abéné) are on the coast with good beaches. Each village manages its own *campement*, with profits used to fund health clinics, schools or other community projects. The success of the scheme has inspired around 20 private *campements*. These are often in competition with the village projects, although they are still locally owned. $5 per night (accommodation and food). There are good descriptions and travel details for both official and private *campements* in *The Rough Guide to West Africa*.

■ Adama Goudiaby, Director, Campements Rural Intégrés, Centre Artisanal, BP567 Ziguinchor, Casamance

🕿 991-1980 📠 991-2804

Crossing Cultures Programme   TOUR/VOL

Arranges village stays in Senegal with study courses in arts and traditional culture on request (dance, medicine, etc). Volunteering opportunities.

■ Janet L Ghattas: Intercultural Dimensions Inc, PO Box 391437, Cambridge, MA 02139-0015, US

☎ 617-864 8442   ✆ 617-868 1273

✉ janetid@aol.com

Karamba Ltd   TOUR

Music and dance holidays based in the village of Abéné in southern Senegal. Djembe, sabar, talking drum, kora workshops with local musicians. For all levels from complete beginner to experienced. As well as music, there is a good beach, canoeing, birdlife, excursions to markets and the chance to see rural West African life. 14-day tour: £785, excluding flights.

■ Gary Newland: Ollands Lodge, Heydon, Norwich, Norfolk NR11 6RB, UK

☎ + ✆ 01603-872402

🌐 www.karamba.co.uk   ✉ karamba@gn.apc.org

SOLOMON ISLANDS

International dialling code +677.

Scuba divers will know that the Solomon Islands are one of the world's best diving and snorkelling locations, with stunning reefs and World War II wreckages in abundance. And you're never going to feel crowded at your dive site; if you see someone else down at 20 metres it's most likely to be a Solomon Islander free-diving for his dinner. Above water, things are equally uncrowded. Here, the main attractions are magnificent tropical forests, rich birdlife, and uncrowded white-sand beaches. Marovo Lagoon, in particular, is a beautiful lagoon with World Heritage status.

Conditions for tourists are usually fairly basic. But the friendly welcome, fascinating local customs and the beauty of the lagoons, hills and rainforests are well worth a little discomfort. Travel is by boat, canoes and small inter-island planes – only on the islands of Malaita and Guadalcanal will you find some rough roads, serviced by trucks and minibuses.

The vast majority of Solomon Islanders live by fishing and farming. There has been logging of the rainforest that once covered most of the islands, although this has slowed under the current government and there are still areas of superb primary forest. The country is normally the epitome of peacefulness. Recently, however, the island of Guadalcanal (which includes the capital, Honiara) was unsafe due to an inter-island dispute – check the situation before visiting. The main tourist region of Western Province is unaffected.

Makira Hill Tribes Tour   TOUR

An adventurous week-long trek into the Makira highlands passing through beautiful rainforest. Excellent birdwatching. The villages in the highlands are more traditional and less Christian than the coastal villages. The project was developed by Conservation International.

- ■ Solomon Sights and Sounds: destsolo@welkam.solomon.com.sb (or contact the Solomon Islands Development Trust, see below)
- ■ In the US: Conservation International (see Responsible tour operators)
- ■ In Australia: One World Travel (see Responsible tour operators) or Ecotour Travel in Sydney (see Australia)

Solomon Islands Visitors Bureau   ORG

Can provide details of village stays and community-run lodges.

- ■ Wilson Maelaua
- ✆ 22442   ✆ 23986
- ✉ visitors@welkam.solomon.com.sb

Solomon Islands Development Trust   ORG

- ■ Silverio Wale/Francis Tarihao
- ✆ 21131

Solomons Village Stay   ACCOM+

An agency that organizes stays with local families, mostly in coastal villages. Fishing, bushwalking, canoeing, snorkelling (although you usually have to take your own gear), swimming, climbing and caving.

- ■ Solomon Islands Visitors Bureau (see above)

Vanua Rapita Lodge   ACCOM+

A community-owned lodge in a beautiful and peaceful location on Marovo Lagoon. The lodge offers access to excellent snorkelling and diving (there is a dive lodge nearby), plus guided rainforest walks, river trips, snorkelling, fishing, crocodile-spotting, village tours and local culture. Supported by WWF. British Airways Tourism for Tomorrow Awards, highly commended 1998.

- ■ Vanua Rapita Lodge, Seghe Postal Agency, Marovo Lagoon, Solomon Islands
- ✆ 60191   ✆ 60294
- ■ Solomon Islands Visitors Bureau (see above)

SOUTH AFRICA

International dialling code +27.
The end of apartheid put South Africa back on the tourism map and it has rapidly become one of Africa's most popular destinations. Five times the size of Britain, South Africa has the best hotels, transport and roads in Africa, plus some of the continent's best scenery and game parks.

Cape Town is the most attractive South African city for tourists with good nightlife and a spectacular setting. Near Cape Town, there is excellent whale-watching, plus popular touring around the Paarl and Stellenbosch vineyards and the scenic Garden Route. Further north, towards Namibia, there are austere rust-red deserts, with spring wildflowers in August and September and the Kalahari-Gemsbok National Park. Just across the border in southern Namibia is Fish Canyon, southern Africa's Grand Canyon.

Some of South Africa's best natural attractions are in the north-west, towards Mozambique. In particular, Kwazulu Natal contains the beautiful Drakensberg mountains, which offer superb scenery and hiking. The province's Indian Ocean coastline, especially in the far north, has kilometres of deserted beaches and wild coastline, with great surfing and coral reefs. Hluhluwe-Umfolozi is one of the country's best game reserves. North of Swaziland, in Northern Province, the famous Kruger National Park – the size of Wales – is one of the continent's premier safari parks.

South Africa's transformation from apartheid pariah to rainbow nation democracy has been remarkable but there are still problems, including a high crime rate. However, South Africa is little different from, say, the US – some areas are safe while others aren't. The legacy of apartheid means that most hotels, etc, are in predominantly white areas and were developed for white South African holidaymakers. Unless you make an effort – by taking a township tour, for instance – most of your money still goes to white South Africans and you won't see much of everyday life for the black majority, especially in urban areas.

Asijiki Tour Enterprises   TOUR
Two-day trips to Robben Island, including a guided tour of the prison by an ex-political prisoner, plus campfire supper and overnight homestay: R440.

■ Robben Island, Strand Towers, 66 Strand St, Cape Town 8001

❶ 083-326 7601; 083-593 9185 ❶ 083-419 2386

Calabash Lodge and Tours   ACCOM/DAY
Day tours and guesthouse in Port Elizabeth. Tours include townships and community projects.

■ 8 Dollery Street, Central Port Elizabeth, 6001

❶ 041-556 162

CCAfrica (formerly Conservation Corporation Africa)
LUXURY/SAFARI

CCAfrica's philosophy is unashamed luxury with a green conscience. The company owns over 20 upmarket safari lodges in Southern and East Africa, including **Phinda Reserve** and a lodge in **Madikwe Reserve** in South Africa; **Londolozi Camp** in Kruger National Park, South Africa; **Kichwa Tembo** in southern Kenya; **Mnemba Island** on Zanzibar; and **Klein's Camp** on the Serengeti in Tanzania. With assets and revenue exceeding $60 million, Conservation Corporation is hardly community-based, but it has shown a commitment to local communities that is rare for a company of its size and its Rural Investment Fund has given over $1 million to villages near its lodges.

◾ CCAfrica: Private Bag X27, Benmore 2010

☏ 011-775 0000 **✆** 011-784 7667

Ⓦ www.ccafrica.com **ℯ** information@ccafrica **ℯ** reservations@conscorp.ca.za

◾ In the UK: Discovery Initiatives (see Responsible tour operators) and Rainbow Tours (see below) are agents for Phinda Reserve

Eco-Escapes
TOUR

Tours to the Transkei region of South Africa in partnership with local Pondo and Xhosa communities, who provide lodging, food and guides. Tours from four to ten days, including local culture plus coastal hikes along a wild stretch of the Indian Ocean, waterfalls, beaches, etc. One trip focuses on traditional healing. Tours start from Durban.

◾ Neville Botha: 57 River Drive, Carrington Heights, Durban 4001

☏ + **✆** 031-261 7232

Ⓦ www.icon.co.za/~surfsa/eco.htm **ℯ** surfsa@icon.co.za

Isinamva Cultural Village (Mount Frere, Eastern Cape)
TOUR

A group of villages in a remote part of the Eastern Cape. You can stay overnight in the Kraals, help prepare traditional food, feed the animals and experience Xhosa life and hospitality. Four people minimum.

◾ PO Box 72, Mount Frere, 5090

☏ 039-255 0427

◾ East Cape Tourism Board

☏ 040-635 2115

ℯ judy@ectourism.org.za

◾ In the UK: Rainbow Tours (see below)

Lake Sibaya Lodge ACCOM/SAFARI

An upmarket lodge and community-run nature conservancy on the shores of Lake Sibaya in Maputaland, Kwa-Zulu Natal Province. Activities include canoe trips on the lake and sunset sailing trips in dhows, plus fishing, guided or unguided bushwalks and good bird and wildlife. There is turtle-watching and beaches nearby on the Indian Ocean coast, including Kosi Bay. The local community owns 50 per cent of the camp with profits funding local village projects. R595 per night. This project incorporates the former **Camp Abandon**.

■ PO Box 19233, Fishershill 1408, Johannesburg

☎ 011-616 9950 ✆ 011-616 8232

✉ sibayi@iafrica.com Or PO Box 1194, Kloof 3640, Durban

☎ 031-763 4267

■ In the UK: Rainbow Tours (see below)

Masithandane (Grahamstown) DAY

Near Port Elizabeth in the Eastern Cape, this cooperative organizes township tours and serves Xhosa lunches to tourists. Local women also turn plastic litter into hats, bags and mats for sale to tourists and produce traditional Xhosa beadwork. It is also possible to visit Mgwali Village, 25 kilometres east of Stutterheim.

■ Erica McNulty, PO Box 2240, Grahamstown, 6140

☎ 046-622 8735; 046-622 5944

■ East Cape Tourism Board

☎ 0406-352 115

✉ judy@ectourism.org.za

■ In the UK: Rainbow Tours (see below)

Rainbow Tours TOUR

Tours and self-drive itineraries to South Africa, Zimbabwe, Mozambique and Lesotho. Tours available include a 16-day introduction to South Africa, plus shorter trips. Also customized itineraries, including wildlife parks, Indian Ocean beaches and visits to local community projects. Rainbow works with a number of community-based lodges, hotels and local businesses and can include township tours in your itinerary. ATOL-bonded. Brochure available.

■ Roger Diski: Canon Collins House, 64 Essex Rd, London N1 8LR, UK

☎ 020-7226 1004 ✆ 020-7226 2621

✉ rainbow@gn.apc.org

144

- South Africa and Zimbabwe self-drive specialists
- Community tourism projects
- Kruger Park, safari lodges and camping safaris
- Guided cultural tours - for a unique insight into South Africa in transition
- Also Mozambique, Madagascar and Botswana

PHONE FOR BROCHURE 020-7226 1004

Shiluvari Lakeside Lodge /Kuvona Cultural Tours ACCOM/DAY

A guesthouse in the Northern Province. Also tours to local villages to see crafts-people working and to learn about local life. Double rooms from R250.

■ PO Box 560, Louis Trichardt 0920, Northern Province

📞 015-556 3406 📠 015-556 3413

Tsweleni Guest House ACCOM

A small community-based guesthouse on the Wildcoast at Mpande. Run with Eco-Escapes (see above). R20 per night.

■ Neville Botha, 57 River Drive, Carrington Heights, Durban 4001

📞 031-261 7232; 083-306 8669 📠 031-261 7232

📧 nevil_transkei@hotmail.com

Wilderness Safaris LUXURY/SAFARI

A large commercial wildlife tour operator. Some of its lodges involve local communities. **Ndumo Wilderness Camp** in Maputaland (northern KwaZulu) is jointly owned by Wilderness, a local Thonga village and the KwaZulu Department of Nature Conservation. It has some of Africa's best birdwatching (with over 400 species) plus good wildlife. **Rocktail Bay Lodge**, also co-owned by the local community, is an away-from-it-all lodge on a stretch of wild Maputaland coast, with deserted beaches, good birdwatching, wildlife, snorkelling. Wilderness also market **Ndunu Safari Lodge** in Zimbabwe (see below) and **Damaraland** and **Llanshulu Lodges** in Namibia (see above) – all upmarket safari lodges.

■ PO Box 651171, Benmore 2010

📞 884-1458; 884-4633 📠 883-6355

🌐 www.african-safari.com/wildrnes.htm 📧 info@sdn.wilderness.co.na

■ In the UK: Rainbow Tours (see above)

SRI LANKA

International dialling code +94.
The Garden of Eden, the Land of Serendipity, colonial Ceylon, war zone… you could be forgiven for being confused about Sri Lanka. However, the civil war mainly affects the northern tip of the island. The rest of the country is peaceful: less hectic than neighbouring India with fine beaches – especially on the south and west coasts – and cool hills covered with tea plantations. Although there are Hindu, Muslim and Christian communities, Sri Lanka is predominantly a Buddhist country. The Temple of the Sacred Tooth (one of the Buddha's) in Kandy is its foremost religious monument.

Forests for People, Tanamalvila   ACCOM+
Rustic accommodation in a conservation project near Tanamalvila village in Lower Uva. Guided treks and walks to rainforest and dry zones.

■ c/o Woodlands Network (see below)

Forest Park Country Home, Keppetipola   ACCOM+
A guesthouse in the grounds of a former colonial hunting lodge between Nuwara-Eliya and Bandarawela. Walking and trekking, plus village life and organic farming. Volunteer opportunities.

❶ 072-666 608 or c/o Woodlands Network (see below)

Green Field Bio Plantation, Haputale   ACCOM+
A project to diversify a tea plantation with mixed agriculture and tourism, including accommodation, restaurant, shop and information centre. Magnificent scenery, walking, climbing, birdwatching. On the Colombo-Kandy-Badulla 'tea railway' line. Also volunteer opportunities.

❶ + ❶ 057-68101 or c/o Woodlands Network (see below)

Jungle Exploration Home/JP Walks and Climbs   ACCOM+
Rural accommodation plus guided jungle walks in a small village near Wellawaya in the Lower Uva dry zone, on the road to Buttala. Handapanagala Lake, with its elephant herd, is within walking distance.

❶ 072-658 823 or c/o Woodlands Network (see below)

Karuna Sevana (Haven of Kindness)   ACCOM
Accommodation near Colombo (3 kilometres from the airport) in a community project that also provides vocational training for abandoned boys.

■ Centre for Society and Religion, Colombo.

❶ 01-695425 ❶ 01-682064

❷ csrlibra@slt.lk

Turtle Watch, Rekawa   DAY

In a project initiated by the Turtle Conservation Project, an international wildlife agency, the villagers of Rekawa are paid to protect the nests of green sea turtles and earn money from a Turtle Watch tourist attraction. British Airways Tourism for Tomorrow Awards, highly commended 1998.

■ Turtle Conservation Project, 73 Hambanota Road, Tangalle

❶ 047-40581

Woodlands Network   ACCOM+/AGRI/ORG/TOUR

ToDo! Award winner

An organization run by local women that can arrange stays in guesthouses or with families, mainly in rural villages in Uva province, where you can experience day-to-day life while contributing to the local economy. Uva Province, in Sri Lanka's interior, is an attractive region of hills, forests, waterfalls and tea estates. Running through the province, the Colombo–Kandy–Badulla 'tea railway' is a scenic highland train journey. Woodlands Network is not a travel agency but provides visitor information for many local guesthouses, homestays, guiding services and community-based 'eco-centres'. (A few of these are listed separately, see above.) With advance notice they can also suggest tailor-made itineraries on themes including walking/trekking, agritourism (tea, organic farming, conservation, reforestation) culture (music, dance, handicrafts), Buddhism and Ayurvedic medicine. Also volunteer opportunities. Woodlands Network produces a guidebook to Uva with some recommended travel itineraries.

■ Harry Haas/Sarojinie Ellawela: 30/6 Esplanade Road, (BD) 90100 Bandarawela

❶ + ❶ 057-22735; 057-22712

❷ haas@personal.is.lk

■ In the UK: Travel Friends International (see Responsible tour operators)

SWAZILAND

International dialling code +268.

Like many other Southern African nations, the main focus of tourism in tiny Swaziland is wildlife in national parks such as Mkhaya. Most of the country, however, is agricultural land: the project below also allows you to experience rural Swazi life.

Woza Nawe Tours/Liphupho Lami   ACCOM+/TOUR

Woza Nawe Tours run 4WD tours around Swaziland with a community focus. Tours feature visits to markets, schools and community projects as well as walking and cycling in the attractive hills around Kaphunga, a village 65 kilometres south of Manzini. Under the same management, **Liphupho Lami homestead** provides accommodation on a 1600 hectares community-owned farm in Kaphunga.

■ Mxolisi Mdluli, PO Box 2140, Manzini M100

❶ 52-83117

ⓔ mzn136@postcafe.co.sz

TANZANIA

International dialling code +255.
Like Kenya, Tanzania boasts magnificent wildlife, Indian Ocean beaches, Rift Valley lakes, tribal cultures and Swahili towns... but with far fewer tourists. The Swahili island/town of Zanzibar has long been a favourite among backpackers for its enticing blend of beaches and Swahili culture, and is now on the verge of mass tourist development.

On the mainland, Tanzania's wildlife viewing is, if anything, superior to Kenya. Most tourists stick close to the Kenyan border, in the 'Northern Safari Circuit'. This includes Ngorogoro Crater – a 16-kilometre wide volcanic crater packed with wildlife (and tourists!) – the Serengeti National Park and Mount Kilimanjaro, Africa's highest peak.

However, there is good wildlife viewing, national parks and scenery throughout the country, as well as many interesting local cultures and the opportunity to see rural East African life away from the tourist regions.

Cultural Tourism Programme   BUDGET/ORG/TOUR
A joint project of the Tanzania Tourist Board and SNV (a Dutch development NGO) to develop village-based cultural tours, mainly in northern Tanzania. Profits go towards village projects such as schools, irrigation canals and cattle dips. There are currently 14 projects, all led by local people. These are the **Usambara Mountains**, the **Northern** and **Southern Pare Mountains**, **Longido**, **Ng'iresi**, **Mto wa Mbu**, **Engaruka**, **Mamba and Marangu**, **Mkuru**, **Ilkiding'a**, **Mbeya**, **Gezaolole**, **Amani and Mulala**. Activities include walking safaris, hiking in forests and hills, learning about local culture, visiting village projects and farms, birdwatching, explanations of medicinal plant use, dancing, caves, waterfalls and ancient ruins. Camping and homestays. At Mkuru, there are camel safaris. The programme has been running since 1995.

■ Thomas Ole Sikar, Cultural Tourism Programme: AICC, Serengeti Wing, Room 643-645 (Postal: PO Box 10455), Arusha

❶ + ❶ 057-7515

ⓦ www.infojep.com/culturaltours ⓦ www.habari.co.tz/culturetours

ⓔ tourinfo@habari.co.tz

■ or the Tourist Information Centres in Arusha (Boma Road, tel: 057-3842/3), Dar es Salaam (Samora Avenue, tel: 051-120 373) and Lushoto (tel: Lushoto 132)

■ In the UK: Simply Tanzania (See Responsible tour operators)

Tailor-made tours off the beaten track. Development projects, cultural tourism, remote tourist sites. Your chance to see the real Tanzania.

Simply Tanzania Tour Company

54 Cotesbach Road, London E5 9QJ. Tel/fax: 020-8986 0615
enquiries@simplytanzania.freeserve.co.uk
www.simplytanzania.freeserve.co.uk

Dorobo Tours and Safaris   SAFARI+

A private operator with an good record of consulting and supporting local communities. They run camping, wildlife viewing and walking trips with local Dorobo, Maasai, Hadza and Datoga people. Destinations include the wildlife-rich **Soitorgoss** area on the eastern Serengeti. Dorobo Safaris have also set up a charitable fund to promote community-based projects. Tailor-made itineraries available. $180–$300 per day.

■ David, Thad or Mike Peterson: PO Box 2534, Arusha

☎ 57-2300 ☎ 57-8336

✉ dorobo@yako.habari.co.tz

IntoAfrica   SAFARI/TOUR

Safaris in northern Tanzania. Tours feature the normal wildlife, plus opportunities to meet local people and use local guides. The company pays a negotiated fee per visitor to local communities and donates to community funds. Two-week tours from £1431. Also Mount Kilimanjaro hikes.

■ Chris Morris: 59 Langdon Street, Sheffield S11 8BH, UK

☎ 0114-255 5610

🌐 www.intoafrica.co.uk ✉ enquiry@intoafrica.co.uk

■ IntoAfrica Eco-Travel: PO Box 50484, Nairobi, Kenya

Oliver's Camp   SAFARI

A private safari camp in Tarangire National Park near Arusha in northern Tanzania, with similar wildlife to the Serengeti. The camp owners have set up a wildlife conservation area with two Maasai villages (Loboir Soit and Emboreet). They pay the villages a $12 fee per tourist per day: between 1993 and 1997 this amounted over $40,000.

■ PO Box 425, Arusha

☎ 57-4116 ☎ 57-8548

🌐 www.safaritanz.com ✉ olivers@habari.co.tz

Simply Tanzania Tour Company   SAFARI/TOUR

Tailor-made 4WD tours run by an ex-VSO field director for Tanzania. Tours combine wildlife safaris with off-the-beaten-track destinations and visits to communities and development projects. From £1400 for a two-week tour. Shorter trips available.

■ Tony Janes: 54 Cotesbach Road, Clapton, London E5 9QJ, UK

✆ + ✆ 020-8986 0615

🌐 www.simplytanzania.freeserve.co.uk ✉ tjanes@simplytanzania.freeserve.co.uk

Sisi Kwa Sisi   BUDGET/ORG/TOUR

A community-based organization developing tourist facilities in the town of Mbeya near the border with Zambia and Malawi, including guides, homestays and a guesthouse. Nearby attractions include mountains, bush and forest hikes with good Rift Valley scenery, hot springs, etc. There are also visits to traditional healers and opportunities to learn about local life and customs.

■ Nicholas Amandus Ntinda: PO Box 2869, Mbeye (office in Mbeye, near bus station next to Japan-Tanzania Monument)

Trade Aid Mikindani   DAY

A project supported by a British NGO to restore a colonial German fort in the town of Mikindani on the southern coast, to encourage local tourism.

■ PO Box 993, Mtwara

✆ 059-333 875

✉ tradeaid@raha.com

■ In the UK: Trade Aid UK: Burgate Court, Burgate, Hampshire, England, UK

✆ 01425-657 774

✉ tradeaid@netcomuk.co.uk

Zanzibar Travel   TOUR

A UK-based tour operator that uses locally owned hotels and operators and includes village tours, meals with families, etc.

■ Michael Sweeney: Reynards House, Selkirk Gardens, Cheltenham, Gloucestershire GL52 5LY, UK

✆ + ✆ 01242-222 027

✉ sweeney@cotswoldgroup.demon.co.uk

THAILAND

International dialling code +66.

Thailand is one of the most popular destinations in Asia for British tourists. They are attracted by a superb cuisine, a rich and exotic culture, historic temples and palaces and a friendly and proud people. There are fascinating hill tribes and forested mountains in the north, and tropical islands such as Ko Samui or the islands of Krabi Bay in the south.

The Thais, the only South-East Asian people not to have been colonized, are tough, business-like and independent, with a resilient cultural identity. Tourism has put a lot of money into the Thai economy without destroying Thai culture, and there are many locally run guesthouses and tour agencies. On the other hand, it's estimated that 60 per cent of tourist spending in Thailand leaves the country, while the over-expansion of the Thai economy (not solely due to tourism) has led to a recent economic crash.

Thailand has also become a prime destination for sex tourism, with young girls and children being forced into prostitution and a serious AIDS problem. In the UK, **ECPAT** (see 'Responsible tourism organizations and resources' in Section Three of this book) is a campaign to end sex tourism.

Another area where responsible tourism is important is trekking to the northern hill tribes. Tourists visiting hill tribes should seek out responsible guides. Does the guide have permission to take tourists into tribal villages? Is he doing anything to ensure that the people you visit benefit from your presence? Are visitor numbers kept low to minimize impact? Also, trekkers – especially backpackers – are frequently offered opium in hill-tribe villages. Remember that the village boys assigned to smoke with tourists often end up as addicts.

In north-west Thailand, the 'long-necked women' of the Padaung tribe wear neck rings that stretch their necks. These cause serious health problems and the practice would probably have died but for their perceived value as a tourist attraction. While this human zoo brings money into the local economy, little of it goes to the Padaung themselves. We suggest that you don't visit Padaung long-necked women.

The southern island of Ko Phan Kgan has become a centre for rave tourism, famous on the backpacker circuit for its full-moon parties every month. The 'rave' area is relatively small and the rest of the island is peaceful. Remember that a number of foreigners are enjoying stays in Thai prisons for drug possession.

Beyond the beaches, Thailand offers some fascinating cultural opportunities. You can go on silent meditation retreats in Buddhist monasteries, learn Thai cookery, Thai massage or even Thai boxing.

Khao Nor Chuchi Lowland Forest Project ACCOM+/TOUR

A rural development and reforestaton project 60 kilometres south of Krabi in southern Thailand. Accommodation in thatched huts, food and activities including walking trails, swimming in forest pools, local village activities such as rubber-tapping, hot springs. 250Baht per day. Trips can be arranged through Chan Phen travel agency in Krabi.

■ Chan Phen travel agency: Thanon Utarakit, Krabi

Lisu Lodge ACCOM+

A small, rustic lodge in a Lisu village near Chang Mai that works closely with the local community. Rafting, biking, elephant rides,

■ East West Siam: Building One, 11th Floor, 99 Wireless Road, Pathumwan, Bangkok 10330

☎ 02-256 6153 ✆ 02-256 6665

🌐 www.east-west.com ✉ siamex@mozart.inet.co.th

PDA Tours & Travel CENTRE/TOUR

PDA Tours & Travel is the trekking company of the non-profit **PDA (Population and Community Development Association)** in Chiang Rai. Profits from treks go to hill-tribe development projects. The trekking agency is based in the **Hilltribe Education Centre**, which also contains a museum on hilltribe culture and a crafts shop.

■ Hilltribe Education Centre: 620/1 Thanon Thanalai, Chiang Rai

☏ 053-719 167; 053-711 475 ✆ 053-718 869

ⓔ crpda@chiangrai.a-net.net.th

PRLC (Project for Recovery of Life and Culture)   TOUR
The **PRLC** is an NGO working to improve living standards in hill-tribe villages in northern Thailand. They have been helping hill-tribe communities develop tourism facilities: the Karen village of **Baan Huay Hee** was the first to take in visitors. Homestays, hiking in the surrounding hills and forests, learn about local farming techniques. PRLC run treks from Mae Hong Son which includes stays in two other villages – **Baan Huay Tong Kaw** and **Baan Huay Kung** – plus rafting, elephant rides, birdwatching, forest walks. Hard or easy trekking. Unlike standard hill-tribe treks, the primary aims are to benefit the villagers and to give tourists more insight into local life. Four-day trek: $125.

■ Mr Tawatchai Rattanasorn, Project for Recovery of Life and Culture: 54/1 Singhanart Bamrung Road, Tambon Jongkham, Muang, Mae Hong Son 5800

☏ + ✆ 053-612 338

■ Also marketed by TVS-REST (see below)

Symbiosis   TOUR
A UK-based tour operator that runs a Thailand trip focusing on village life and traditional herbal medicine, including visits to herbal doctors in the village of Ban Yang Luang in Mae Chaem province, plus homestays and visits to hilltribe villages in Mae Salong province in northern Thailand. The tour is organized with a local development NGO that works in the villages.

■ 205 St John's Hill, London, SW11 1TH, UK

☏ 020-7924 5906 ✆ 020-7924 5907

ⓦ www.symbiosis-travel.co.uk ⓔ info@symbiosis-travel.co.uk

Thai Tribal Crafts/Hill-Tribe Products Promotion Centre, Chiang Mai   CENTRE
Two non-profit outlets for hill-tribe crafts in Chiang Mai are Thai Tribal Crafts and Hill-Tribe Products Promotion Centre. Both have a good selection and good quality and more of your money goes to the actual craftspeople and/or hill-tribe welfare projects.

■ Thai Tribal Crafts: 208 Thanon Bamrungrat, near McCormick Hospital

☏ 053-241 043

■ Hill-Tribe Products Promotion Centre: 21/17 Thanon Suthep, near Wat Suan Dawk

☏ 053-277 743

TVS-REST (Responsible, Ecological and Social Tourism) ORG/TOUR
Tours are run by the Thai Volunteer Service – an NGO that trains young Thais
for voluntary work on social and community projects. The tour programme
features community-based tours and homestays in rural villages, from three
days to three weeks. Opportunities to learn about local farming, Thai cookery,
visits to floating markets, Thai puppetry, trekking, etc. Trips in northern
Thailand include visits to Karen, Hmong and Mmien villages, with the chance
to learn much more about their lives than on commercial 'hill-tribe treks'.

■ 409 Soi Rohitsook, Pracharaj-Bampen Road, Huay-Khwang, Bangkok 10320

❶ 02-691 0437 ❶ 02-690 2796

Ⓦ www.welcome.to/tvs Ⓔ tvsrest@asiaaccess.net.th

Yat Fon/Ban Tung Laem Sai   ACCOM+
Ban Tung Laem Sai is a Thai-Muslim fishing village in Trang Province in the far
south of Thailand. A local non-profit agency, **Yat Fon**, organizes homestays in
the village, where you see local life and learn about conservation and management of the local ecosystem of coral reefs, and mangroves.

■ Khun Suwit

❶ 075-219 737

UGANDA

International dialling code +256.
Lush and green, fertile Uganda is one of East Africa's bread-baskets. Its people
suffered the dictatorships of Idi Amin and Milton Obote in the 1970s and 1980s,
but since Yoweri Museveni ousted Obote in 1986 things have got better, with
democratic elections and economic growth. The two outstanding problems
today are the AIDS epidemic and instability in neighbouring Rwanda, southern
Sudan and the Democratic Republic of Congo (formerly Zaire). Uganda itself is
generally safe and friendly, but check the situation with local sources (such as
tour operators or UCOTA, below) before visiting western Uganda in particular.
At the time of writing, the Rwenzori National Park was closed to visitors.

This western region includes some of the country's natural highlights: the
Bwindi and Mgahinga National Parks are hilly, forested parks famous for their
gorilla-watching. The Rwenzori Mountains – the fabled 'Mountains of the
Moon' – are a 5000 metre snow-capped range that offers great (although
tough) trekking. Elsewhere, there is good trekking in Mount Elgon National
Park in eastern Uganda and the spectacular Murchison Falls in the north-west.

Uganda also has a strong cultural heritage and part of its appeal is the
chance to experience East African life away from Kenya's tourist honeypots.

UCOTA (Uganda Community Tourism Association)   ORG/ACCOM+
An association providing training and marketing for community tourism
projects in Uganda. The following are some UCOTA members that have
accommodation (usually in thatched huts called *bandas*) and camping facilities: **Buhoma Rest Camp** in Bwindi National Park; **Amajambwere Iwacu** in
Mgahinga National Park; **Kaniyo Pabidi** and **Busingiro** in the Budongo Forest.
The **Abanya Rwenzori Mountaineering Association** provides accommodation
and guides for treks into the Rwenzori. The **Kibale Association for Rural and
Environmental Development (KAFRED)** offers tours in the Bigodi Wetland
Sanctuary in west Uganda. Most projects also include women's groups who
produce local handicrafts. There are other projects not listed here – contact
UCOTA for more information.

■ Elissa Williams, UCOTA: PO Box 27159, Kampala

❶ 41-230 805

🄴 prof@swiftuganda.com 🄴 ucota@swiftuganda.com

US – NATIVE AMERICAN TOURISM

International dialling code +1.
Statistics on health, mental illness, suicides, etc, show that Native Americans
share many of the problems of poor people in developing countries, despite living
in one of the world's wealthiest nations. In this, there is a clear parallel with other
First Nations peoples, such as Aboriginal Australians. The situation is especially
bad on the 300 or so reservations, which are home to roughly a quarter of the
Native American population (or 437,000 people), with high unemployment,
alcoholism, poverty and substandard health and educational facilities.

But it is the reservation communities, especially in the South-West, that
attract tourists. Traditional Native American culture tends to be strongest today
in these desert and mountain regions, and these are also some of the most
scenic parts of the US.

The South-West (Arizona, New Mexico, Utah and Colorado), with its
stunning canyons, sculpted rocks and painted deserts, is also the heart of contemporary Native America. The Navajo in Arizona are the largest Native American
nation and Navajoland – which includes the dramatic rock spires of Monument
Valley and ancient cliff-dwelling sites such as Canyon de Chelly – is the largest
tribal territory in the US. Other South-West tribes involved in tourism include
the Hopi, Zuni, Pueblo, Apache, Hualapai and Havasupai. There is also Native
American peoples in Oklahoma, Montana, South Dakota and Alaska.

Many reservations, especially in the South-West, attract large numbers of
visitors – for instance, Taos and Acoma pueblos or the Hopi mesa-top villages.
Where the tribe itself manages the tourist facilities, tourist money is usually
reinvested in tribal programmes and services. However, it can be difficult for
reservation communities to retain a degree of privacy and normality, and to

prevent meaningful ceremonies from descending into tourist attractions. Tours are sometimes run to coincide with fairs (or 'pow-wows'), which provide opportunities to see traditional dances and costumes. At other times it is unreasonable to expect – as most tourists seem to – that a brief half-day visit will be packed with ceremonies, ritual dances, sweat-lodges and so on, or that everyone you meet will be wearing a feathered head-dress.

The listings below are just a selection of Native American tourism. Good sources of further information include the **Navajo Tourism Department** (see below) which publishes lists of Native American guides; the book *Indian America* by Eagle/Walking Turtle (John Muir Publications, Santa Fe, New Mexico, 4th ed, 1995); the *Rough Guide to Southwest USA*; plus *Native Peoples of Alaska: A Traveler's Guide to Land, Art and Culture* and *Native Peoples of the Northwest: A Traveler's Guide to Land, Art and Culture* both by Jan Halliday (available from www.amazon.com or from the author at halliday@olympus.net).

Alaska

Native Americans make up 16 per cent of the Alaskan population and, along with the South-West, Alaska is the richest region in the US for Native American culture and tourism. Alaska is also a superb outdoors destination with vast tracts of wilderness, pristine forests and rivers, soaring mountains (including Mount McKinley, the US's highest peak), frozen tundra and volcanos, plus great wildlife and whalewatching. Alaska has more coastline than all the other US States combined, with hundreds of inlets and strings of islands that reach almost as far as Japan and Siberia. The new 26-acre **Alaska Native Heritage Center** in Anchorage is a good place to start exploring Native Alaskan culture, with art galleries, history displays and dance and theatre performances (tel: 907-263 5170; 1-800-315 6608; www.alaskanative.net). The **Kodiak Native Tourism Association** (tel: 907-486 6014; 1-888-288 5736) markets Native-run lodges, museums, fishing and cultural tours on Kodiak Island, south-west of Anchorage. Other Native tourism in the state includes **Chugach Heritage Center** (tel: 907-224 5065) in Seward; **Eklutna Historical Park** (tel: 907-688 3824) near Anchorage; day tours in **Wrangell** on the Stikine river; **Saxman Native Village** – featuring a collection of giant Tlingit totem poles – near Ketchikan (Cape Fox Tours, tel: 907-225 4846); and the **Totem Heritage Center** in Ketchikan (Ketchikan Indian Corporation, tel: 907-225 5158). In the state's interior, **Alexander's River Adventure**, run by a Native Athabascan family, offers day trips from Fairbanks to a salmon-fishing camp on the Tanana River for $99 or $125 (tel: 907-474 3924). In Barrow, 500 kilometres above the Arctic Circle, there is **Tundra Tours** (two-day tour: $600 from Anchorage, tel: 907-478 8520, www.alaskaone.com/topworld) and the **Inupiat Heritage Center** (tel: 907-852 0422). Other Native tourism ventures in northern Alaska include **Tour Arctic** (three-day tours $544); the Museum of the Arctic in **Kotzebue** (tel: 907-442 3747); and **Gambell Village Tours** (tel: 907-276 7568) on St Lawrence Island – an island within sight of Siberia. (These are all Eskimo communities.) Most tours in Alaska only operate between May and September. (See also **Athabasca Cultural Journeys**, **St Paul Island** and **Yukon River Tours**, below.)

■ Alaska Native Tourism Council: 1577 C Street, Suite 304, Anchorage AK 99501

☎ 907-274 5400 ✆ 907-263 9971

✉ avi@ruralak.org

■ Alaska Airlines Vacations (for Barrow, Kotzebue, Kodiak)

☎ 1-800-468 2248

■ Southeast Alaska Visitor Center (for Saxman, Wrangell, Ketchikan): Ketchikan

☎ 907-228 6214

Athabasca Cultural Journeys   TOUR
Three-day camping trips in the interior, starting from the Athabascan village of Huslia and visiting a camp in the Koyukuk National Wildlife Refuge. Superb scenery and wildlife including moose, caribou, bear, wolf, otter, beaver, eagles and owls. Hiking, fishing and boat trips. Three-day tour: $1650.

■ PO Box 72, Huslia, Alaska AK99746

☎ 907-829 2261; 1-800-937 0899

ATTA (Alliance of Tribal Tourism Advocates)   ORG
ATTA is an umbrella association promoting tourism for nine tribes in South Dakota. Hunting, fishing, tipi stays and hiking.

■ Daphne Cook, Oglala Sioux Tribe: PO Box 3008, Pine Ridge, SD 57770

☎ 605 867-5771; 605-455 2094 ✆ 605-867 1471

🌐 www.atta.indian.com

■ Ronald L Neiss, Rosebud Sioux Tribe: PO Box 430, Rosebud, SD 57570

☎ 605 747 2381; 605-747 5205 ✆ 605-747 2243

✉ rstuc@gwtc.net

Bear Print International   TOUR
Bear Print produces AIM4Awareness, the magazine of the American Indian Movement and publishes *The Trail of Many Spirits* by Serle Chapman, a highly-praised book about the history and contemporary culture of Native America. They also run tours to Native American lands and communities with tribal leaders, spokespeople and prominent Native American actors and artists. Tours aim to give a real insight into the history and lives of Native Americans, rather than the tourist stereotypes. Trips are arranged to different regions and tribes, including the Navajo, Lakota (Sioux), Cheyenne and Blackfeet.

■ Sarah Gilbertson: PO Box 244, Cambridge CB5 8YL, UK

☎ 01924-840 111

✉ bearprint@bun.com

Havasupai Tourist Enterprise   ACCOM+

The Havasu Canyon – a side canyon of the Grand Canyon and one of the most enchanting places in the south-west – is part of the Havasupai reservation. It is a beautiful hidden oasis, famous for it's wonderful turquoise waterfalls. It is located 12 kilometres from the road and access is by foot or mule only. In the canyon, there's a comfortable lodge, riverside campsite and tribally run guiding services.

■ PO Box 10, Supai, AZ 86435

❶ 520-448 2141 (Lodge: 520-448 2111)

Ⓦ www.nbs.nau.edu/tribes/havasupai Ⓔ havasupai@nbs.nau.edu

Hopi mesas/Walpi   ACCOM+/DAY

The Hopi villages are among the most visited Native American communities in the US. They occupy incredible locations on top of three inaccessible mesas. The Hopi preserve their traditional spiritual practices, and their ceremonies used to be a major tourist attraction. Recently, however, the Hopi have decided to close most religious ceremonies to tourists. Motel and camping accommodation is available on the reservation and there are guided tours of **Walpi**, the most spectacularly situated of the villages. Photography is not allowed in the Hopi villages.

■ Hopi Cultural Center, Second Mesa

❶ 520-734 2441x190; 520-734 6648

Hualapai Lodge/Grand Canyon West/River Runners   ACCOM+/DAY

The Hualapai run a lodge in Peach Springs (double room $75), and a 'self-drive visitor facility' with a two-hour guided tour on the rim of the Grand Canyon at Grand Canyon West. They also run whitewater rafting trips through the Grand Canyon (daily, March–September, $160 or $235).

■ Ed Rosenfeld: PO Box 359, Peach Springs, AZ 86434

❶ 520-769 2419x21 (1-888-255-9550) ❻ 520-769 2410

Largo NavajoLand Tours   TOUR

Navajo-owned company that offers eight-day tours of the south-west, using Indian-owned accommodation and guides. There are 'soft' tours (travelling by car, staying in motels) or more adventurous trips where you camp or sleep in *hogans* (log huts) plus horseriding, hiking, etc. Customized itineraries available. John Largo is also involved in the Dine Bi Keyah (Navajo) Tourism Association and will provide information on other Navajo tourism facilities.

■ John Largo

❶ + ❻ 505-8630050 (1-888-726 9084)

Ⓦ www.navajolandtours.com Ⓔ jlargo@cia-g.com

Moccasin Tracks Tours   TOUR
Tours to the San Carlos Apache and Fort Apache Reservations in Arizona led by an Apache story-teller. Rodeos, camping, ceremonial dances and archaeological sites.

■ Irma Bell Kitcheyan: PO Box 80982, Phoenix, AZ 85060-0982

❶ 602-294 9320

Ⓦ www.ncaied.org/moccasintrackstour

Navajo Tourism Department   ORG
Navajoland is the largest Native American reserve in the US and includes some spectacular scenery, such as Monument Valley (made famous by John Ford's classic Westerns) and the cliff dwellings of Canyon de Chelly. We don't have space to list all Navajo guides: many are based at the entrance to Monument Valley. They offer jeep tours of the Valley, and many will also do longer hiking and camping tours. The Navajo Tourism Department has a list of Navajo guides.

■ Navajoland Tourism: Economic Development Building, Highway 264 (Postal: PO Box 663), Window Rock, AZ 86515

❶ 520-871-6436; 520-871 7371 ❶ 520-871-7381

Ⓦ www.navajoland.com

Pueblos, New Mexico   DAY/TOUR
There are 19 Pueblo communities in New Mexico, mostly along the Rio Grande near Santa Fe. Although they do not organize tours, most are open to visitors and have crafts shops. Many charge a small admission fee and a separate fee to take photographs. The best known and most impressive are **Taos** and **Ácoma**, which is known as Sky City because of its spectacular mesa-top location. The Pueblo Cultural Center in Alburquerque has displays on Pueblo culture and visitor information for all the Pueblos. The *Rough Guide to Southwest USA* and *Touring the Pueblos: A Travel Guide* by Ron Swartley ($10.95, Frontier Image Press) are two useful guidebooks. A Santa Fe company, **Nambe Peublo Tours**, organizes tours of the Pueblos.

■ Pueblo Cultural Center: 2401 12th Street NW (one block north of I-40), Albuquerque, New Mexico 87104

❶ 505-843 7270 (1-800-766 4405)

Ⓦ www.indianpueblo.com Ⓔ info@indian.pueblo.com

■ Eight Northern Indian Pueblos

❶ 505-852 4265 (1-800-793 4955)

■ Nambe Pueblo Tours: 112 W San Francisco St, Santa Fe

❶ 505-820 1340 (1-800-946 2623)

Ride with Native Americans DAY/TOUR

A Nez Perce guide who leads horseriding treks into Hell's Canyon, Idaho. For good riders only. Plus Native American history, and wildlife including bear, cougar, eagles.

■ Jon Yearout: PO Box 231, Lapwai, Idaho 83540

☏ 208-843 2452

St Paul Island TOUR

Tours from three to eight days to remote **St Paul Island**, 450 kilometres off the Alaskan mainland, run by the Native Aleut people of the island. St Paul is a spectacular wildlife and birdwatching destination: the island's fur seal and seabird rookeries are among the largest in the world with over 800,000 seals and more than a million seabirds. Plus fishing, reindeer and a chance to experience life on this remote island. From $900 to $1640, including flight from Anchorage.

■ Reeve Aleutian Airways

☏ 1-800-544 2248

■ Alaska's Southwest

☏ 562 7380

✉ pribilof@alaska.net

Totem Pole Tours DAY/TOUR

Run by Vergil Bedoni, a Navajo guide. Jeep, horseback and camping tours in Monument Valley and NavajoLand. Can also arrange homestays with Navajo families and Navajo culture tours (stories, plant medicine, etc). $75 per day or $25 for a two hour tour.

■ Vergil Bedoni: PO Box 360579, Monument Valley, Utah 84536-0579

☏ 435-727 3313 (1-800-345 8687) ☏ 435-727 3315

🌐 www.moab-utah.com/totempole ✉ vbedoni@aol.com

Ute Mountain Ute Tribal Park DAY/TOUR

A tribally run park in south-west Colorado near the Four Corners state junction. It features Anasazi cliff villages (comparable to nearby Mesa Verde but less visited) and spectacular South-West scenery. Day tours and longer camping and hiking trips. June-September. Day tour: $25.

■ PO Box 109, Towaoc, CO 81344

☏ 303-565 3751 (1-800-847 5485) ☏ 303-565 7412

🌐 http://swcolo.org/Tourism/Archaeology/UteMtTribalPark.html ✉ utepark@fone.net

Walk Softly Tours TOUR

Tours to Navajoland and the Hopi mesas, etc, in Arizona. A non-Indian company but one that uses Indian-owned tours, accommodation and guides. Navajo/Hopi culture, arts and crafts, visits to Canyon de Chelly, Monument Valley, etc.

■ PO Box 6371, Scottsdale, AZ 85261-6371

🕿 602-473 1148 🖷 602-473 1149

🆆 www.walksoftlytours.com 🄴 roundup@goodnet.com 🄴 jriley@amug.org

■ In the UK: Tribes Travel (see Responsible tour operators)

Yukon River Tours DAY/TOUR

Day and overnight boat trips on Alaska's unspoiled Yukon River, three hours north of Fairbanks on the Dalton Highway. Opportunities for hiking, canoeing, fishing, birdwatching. Owned and operated by the Athabascan community of Stevens Village. There is also an Athabascan cultural centre/museum.

■ David Lacey: 214 Second Avenue, Fairbanks, Alaska, AK 99701-4811

🕿 907-474 8224 🖷 907 452 7162

🆆 www.mosquitonet.com/~dlacey/yrt.html 🄴 dlacey@mosquitonet.com

VENEZUELA *

International dialling code +58.

Venezuela is another South American country with many natural highlights, including coral reefs, palm-fringed Caribbean beaches, wildlife-rich plains, snow-capped mountains and tropical rainforest. Most Venezuelans live near the Caribbean coast, with its lovely (but littered) beaches and good coastal national parks, such as Morrocoy and Mochima or the coral reefs of the Islas Los Roques. Isla Margarita, in the Caribbean, is the country's most developed beach destination.

Merida is a pleasant town in the Andes with good hiking and many tour agencies and backpacker hostels. Merida also boasts the world's longest cable car in the world and an ice-cream parlour that claims to serve the widest range of flavours on earth.

More adventurous destinations lie to the south. Los Llanos, an open savannah comparable to the plains of East Africa, is one of the best place in South America to see wildlife. There are the wild, rarely-visited, roadless rainforests

---

* *Publisher's update:* In December 1999, flash floods followed by mudslides killed thousands of people and wiped out entire towns along Venezuela's northern coastline. Widespread damage to the country's infrastructure will take some time to repair. Road access is restricted and, as of 6th January 2000, domestic flights were running at 30 per cent of their usual capacity.

of Amazonas in the south and the Orinoco Delta on the Atlantic coast, home to mainly indigenous communities. The vast, hauntingly beautiful, thinly populated Gran Sabana in the far south is a mixture of rainforest and open plains interspersed by ancient *tepuis* – towering flat-topped mountains with sheer cliffs on all sides. Huge waterfalls fall over these cliffs, including Angel Falls, the world's tallest. On the border with Brazil is Roraima, the highest of the *tepuis*, which reputedly inspired Arthur Conan Doyle's novel, *The Lost World*. The Gran Sabana is the homeland of the indigenous Pemon.

Canaima/Angel Falls region

Canaima, in the Gran Sabana, is the main tourist base for visiting the Angel Falls. Many tour agencies in Caracas, Porlamar, Cuidad Bolivar and Canaima offer trips to the falls but this listing highlights Pemon-run tourism. In Canaima itself, two Pemon agencies are **Kamaracoto** and **Excursiones Churum Vena**. (Kamarocoto also have offices in Cuidad Bolivar, tel: 085-27680). These agencies offer six-day river trips to Angel Falls (from $200, May–December) which finish in the community of **Kamarata**. In Kamarata, **Aicha Vena Tours** (Tito Abati, tel: 086-620443) does the same route the other way round. There are also community-owned cabañas in **Kavak**, a Pemon settlement close to the impressive Kavak Canyon. A Pemon guide in Kavak is Marino Sandoval of **Excursiones Pemon**. From either Kamarata (ask for **Lino**, the English teacher) or Kavak, you can organize 10-day treks to the top of Auyantepuy, the Angel Falls tepuy – an adventurous trip that involves tough hiking. There are no roads in this region: flights to Canaima or Kavak (from Caracas, Porlamar or Cuidad Bolivar) cost approximately $70.

Corpomedina CA/Proyecto Paria ACCOM/ORG/TOUR

ToDo! Award winner

A community-owned company on the Paria peninsula in north-east Venezuela. The peninsula has beautiful tropical beaches, rainforest in the mountains behind the coast and a superb wet savannah on the coastal plains. Corpomedina embraces a network of community tourism projects that employ 142 local people and reinvest profits in the local community. These include two small beach resorts. **Playa Medina** is the more upmarket of the two, with eight cabañas on a beautiful secluded beach (double rooms: $158 including meals). The other, **Playa Puipu**y, is cheaper. There is also a small hotel, **Posada La Colina**, in Carúpano, which is the main town of the peninsula. The Posada will organize transfers to the beaches, plus trips to other tourism projects in Paria including the **Jardin Botanico El Pilar**, the hot mineral springs of **Agua Sana** where there is a small hotel; and a buffalo ranch called **Hato Rio de Agua** where there is (solar-powered) accommodation, horseriding and canoe trips to spot crocodiles and water buffalo. Tours can also be arranged to the Orinoco Delta and the amazing Cueva del Guácharo, a vast cave system that is home to thousands of guácharos (oil birds). Carúpano itself is known for having

Venezuela's most traditional and colourful Carnival. Another Corpomedina offshoot, **Proyecto Paria**, provides micro-credit and business support to small local businesses. Apart from at Playa Medina, accommodation is $50 per night for a double room with breakfasts. **Vuelta Larga**, near El Pilar, is another buffalo-ranch/lodge on the Paria peninsula (although not connected with Corpomedina). The owner, Klaus Múller, organizes tours to nearby cloudforest and works with indigenous Warao communities.

■ Wilfried Merle, Corpomedina: Callejon Santa Rosa 9, Casa del Cable, Carúpano, Estado Sucre

🕓 094-320 527 🕓 094-312 067

🅴 wilfried@telcel.net.ve

■ Playas Medina and Puipuy

🕓 094-315 241

■ Klaus Muller, Vuelta Larga: Calle Bolivar 8, Guaraúnos

🕓 094-69052; 094-647 292

Roraima (San Francisco de Yuruani/Paraitepui)   BUDGET/TOUR
Roraima lies on the southern edge of the Gran Sabana, on the border with Brazil and Guayana. Pemon guides can be hired for the six-day hike to the top of Roraima in the villages of **San Francisco de Yuruani** or **Paraitepui**. In Paraitepui, ask for 'el Capitan': men from the village work as guides on a rota system with communally-agreed rates (currently $15 per day). In San Francisco, **Roraima Tours** is a Pemon-run agency.

■ Roraima Tours: Ana Ferna'ndez

🕓 088-951 283

ZAMBIA

International dialling code +260.
Zambia is one of the less-established Southern African destinations, but its wildlife compares favourably with its neighbours. With plains and woodlands enclosed by steep escarpment walls, the Luangwa valley is one of Africa's richest wildlife areas. Two national parks (North and South Luangwa National Parks) contain huge herds of elephant and buffalo, lion, leopard, hyena, impala, etc. These parks are particularly known for walking safaris, which were pioneered here. Zambia's other big attraction is, of course, the Victoria Falls, which it shares with Zimbabwe.

Zambia is a poor country with high unemployment, a national economy crippled by debt repayments, a crumbling mining industry and an alarming AIDS problem. The government sees tourism as an important potential income earner.

Kawaza Village ACCOM+/DAY

A Kunda (Bantu-speaking) village in the Luangwa Valley. The village works with Robin Pope Safaris – a safari operator in the South Luangwa National Park. Visitors can meet craftspeople, the chief or the traditional healer, visit the local school or tour neighbouring villages with local guides. Dancing, drumming and story-telling are featured. Day trips and overnight stays in local-style huts. $20 per night including food and activities. Camping: $12. The project is run by an elected team of villagers.

■ Kawaza Village Tourism Project: PO Box 15, Mfuwe

Ⓦ www.ftsl.demon.co.uk/kvtp.htm

■ Robin Pope Safaris: PO Box 80, Mfuwe

Ⓣ 062-45090 Ⓕ 062-45051 rps@super-hub.com

Ⓔ popesaf@zamnet.zm

■ In the UK: Sunvil and Discovery Initiatives (see Responsible tour operators)

Mukuni Village/Songwe Point DAY

Songwe Point is a hotel overlooking the Victoria Falls from the Zambia side, which has been designed to look like a traditional village. Activities include tours to Mukuni village, which – despite being over 700 years old – is a real village. There are other interesting archaeological sites nearby. The local community owns a share of the business. Visits can be booked from the Victoria Falls Safari Lodge, just across the border in Zimbabwe.

■ Victoria Falls Safari Lodge, Zimbabwe

Ⓣ (+263)13-3211 Ⓕ (+263)13 3211

■ In the UK: Rainbow Tours (see Responsible tour operators)

Nsendamila Village DAY

Another Kunda village near the South Luangwa National Park. Nsendamila offers day trips rather than overnight stays, but also affords visitors a taste of rural Zambian life. $5 entry.

■ Ask for directions from Mfuwe

ZIMBABWE

International dialling code +263.
Incoming foreign tourism supports an estimated 100,000 jobs in Zimbabwe, and a third of all visitors are British. As in most African countries, safaris are the mainstay of tourism in Zimbabwe: over 95 per cent of Zimbabwe tourism is nature based. Hwange National Park is the star, with over 100 animal species

and huge elephant herds. The country has other attractions, of course. Most tourists find time to visit the mighty Victoria Falls, and the adventurous among them bungee-jump or whitewater raft on the Zambezi River near the Falls. In Great Zimbabwe, too, the country has one of Africa's most impressive and mysterious archaeological sites. The Chimanimani mountains in the eastern highlands have lovely hiking, while the Matobo Hills National Park contains a unique landscape of giant scattered boulders, as well as rock art.

CAMPFIRE (Communal Areas Management Programme for Indigenous Resources) ORG

The CAMPFIRE scheme was set up by the Zimbabwean government to promote development of Zimbabwe's rural villages. Although a state programme, the emphasis is on decentralized village management. In the past, CAMPFIRE villages concentrated on selling hunting permits as a source of income, but some communities are now moving into safari and cultural tourism. CAMPFIRE lodges listed here include **Chesvingo**, **Mavuradonha**, **Sunungukai**, **Sanyati Bridge**, **Mahenye** and **Chilo** (see Gonarezhou National Park, below) but more are being developed: contact the CAMPFIRE Association for information.

■ CAMPFIRE Association: 15 Philipps Avenue, Belgravia, Harare

☎ 04-72 957 ☏ 04-795 150

ⓦ www.campfire-zimbabwe.org ⓔ campfir@id.co.zw or

■ Steve Kasere: Mukuvisi Woodlands, (Postal: PO Box 661), Harare

☎ 04-747 422 ☏ 04-747 470

■ Africa Resources Trust: PO Box HG690, Highlands, Harare

☎ 04-732 625 ☏ 04-739 163

■ In the UK: Keith Madders/Christine Lippai: Zimbabwe Trust, The Old Lodge, Christchurch Road, Epsom, Surrey KT19 8NE, UK

☎ 01372-741237

ⓔ christine.lippai@virgin.net ⓔ keith.madders@virgin.net

Chesvingo Lakeside Village (Masvingo) ACCOM+/BUDGET

Near Great Zimbabwe, with attractive lake and mountain scenery. Simple lodgings, guided walks, rock art. Run by the local Shona community.

■ PO Box 773, Masvingo

☎ 039-7157

■ Travel World: Masvingo

☎ 039-62131 ☏ 039-64205

Chilangililo   ACCOM/DAY

A Tongan cooperative in Binga by Lake Kariba. Chilangililo offers low-cost stays in traditional slilt houses on the lakeshore, plus guided visits to Tonga villages and local handicrafts.

■ Private Bag 5713, Binga

❶ 115-2407

✉ windwaai@cis.co.za (Peta Jones)

Emadwaleni (Matobo Hills, Bulawayo)   ACCOM+

Overnight stays in a Ndebele village in the Matobo Hills outside Bulawayo, with traditional Ndebele food and guided tours including visits to craftspeople such as the blacksmith and the traditional doctor. Also walking safaris, horseback trails.

■ Emadwaleni Tours and Village, 1 McNeillie Road, Riverside, Bulawayo

❶ + ❶ 09-48889

■ In the UK: Rainbow Tours (see Responsible tour operators)

Gonarezhou National Park/Savé Valley/River Lodges of Africa
SAFARI

In south-east Zimbabwe near Chireszi and the Mozambique border, **Gonarezhou National Park** comprises 5000 square kilometres of wilderness with good wildlife, birdwatching, sandstone cliffs, waterfalls and forest. In the park, **Mahenye** and **Chilo** are lodges co-owned by local communities in the CAMPFIRE programme. Chilo is the larger and more upmarket of the two. The lodges are managed by a commercial company called **River Lodges of Africa**, run by Clive Stockil (a conservationist involved in the creation of CAMPFIRE). Guests at the lodges can visit local Shangaan villages. **Senuko Lodge**, in the nearby **Savé Valley Conservancy**, is also owned by River Lodges of Africa. Although not a CAMPFIRE project, the Savé Valley Conservancy Trust works to involve and benefit local communities. At over 3000 square kilometres, Savé is the largest private wildlife reserve in Africa and wildlife includes cheetah, leopard and black rhino.

■ River Lodges of Africa: Private Bag 7013, Chiredzi

❶ 031-3129; 031-3139 ❶ 031-3179

✉ senuko@svc.icon.co.zw

Inyathi Valley (Victoria Falls)   ACCOM/BUDGET

Rondavel and dormitory accommodation, especially for school and youth groups, developed by ex-combatants through the Zimbabwe Project Trust.

■ Ronnie Patel: PO Box CT300, Victoria Falls

❶ 013-4481 (Zimbabwe Project Trust: Tel: 09-68804)

■ In the UK: Rainbow Tours (see Responsible tour operators)

Kunzwana Trust/Siachilaba Community Tourism Project   TOUR

Kunzwana Trust is a non-profit organization which promotes Zimbabwe's indigenous music. The Trust arranges two and three-day trips to the Tonga village of **Siachilaba**, near Binga in north-west Zimbabwe, with a special emphasis on local music. Attractions include music performances, local crafts (basketwork, beadwork, drums), plus a chance to experience daily village life, visit community projects, etc. Can be combined with Hwange National Park and Victoria Falls.

■ Kunzwana Trust: Penny Yon, 4 Nettleton Road, Braeside, Harare (Postal: PO Box MP349, Mount Pleasant, Harare)

☎ + ✆ 04-742065

✉ kunzwana@pci.co.zw

Mavuradonha Wilderness Camp   ACCOM/SAFARI

A community-owned camp in the 500 square kilometre Mavuradonha Wilderness Area in northern Zimbabwe. Simple A-frame huts and camping spaces. Good wildlife viewing and birdlife, plus excellent hiking on marked trails through rugged, mountainous countryside. Local guides available. The camp is now managed by the **Zimbabwe Wildlife Society** who pay 10 per cent of takings back to the community.

■ Wildlife Society of Zimbabwe: PO Box 3497, Harare

☎ 04-700 451

■ CAMPFIRE: see above

Monde Village (Victoria Falls)   ACCOM/DAY

Guided tours of this village, 13 kilometres from Victoria Falls. Local customs, history, architecture, etc. There is also simple accommodation in the village.

■ Steve Bolnick, Baobab Safaris: PO Box 196, Victoria Falls

☎ 013-4283

✉ safaris@telconet.co.zw

■ In the UK: Rainbow Tours (see Responsible tour operators)

Nduna Safari Lodge   SAFARI

A luxury safari lodge on the border with Mozambique, owned by the Malilangwe Conservation Trust. Money from tourism is reinvested in the reserve and in community projects.

■ Wilderness Safaris (see South Africa)

Sanyati Bridge Camp   ACCOM+

Community-run accommodation (self-catering rondavels and campsites) on the road between Karoi and the Bumi Hills, beside the Matusadona National Park. Attractions include game viewing, bush walking in rugged countryside, good birdlife, fishing and trips to local villages. Restaurant and crafts shop. Profits go to community projects such as schools and health clinics. Rondavals: $60 per night. Camping: $20.

■ Zambezi Society: Mukuvisi Woodlands, cnr Glenara Avenue and Hillside Road, Harare

❶ 04-731 596

Sunungukai Camp   ACCOM+

The first CAMPFIRE tourism project to be fully run by local communities. Sunungukai, in northern Zimbabwe on the edge of the Umfurudzi Safari Area, consists of four traditional-style chalets and offers rugged hiking, fishing, birdwatching and wildlife plus the chance to see Bushman paintings, meet traditional healers, experience village life and buy local crafts. The camp is run by a locally elected committee. $10 per night.

■ CAMPFIRE: (see above)

HOLIDAY-FINDER INDEX

This index will help you find holidays that match your own interests. Projects may be listed in more than one category. These indexes are selective: just because a project is not listed under 'birdwatching', for instance, doesn't mean that you won't see *any* birds there, but we've tried to highlight the projects that offer the best in each category, or ones that place a particular emphasis on that type of activity.

AGRITOURISM

Agritourism means participating in or learning about local farming methods and related traditions and lifestyles.

Costa Rica	COOPRENA
Guatemala	Eco-Escuela (Bio Itza School), PRODEFOR
India	Alternative Travels, ROSE
Indonesia	Mitra Bali
Mexico	Las Canadas, Maya Ik (Nacajuc)
Peru	Granja Porcon
Sri Lanka	Woodlands Network
Tanzania	Cultural Tourism Programme
Thailand	TVS-Rest

ARCHAEOLOGICAL SITES

Ecuador	Huacamayos
Egypt	Wind, Sand & Stars
Ethiopia	Experience Ethiopia
Guatemala	Agua Selva, Montes Azules, Pro-Peten/EcoMaya
Indonesia	Bina Swadaya
Peru	Llama Trek, Ollantaytambo Heritage Trails
Tanzania	Trade Aid Mikindani
US	Hopi mesas, Ute Mountain Ute
Zimbabwe	Mukuni

ARTS AND CRAFTS

Many community projects have shops selling local paintings, crafts, etc.

Belize	Toledo Ecotourism Association
Canada	Anishinabe Experience, Shawenequanape Kipichewin, Tours Innu
Gambia	Tumani Tenda
Guatemala	Totonicapan
Indonesia	Bina Swadaya, Mitra Bali, Sua Bali
Kenya	Tawasal Institute
Mexico	Union de Museos Comunitarios de Oaxaca
Peru	Willoc
Senegal	Crossing Cultures
Thailand	Thai Tribal Crafts
Zimbabwe	Emadwaleni

BACKPACKERS/BUDGET GUESTHOUSES

Australia	Darlgunaya Backpackers
Guatemala	Hotel Backpackers
Mexico	Agua Selva, Maruata 2000, Tourist Yu'u
Namibia	Aba Huab, Khowarib, Omatako, Ongongo, Purros, Salambala
New Zealand	Main Street Backpackers
Senegal	Campement Villageois

BEACHES

Australia	Kooljaman, Lombardina
Brazil	Prainha do Canto Verde
Costa Rica	ATEC, Lapa Rios
Egypt	Basata
Mexico	Maruata 2000, San José el Hueyate
Panama	San Blas
Samoa	all listings
Solomon Islands	Vanua Rapita
South Africa	Eco-Escapes, Rainbow, Wilderness Safaris (Rocktail Bay)
Tanzania	Zanzibar Travel
Thailand	TVS, Yat Fon
Venezuela	Corpomedina

BIRDWATCHING

All tours in the Cloudforest and Rainforest sections (below) offer good birdwatching.

Belize	Belize Audubon Society
Ecuador	all listings
Peru	Casa Machiguenga, Manu Wildlife Centre, Tambopata
Mexico	Grupo Ecologico Sierra Gorda, Maya Ik (Rio Lagartos)
South Africa	Wilderness Safaris (Ndumo)
US	St Paul Island
Zimbabwe	Mavuradonha

CANOEING/SEA-KAYAKING

Canada	Nuuhchimi Wiinuu, Tours Innu
Samoa	Eco-Tour Samoa
Solomon Islands	Solomon Islands Village Stay
South Africa	Lake Sibaya

CAVES

Australia	Mimbi Caves
Belize	Toledo Ecotourism Association
Ecuador	Huacamayos
Mexico	Sierra Tarahumara, Union de Museos Comunitarios de Oaxaca

CLOUDFOREST

Ecuador	Bellavista, Fundación Golondrinas, Maquipucuna, Oyacachi
Honduras	El Carbon
Mexico	Grupo Ecologico Sierra Gorda, Las Canadas

CULTURE

Most of the tours in this guide offer contact with local people and insights into local culture – this is one of the big attractions of community-based tourism.

The following place a special emphasis on exploring of local culture.

Australia	Aboriginal Arts and Cultural Centre, Desert Tracks, Manyallaluk, Tiwi Tours, Umorrduk
Botswana	Kalahari Sunset Tours
Canada	Anishinabe Experience, Cowichan, Shawenequanape Kipichewin
Guatemala	Totonicapan
India	Alternative Travels, Insight India, Kolam
Indonesia	Bina Swadaya, Mitra Bali, Sua Bali
Kenya	Tawasal Institute
Mexico	Union de Museos Comunitarios de Oaxaca
Namibia	Lianshulu (Lizauli), Khowarib (Anmire), Tsumkwe
New Zealand	Te Wero Nui
Peru	Ollantaytambo Heritage Trails, Taquile, Willoc, Winaymarka
South Africa	Isinamva
Sri Lanka	Woodlands Network
Tanzania	Cultural Tourism Programme
Thailand	Symbiosis, TVS-Rest
Uganda	UCOTA
US	Bear Print, Moccasin Tracks
Zambia	Kawaza, Nsendamila
Zimbabwe	Kunzwana, Monde Village

DESERT

Australia	Aboriginal Arts and Cultural Centre, Anangu Tours, Desert Tracks
Botswana	Kalahari Sunset Tours
Egypt	Wind, Sand & Stars
Morocco	Tizi-Randonnées
Namibia	all listings
US	Havasupai, Largo Tours, Navajo Tourism Dept, Totem Pole, Walk Softly

DEVELOPMENT PROJECTS

India	Equations, Kolam, Insight India, Project India
Indonesia	Bina Swadaya, Mitra Bali
Kenya	Tawasal
Philippines	Biyaheng Pinoy

South Africa	Calabash, Rainbow
Sri Lanka	Woodlands Network
Tanzania	Simply Tanzania
Thailand	TVS-REST
General Operators	Community Aid Abroad Tours (see page 68)

FISHING

Australia	Kooljaman, Lombardina
Canada	Kanio Kashee Lodge, Tin Wis/Sea Serpent
Costa Rica	ATEC
Solomon Islands	Solomon Islands Village Stay, Vanua Rapita
South Africa	Lake Sibaya
US	Alaska (Alexander's River Adventure, Kodiak Island), Athabasca Cultural Journeys, Yukon River Tours
Zimbabwe	Sanyati Bridge

HEALING (TRADITIONAL, PLANT)

Many of the tours listed under Culture and Rainforest include walks identifying traditional medicinal plants.

Canada	Shawenequanape Kipichewin
Botswana	Kalahari Sunset Tours
Ecuador	RICANCIE
Guatemala	Eco-Escuela (Bio-Itza School)
Honduras	El Carbon
Indonesia	Sua Bali
Mexico	CICE, Las Canadas
Namibia	Purros
South Africa	Eco-Escapes
Sri Lanka	Woodlands Network
Tanzania	Sisi Kwa Sisi
Thailand	Symbiosis

HOMESTAYS AND VILLAGE STAYS

Belize	Toledo Ecotourism Association
Cuba	Casa del Caribe
Honduras	Rio Platano

India	Alternative Travels, Kolam, ROSE
Indonesia	Bina Swadaya, Mitra Bali
Kenya	Tawasal
Kyrgyzstan	Karokol Intercultural Programme
Peru	Amananti, Taquile, Winaymarka
Philippines	Biyaheng Pinoy
Samoa	all listings
Senegal	Campement Villageois, Crossing Cultures
Solomon Islands	Solomon Islands Village Stays
Sri Lanka	Woodlands Network
South Africa	Isinamva
Tanzania	Cultural Tourism Programme, Sisi Kwa Sisi
Thailand	TVS-Rest
Zambia	Kawaza
Zimbabwe	Chilangililo, Emadwaleni

HORSERIDING

Belize	Toledo Ecotourism Association
Canada	Quaaout Lodge
Ecuador	Casa Mojanda, Fundación Golondrinas, Oyacachi
India	Alternative Travels
Mexico	Grupo Ecologico Serra Gorda
US	Largo Navajoland Tours, Ride with Native Americans, Totem Pole

LANGUAGE SCHOOLS

Guatemala	Eco-Escuela, Proyecto Linguistico Quetzalteco
Cuba	Caledonia Languages Abroad

LUXURY

Botswana	Uncharted Africa
Costa Rica	Lapa Rios
Ecuador	Kapawi
Namibia	Damaraland
South Africa	CCAfrica, Wilderness Safaris
Zimbabwe	Nduna

MUSIC AND DANCE

Cuba	Caledonia Languages Abroad, Karamba
Gambia	Tumani Tenda
Senegal	Karamba
Zimbabwe	Kunzwana

RAINFOREST

Belize	Toledo Ecotourism Association
Bolivia	Chalalan
Brazil	ASPEC
Costa Rica	ATEC, Lapa Rios
Ecuador	most listings
Guatemala	Pro-Peten/EcoMaya
Honduras	all listings
Indonesia	Bina Swadaya
Mexico	Montes Azules
Peru	Casa Machiguenga, InkaNatura, Tambopata
Philippines	Aeta
Solomon Islands	Makira Hill Tribes Trek
Venezuela	Canaima

SAFARIS AND WILDLIFE

Most tours in the Rainforest section (above) also feature good wildlife

Botswana	most listings
Kenya	most listings
Tanzania	most listings
Namibia	most listings
South Africa	most listings
US	St Paul Island, Athabasca Cultural Journeys
Zambia	most listings
Zimbabwe	most listings

SNORKELLING AND DIVING

Costa Rica	ATEC
Indonesia	Togean Ecotourism Network

Panama	San Blas
Samoa	all listings
Solomon Islands	Solomon Islands Village Stay, Vanua Rapita
South Africa	Wilderness Safaris (Rocktail Bay)
Thailand	RVS-REST

TREKKING/HIKING

Ecuador	Fundación Golondrinas, Oyacachi
India	Dhami Dham, Tashila Tours
Mexico	Sierra Tarahumara
Morocco	Tizi-Randonnées
Nepal	all listings
Pakistan	Full Moon Night Trekking
Peru	Llama Trek
Solomon Islands	Makira
Tanzania	IntoAfrica
Thailand	TVS-Rest, PDA, PRLC
Uganda	UCOTA
Venezuela	Canaima, Roraima
Zimbabwe	Mavuradonha

TRIBAL CULTURE/LIFESTYLES

Australia	Anangu, Desert Tracks, Manyullaluk, Peppimenarti, Umdorruk
Botswana	Kalahari Sunset Safaris
Canada	all listings
Ecuador	all rainforest tours
Kenya	Tawasal Institute
Malaysia	Ulu Ai
Namibia	Tsumkwe
Philippines	Aeta
Solomon Islands	Makira Hill Tribes Trek
Thailand	TVS-Rest, Symbiosis
US	Bear Print

URBAN TOURS

Australia	Dharawal Tours, Sydney Aboriginal Discoveries
Philippines	Biyaheng Pinoy
South Africa	Calabash, Rainbow

VOLUNTEERING

We list a few short volunteer placements (a month or less) which can be fitted into a holiday, but not long-term placements such as VSO.

Costa Rica	COOPRENA
Kyrgyzstan	Intercultural Programme
Ecuador	Fundación Golondrinas
India	Project India, ROSE
Senegal	Crossing Cultures
Sri Lanka	Woodlands Network
General Operators	Cross-Cultural Solutions (see page 66), Earthwatch (see page 60), IVEX (see page 66)

WHALEWATCHING

Canada	Sea Serpent, Tours Innu
New Zealand	Whale-Watch Kaikoura

WOMEN

Many projects offer insights into the situation of women in different societies, and a number of projects in the book, such as Woodlands Network in Sri Lanka, specifically involve women's groups, but this tour focuses specifically on women's issues.

India	Project India/Cross-Cultural Solutions

SECTION THREE

USEFUL INFORMATION

RESPONSIBLE TOURISM ORGANIZATIONS AND RESOURCES

CATEGORIES

Organizations and websites

- Members of TEN (Third World Tourism European Network)
- Responsible tourism: the West
- Responsible tourism: developing world
- Ecotourism
- General travel
- Environment and conservation
- Indigenous people
- UK-based development organizations

Books

- Academic, textbooks
- Guidebooks, magazines

KEY
■ contact name/address ❶ telephone ❶ fax Ⓦ website ❷ email

TOURISM CONCERN

■ Stapleton House, 277–281 Holloway Road, London N7 8HN, UK

❶ 020-7753 3330 ❶ 020-7753 3331

Ⓦ www.tourismconcern.org.uk ❷ info@tourismconcern.org.uk

MEMBERS OF TEN (THIRD WORLD TOURISM EUROPEAN NETWORK)

TEN is a loose association of NGOs with interests similar to those of Tourism Concern.

Arbeitskreis Tourismus und Entwicklung
Swiss NGO working for responsible tourism.

■ Missionsstrasse 21, CH-4003, Basel, Switzerland

☏ +41 (0)61-2614 742 ☏ +41 (0)61-261 4721

ⓦ www.akte.ch ⓔ info@akte.ch

Associazione RAM
Italian NGO working for fair trade and responsible tourism. They also run trips in Nepal, India, Thailand, Bangladesh and Italy.

■ Renzo Garrone, Via Mortola 15, I-16030 San Rocco di Camogli (GE), Italy

☏ + ☏ +39 (0)185 773 061

ⓔ ramcatrg@rapallo.newnetworks.it

Informatie Verre Reizen
Dutch NGO working for responsible tourism.

■ PO Box 1504, NL-6501 Nijmegen, The Netherlands

☏ +31 (0)24-355 2534 ☏ +31 (0)24 355 2473

ⓔ IVR@xs4all.nl

respect/Austrian Centre for Tourism and Development
Austrian campaign for more sustainable tourism.

■ Christian Baumgartner: Diefenbachgasse 36/3, A-1150, Wien, Austria

☏ +43 (0)1-895 6245 ☏ +43 (0)1-812 9789

ⓦ www.respect.at ⓔ office@respect.at

Stichting Retour (Retour Foundation)
Dutch responsible-tourism NGO and non-profit consultancy. Consultancy income is reinvested into campaigns/projects supporting communities affected by tourism.

■ PO Box 1570, 6501 BN Nijmegen, The Netherlands

☏ + ☏ +31 (0)24-360 6224

ⓦ www.do.nl/retour ⓔ retour@do.nl

Studienkreis fur Tourismus und Entwicklung
German responsible-tourism NGO. Organizes the ToDo! Awards.

■ Kapellenweg 3, D-82541 Ammerland, Germany

● +49 (0)8177 1783 ● +49 (0)8177 1349

Ⓦ www.studienkreis.org Ⓔ studienkreistourismus@compuserve.com

Tourism Watch
German responsible-tourism NGO.

■ Nikolaus-Otto-Str 13, D-70771 Leinfelden-Echterdingen, Germany

● +49 (0)711-7989 281/2 ● +49 (0)711-7989 283

Ⓦ www.tourism-watch.org Ⓔ tourism-watch@due.org

Transverses
French responsible tourism NGO.

■ 7 rue Heyrault, F-92100, Boulogne, France

● + ● +33 (0)1-4910 9084

OTHER RESPONSIBLE TOURISM ORGANIZATIONS AND WEBSITES

ACT (Action for Conservation through Tourism)
A charity that helps local communities, NGOs, governments and tour opera-tors to develop and market sustainable tourism projects that benefit local communities.

■ Sue Hurdle: ACT, CREATE Centre, Smeaton Road, Bristol BS1 6XN, UK

● 0117-927 3049 ● 0117-930 0076

Ⓔ act@gn.apc.org

C.E.R.T. (Centre for Environmentally Responsible Tourism)
Runs an award-scheme for 'tour operators working towards high environmen-tal standards'.

■ Peter Chipperfield: Indaba House, 1 Hydeway, Thundersley, Essex SS7 3BE, UK

● 01268-795 772 ● 01268-759 834

Ⓦ www.c-e-r-t.org Ⓔ certdesk@aol.com

ECPAT UK (formerly The Coalition on Child Prostitution and Tourism)

A campaign to end child prostitution, pornography and trafficking, including child-sex tourism in Thailand, the Philippines, the Caribbean, Kenya etc.

■ The Stable Yard, Broomgrove Road, London SW9 9TL, UK

✆ 020-7501 8927 ✆ 020-7738 4110

ⓦ www.ecpatuk.freeserve.co.uk ⓔ ecpatuk@antislavery.org

Partners in Responsible Tourism

US-based tourism campaign organization.

■ PO Box 419085-322, San Francisco, California CA94141, US

✆ + ✆ +1 415-273 1430

ⓦ www2.pirt.org/pirt/ ⓔ bapit@aol.com

RTN (Responsible Tourism Network)

Australian networking organization linked to Community Aid Abroad Tours (see Responsible tour operators).

■ Brian Witty: PO Box 34 Rundle Mall, South Australia 5000

✆ +61 (0)8-8232 2727 (1800-814 848) ✆ +61 (0)8-8232 2808

ⓦ www.caa.org.au/travel/ ⓔ info@tours.caa.org.au

RESPONSIBLE TOURISM ORGANIZATIONS IN DEVELOPING COUNTRIES

ACAP (Annapurna Conservation Area Project)

A project of the King Mahendra Trust for Nature Conservation (KMTNC), the ACAP uses trekking fees to protect the local environment and culture and to fund community schemes. With Tourism Concern, ACAP has published the Himalayan Code providing guidelines for responsible trekking in Nepal.

■ PO Box 183, Pokhara, Nepal

✆ +977 (0)61-21102; 61-28202 ✆ +977 (0)61-28203

ⓔ acap@mos.com.np

ASEC (Asociacion Ecuatoriana de Ecotourismo)

ASEC have published guidelines for ecotourism operators in Ecuador.

■ Diego Andrade-Ubidia, Director Ejecutivo, ASEC, PO Box 17211798, Quito, Ecuador

✆ + ✆ +593 (0)2-466 295; 245 055

ⓔ asec@accessinter.net

Bina Swadaya

An Indonesian community-development NGO. They also run tours (see 'Local tour operators by country: Indonesia').

■ Wisma Jana Karya, Jl Gunung Sahari III/7, Jakarta Pusat 10610 (PO Box 1456, Jakarta 10014), Indonesia

☏ +62 (0)21-420 4402; +62 (0)21-425 5354 ☏ +62 (0)21-420 8412

✉ bst@cbn.net.id

Ecumenical Coalition on Third World Tourism

This Christian-based NGO was a founding light of the responsible tourism movement. It was set up at the 1980 conference in Manila, which published the Manila Declaration on World Tourism criticizing the impact of tourism in the developing world. The NGO published the magazine, Contours. Now based in Hong Kong.

■ Mr Tan Chi Kiong: CCA Centre, 96 2nd District, Pak Tin Village, Mei Tin Road, Shatin, NT, Hong Kong SAR

☏ +852 (0)269 4378

✉ contours@pacific.net.hk

Equations

Indian responsible-tourism organization.

■ 198, 2nd Cross, Church Road, New Thippasandra, Bangalore 560 075, India

☏ +91 (0)80-529 2905 ☏ +91 (0)80-528 2313

🌐 www.equitabletourism.org ✉ admin@equations.ilban.ernet.in

Gambia Tourism Concern

Campaigns to bring more of the benefits of tourism in The Gambia to local people.

■ Adama Bah: Bakadaji Hotel, PO Box 2066, Serrekunda, The Gambia

☏ +220 (0)462 057 ☏ +220 (0)462 307

✉ concern@qanet.gm

IID (Initiatives for International Dialogue)

Philippine NGO that campaigns for more responsible tourism and promotes alternative tourism projects, as well as exchanges with people from other developing countries.

■ 27d Rosario Townhouse, Galaxy Street, GSIS Heights, Matina, Davao City, Philippines

☏ +63 (0)82-299 2574 ☏ +63 (0)82-299 2052

🌐 www.skyinet.net/~iiddvo ✉ iid@skyinet.net

INDECON (Indonesian Ecotourism Network)

A network set up by the Institute for Indonesian Tourism Studies, Bina Swadaya Foundation and Conservation International, to promote responsible ecotourism in Indonesia.

- ■ Ary Suhandi: Centre for Indonesian Ecotourism Research, Jl Taman Margasatwa 61, Pasar Minggu, Jakarta 12540, Indonesia
- ☎ +62 (0)21-7883 8624; 7883 8626 ✆ +62 (0)21-780 0265; 794 7731
- ⦿ http://indecon.i-2.co.id ✉ indecon@cbn.net.id ✉ indecon@indosat@net.id

IPPG (International Porter Protection Group)

A campaign to improve conditions and safety for trekking porters in the Himalaya.

- ■ In Nepal: Prakash Adhikari, Himalayan Rescue Association (HRA), PO Box 4944, Thamel, Kathmandu
- ✉ hra@aidpost.mos.com.np
- ■ In Australia: Dr Jim Duff: PO Box 53, Repton, NSW 2454
- ☎ +61 (0)2-665 3424
- ⦿ www.users.com.au/duffbel/porter.html ✉ duffbel@omcs.com.au
- ■ In the UK: Ed Cartwright
- ☎ +44 (0)20-7223 5180
- ✉ edward.cartwright@oriel.oxford.ac.uk
- ■ In the US: Dr Jim Litch: jlitch@yahoo.com/Ben Ayers: mklayers@together.net

Kathmandu Environmental Educational Project (KEEP)

KEEP is a non-profit organization based in Nepal. It provides advice on low-impact trekking and tourism in Nepal to both Nepalese people and tourists. It also has an information centre in the Thamel district of Kathmandu which it shares with the Himalayan Explorers Club (www.hec.org). This includes trekking information, a library and the Keep Green coffee shop.

- ■ Partemba Sherpa/PT Sherpa Kerung: KEEP, Jyatha Road, Thamel (PO Box 9178), Kathmandu
- ☎ +977 (0)1-259 567; +977 (0)1-259 275 ✆ +977 (0)1-411 533
- ⦿ www.nepal-connect.com/keep ✉ tour@keep.wlink.com.np

Kenya Tourism Concern

Kenyan campaign for more sustainable tourism.

- ■ Samuel Munyi: PO Box 22449, Nairobi
- ☎ +254 (0)2-535 850 ✆ +254 (0)2-557 092

NACOBTA (Namibian Community-Based Tourism Association)

An association representing community tourism projects in Namibia.

■ Andee Davidson/Maxi Louis: PO Box 86099, 18 Lilliencron St, Windhoek, Namibia

☎ +264 (0)61-250 558 📠 +264 (0)61-222 647

📧 nacobta@iafrica.com.na

Save Goa Campaign

A local organization campaigning against the harmful effects of tourism in Goa.

■ Frederick Noranha: near Lourdes Convent, Saligao 403511, Goa, India

UCOTA (Uganda Community Tourism Association)

An association representing community tourism projects in Uganda.

■ Elissa Williams: PO Box 26318, Kampala, Uganda

☎ +256 (0)41-269 982

📧 prof@swiftuganda.com 📧 ucota@swiftuganda.com

ECOTOURISM ORGANIZATIONS AND WEBSITES

About.com

A broad US 'portal' website with a good ecotourism section. (Search the site for 'ecotourism' to find the right section).

🌐 http://about.com

Conservation International

An environmental agency promoting conservation through community development, including a number of tourism projects. As well as information on their own tourism projects (see 'UK/general tour operators'), Conservation International's website has an Eco-Travel Centre listing other community-based ecotours.

■ Jamie Sweeting: 2501 M St NW Suite 200, Washington DC 20037, US

☎ +1 202-973 2264 📠 +1 202-331 9328

🌐 www.ecotour.org 📧 j.sweeting@conservation.org

Earthwise Journeys

A US website that lists 'responsible' tour operators and 'alternatives to mass tourism'.

🌐 www.teleport.com/~earthwyz

ECoNETT (European Community Network on Environmental Travel & Tourism)
The ecotourism website of the World Tourism and Travel Council.

ⓦ www.wttc.org

Ecosource
A good US starting point for ecotourism links and tour operators on the internet.

ⓦ www.ecosourcenetwork.com

Ecotourism Resource Centre
An Australian ecotourism website with some useful links.

ⓦ www.bigvolcano.com.au/ercentre/

The Ecotourism Society
A US-based organization promoting ecotourism, which it defines as 'responsible travel to natural areas that conserves the environment and improves the well-being of local people'. The website contains valuable information and links.

▇ PO Box 755, North Bennington, VT 05257, US

ⓣ +1 802-447 2121 ⓕ +1 802-447 2122

ⓦ www.ecotourism.org ⓔ ecomail@ecotourism.org

Green-Travel
A good starting-point for internet ecotourism links with an on-line ecotourism mail-list for discussion of ecotourism.

ⓦ www.green-travel.com

Planeta Platica
An excellent website on ecotourism in Latin America (particularly Mexico and Central America) maintained by US travel writer Ron Mader.

ⓦ www.planeta.com

STRING (Sustainable Tourism Research Interest Group)
A Canadian website on sustainable tourism, with ecotourism links.

ⓦ www.dkglobal.org/string

GENERAL TRAVEL ORGANIZATIONS, RESOURCES AND WEBSITES

A selective list of general travel resources.

Lonely Planet
Australian travel guidebook publishers. Their website includes useful internet links.

■ PO Box 617, Hawthorn, Victoria 3122, Australia

☏ +61 (0)3-9819 1877 🖷 +61 (0)3-9819 6459

🌐 www.lonelyplanet.com ✉ talk2us@lonelyplanet.com.au

Mountain Institute
Promotes the conservation of mountain regions worldwide.

■ PO Box 907, Franklin, WV 26807, US

☏ +1 304-358 2401 🖷 +1 304 358 2400

🌐 www.mountain.org

Rough Guides
UK travel guidebook publishers. Their website contains text from their guide-books and other internet links, plus a travel magazine.

■ 62–70 Shorts Gardens, London WC2H 9AB, UK

☏ 020-7556 5001 🖷 020-7556 5050

🌐 www.roughguides.com ✉ mail@roughguides.co.uk

SAEC (South American Explorers' Club)
The SAEC has clubhouses/resource centres in Lima, Cuzco and Quito (addresses listed under Ecuador and Peru in 'Local tour operators by country'). As well as acting as a meeting place for travellers, they have excellent information libraries covering all aspects of travel in South America. Their website is also a good source of travel information about the continent.

■ 126 Indian Creek Road, Ithaca, New York 14850, US

☏ +1 607-277 0488 🖷 +1 607-277 6122

🌐 www.samexplo.org ✉ explorer@samexplo.org

Tourism Information Network
A Canadian website with extensive tourism links for academics and researchers.

🌐 http://webhome.idirect.com/tourism

ENVIRONMENTAL ORGANIZATIONS AND WEBSITES

A selective list of environmental organizations that sometimes deal with tourism issues.

CERN (Caribbean Environmental Reporters' Network)
Web news service on environmental issues in the Caribbean.

■ PO Box 461, Bridgetown, Barbados

☎ +1 246-965 5177 ✆ +1 246-965 5198 (UK fax: +44 (0)161-231 0043)

🅦 http://webgate.poptel.org.uk/zadie

Conservation Foundation
UK-based environmental organization. Their website includes a weekly roundup of environmental news, plus links, etc.

■ 1 Kensington Gore, London SW7 2AR, UK

☎ 020-7591 3111 ✆ 020-7591 3110

🅦 www.conservationfoundation.co.uk 🄴 conservef@gn.apc.org

Earth Pledge Foundation
US organization that promotes sustainable development.

■ Leslie Hoffman, executive director: 149 East 38th Street, New York NY 10016, US

☎ +1 212-573 6968 ✆ +1 212-808 9051

🅦 www.earthpledge.org 🄴 lhoffman@earthpledge.org

Environmental News Service
Internet environmental news roundup and search engine, now part of Lycos. Updated daily.

🅦 http://ens.lycos.com

Friends of the Earth (UK)
Environmental pressure group.

■ 26–28 Underwood Street, London N1 7JQ, UK

☎ 020-7490 1555 ✆ 020-7490 0881

🅦 www.foe.co.uk 🄴 info@foe.co.uk

Global Anti-Golf Movement
UK-based campaign against the development of golf courses worldwide.

■ Desmond Fernandez

☎ 01234-351 966

Greenpeace (UK)

UK branch of the environmental pressure group.

■ Canonbury Villas, London N1, UK

☎ 020-7865 8100 📠 020-7865 8200

🌐 www.greenpeace.org.uk ✉ info@uk.greenpeace.org

IIED (International Institute for Environment and Development)

Publishes an online database of literature on the environment and development.

■ 3 Endsleigh Street, London WC1H 0DD, UK

☎ 020-7388 2117 📠 020-7388 2826

🌐 www.iied.org ✉ mailbox@iied.org

International Bicycle Fund

Promotes sustainable transport, including cycling holiday ideas and many links.

■ 4887 Columbia Drive South, Seattle, Washington 98108-1919, US.

☎ +1 206 767 0848

🌐 www.ibike.org ✉ ibike@ibike.org

INDIGENOUS PEOPLES'
ORGANIZATIONS AND WEBSITES

Abya Yala (Fund for Indigenous Self-Development in South and Meso America)

Networking organization for Latin American indigenous peoples. Spanish/English. The website is part of NativeWeb (see below).

■ 678 13th Street, No 100, Oakland, CA 94612, US

☎ +1 510-763 6553 📠 +1 510-763 6588

🌐 www.nativeweb.org/abyayala 🌐 http://ayf.nativeweb.org/ ✉ abyayala@earthlink.net

Coalition for Amazonian Peoples and their Environment

A coalition of 80 organizations and NGOs representing indigenous Amazonian peoples, including links to member organizations' own websites.

■ 1367 Connecticut Avenue, NW Suite 400, Washington DC 20036, US

☎ +1 202-785 3334 📠 +1 202-785 3335

🌐 www.amazoncoalition.org ✉ amazoncoal@igc.org

Cultural Survival
US-based campaign for the rights of indigenous peoples.

■ 94 Mt Auburn Street, Cambridge, Massachusetts 021, US

☎ +1 617-441 5400 ☏ +1 617-441 5417

🌐 www.cs.org ✉ csinc@cs.org

Indigenous Environmental Network
Environmental campaigns/news from US Native American groups.

■ PO Box 485, Bemidji, MN 56601, US

🌐 www.alphacdc.com/ien ✉ ien@igc.apc.org

NativeWeb
Native American networking website.

🌐 www.nativeweb.org

RTProject (Rethinking Tourism Project)
A project of the non-profit Tides Centre, the Rethinking Tourism Project is an indigenous peoples' campaign for a fairer tourism industry which networks among indigenous groups in tourism.

■ Deborah McLaren, director: PO Box 581938, Minneapolis MN 55458-1938, US

☎ + ☏ +1 651-644 9984

🌐 www2.planeta.com/mader/ecotravel/resources/rtp/rtp.html ✉ RTProject@aol.com

Survival
A worldwide organization campaigning for the rights of tribal peoples.

■ 11–15 Emerald Street, London WC1N 3QL, UK

☎ 020-7242 1441 ☏ 020-7242 1771

🌐 www.survival.org.uk ✉ survival@gn.apc.org

UK-BASED DEVELOPMENT ORGANIZATIONS AND WEBSITES

A selective list of UK-based NGOs with a link to tourism, fair trade, development, etc.

ActionAid

Poverty relief agency that works on community-tourism with RICANCIE in Ecuador.

■ Simon Bottery (press): Hamlyn House, Macdonald Road, London N19 5PG, UK

☎ 020-7561 7614 ☏ 020-7281 5146

🌐 www.actionaid.org ✉ mail@actionaid.org.uk

ACTSA (Action for Southern Africa)

UK-based organization working on development issues in Southern Africa. Has a campaign for 'people-first tourism' in the region.

■ Liz Dodd/Aditi Sharma, 28 Penton St, London N1 9SA, UK

☎ 020-7833 3133 ☏ 020-7837 3001

✉ actsa@geo2.poptel.org.uk

IFAT (International Federation for Alternative Trade)

The world's largest network of fair trade organizations.

■ 30 Murdock Road, Bicester, Oxon, OX6 7RF, UK

☎ 01869-249 819 ☏ 01869-246 381

🌐 www.ifat.org ✉ cwills@ifat.org.uk

GreenNet

UK-based webserver featuring the websites of many environment, human rights and development organizations.

🌐 www.gn.apc.org

OneWorld

Another UK-based webserver for many organizations concerned with development, social justice, etc. The OneWorld homepage features environmental and development news, updated daily.

🌐 www.oneworld.org

Oxfam

Works to relieve developing world poverty and is one of the driving forces in the UK fair-trade movement.

■ 274 Banbury Road, Oxford OX2 7DZ, UK

❶ 01865-311 311 ❶ 01865-313 770

Ⓦ www.oxfam.org.uk Ⓔ oxfam@oxfam.org.uk

TWIN/Twin Trading

TWIN (Third World Information Network) is a British development charity. Twin Trading is the fair-trading arm.

■ 1 Curtin Road, London EC2A 3LT, UK

❶ 020-7375 1221 ❶ 020-7375 1337

Ⓔ info@twin.org.uk

VSO (Voluntary Services Overseas)

Places volunteers with development projects in the South. Also campaigns to maximize the benefits of tourism for communities in developing countries.

■ VSO, 317 Putney Bridge Road, London SW15 2PN, UK

❶ (WorldWise campaign) 020-8780 7306

Ⓦ www.vso.org.uk Ⓔ sjames@vso.org.uk (Sharon James, WorldWise campaign)

World Development Movement

Campaigns for changes that benefit the world's poor, such as an end to Third World debt.

■ 25 Beehive Place, Brixton, London SW9 7QR, UK

❶ 020-7737 6215 ❶ 020-7274 8232

Ⓦ www.wdm.org.uk Ⓔ wdm@wdm.org.uk

BOOKS: ACADEMIC, TEXTBOOKS

The books listed below provide more in-depth discussion of the issues raised in this book. (Note that most US discussion of community tourism comes under the heading of ecotourism.) Some of these can be purchased directly from Tourism Concern, along with many other books and study materials on all aspects of tourism. See the resources page on the Tourism Concern website – www.tourismconcern.org.uk.

Beyond the Green Horizon: Principles for Sustainable Tourism
Introduces the principles and issues of sustainable tourism, with case studies.
■ S Eber, ed (Tourism Concern/WWF, 1992. Available from Tourism Concern)

Community Based Sustainable Tourism – Reader/Handbook
A set of two books, produced by an organization in the Philippines, that discuss community tourism and provide useful, easy-to-understand guidelines and advice for anyone wanting to set up their own community tourism project.
■ Corazon T Urquico, ed (ASSET, Philippines 1998. asset@pacific.net.ph)

The Earthscan Reader in Sustainable Tourism
A useful compilation of book extracts, case studies and papers ranging from the Isle of Man to Nepal and Kenya. Includes a study of Zimbabwe's CAMPFIRE scheme.
■ L France, ed (Earthscan, London, 1997)

Ecotourism: A Guide for Planners and Managers, volume 2
Primarily about nature tours, much of this applies to community-based tourism as well. A mix of practical advice and assessment of industry trends. Volume 1 was published in 1993.
■ Lindberg, Epler Wood & Engeldrum, eds (The Ecotourism Society, Vermont, 1998)

Ecotourism and Sustainable Development
Analysis and case studies of ecotourism in the Galapagos, Costa Rica, Cuba, Tanzania, Kenya and South Africa. Discusses how ecotourism relates to local communities.
■ Martha Honey (Island Press, Washington, 1999)

Ecotourism in the Less Developed World
Research paper with case studies of Costa Rica, Kenya, Nepal, Thailand, the Caribbean and South Pacific.
■ D Weaver (CAB International, Wallingford, 1998)

Last Resorts: The Cost of Tourism in the Caribbean
Examines the impacts of tourism on the Caribbean.
■ Polly Pattullo (Latin American Bureau, London, 1996. Available from Tourism Concern)

Rethinking Tourism and Ecotravel

A book critically reassessing tourism, including 'alternative' forms of tourism, with a good list of responsible tourism resources. Written by the director of the Rethinking Tourism Project.

■ Deborah McLaren (Kumarian Press, West Hartford)

✆ +1 860-233 5895

✉ KpBooks@aol.com

Sustainable Tourism: A Geographical Perspective

Readable academic introduction including both environmental and social issues.

■ C Michael Hall and Alan Lew, eds (Longman, London, 1999)

Tourism and Sustainability: New Tourism in the Third World

Explores globalization, sustainability and global power in relation to tourism, and asks whether emerging forms of tourism (including community tourism) will help people in developing countries. Includes primary research from Central America and the Caribbean.

■ M Mowforth and I Munt (Routledge, London, 1998)

Trading Places: Tourism as Trade

An introduction to tourism as a trade industry, with case studies on The Gambia, Kenya, Turkey, Sri Lanka, Barbados, Egypt and the Philippines.

■ Badger et al (Tourism Concern, 1996. Available from Tourism Concern)

BOOKS: GUIDEBOOKS, MAGAZINES

Selected guidebooks that include good information about community-based tourism.

Namibia: The Bradt Travel Guide

Unusually good on community-based tourism for a mainstream guidebook.

■ Chris McIntyre (Bradt Publications, Chalfont St Peter)

Defending the Rainforest: A Guide to Community-Based Ecotourism in the Ecuadorian Amazon

Excellent, ground-breaking guide to indigenous community tourism in Ecuador's Amazon region, essential for anyone visiting the Ecuadorean Amazon or studying indigenous tourism. (Some of these projects are summarized in the Ecuador section of our directory.)

■ Rolf Wesche/Andy Drumm (Accion Amazonia, 1999). Available from Tropic Ecological Adventures: see 'Locally based tours by country: Ecuador'.

The Green Travel Guide
A comprehensive guide to nature-based holidays both in the UK and abroad, from voluntary conservation work in the UK to jungle tours in the South American rainforest, by The Sunday Telegraph's environmental correspondent.

■ Greg Neale (Earthscan, London, 1998)

Indian America
A guide to present-day tribes of the US. Not specifically a tourism guide, but contains contact details and visitor information.

■ Eagle/Walking Turtle (John Muir Publications, Santa Fe, 4th ed, 1995)

Mexico: Adventures in Nature
An excellent guide to ecotourism and community-based tourism in Mexico.

■ Ron Mader (John Muir Publications, Santa Fe, 1998)

is the UK's leading travel magazine, dedicated to people
who are concerned with the cultures and natural history of
the countries that they visit.

With over 120 pages packed with features by award-winning writers
and photographers, *Wanderlust* now has readers in 97 countries.

If you want to join them, a year's subscription (6 issues) costs £16
(UK addresses), and carries a **money-back guarantee**.

For more details or to place a credit card order:
tel: **01753 620426** or fax: 01753 620474
email: info@wanderlust.co.uk   website: www.wanderlust.co.uk
Or write to: PO Box 1832, Windsor SL4 1YT

Wanderlust

A magazine for independent and small-group travellers, which sometimes
features articles about community-based tours.

■ PO Box 1832, Windsor, Berks SL4 6YP, UK

❶ 01753-620 426

Ⓦ www.wanderlust.co.uk Ⓔ info@wanderlust.co.uk

Wild Planet!

Not specifically about community tourism, but a fascinating guidebook for
anyone interested in cultural exploration, detailing over 1000 festivals, events
and celebrations around the world from Rio's carnival to little-known, quirky
village fairs.

■ Tom Clynes (Visible Ink Press, Detroit, 1995)

THE TODO! AWARDS

The ToDo! Awards are the only awards that we know of dedicated specifically to socially responsible tourism. They are open to projects 'whose planning and realization ensure the involvement of the different interests and requirements of local people through participation'. They are presented each year at the International Tourism Exchange in Berlin by the German NGO **Studienkreis fur Tourismus und Entwicklung**. The winners are described in more detail in the Holiday Directory and on the Studienkreis website (www.studienkreis.org). The awards criteria are:

- raising awareness among local people of the impacts of tourism;
- participation of a broad range of local people in tourism;
- good working conditions for local employees, including pay, security, hours, training;
- reinforcement of local culture;
- minimization of the social and cultural damage caused by tourism;
- developing new partnerships between the tourist industry and local people;
- helping to develop socially responsible tourism in destination areas;
- environmental sustainability.

TODO! AWARDS ORGANIZER

Studienkreis für Tourismus und Entwicklung

■ Kapellenweg 3, D-82541 Ammerland, Germany

① +49 (0)8177 1783 ① +49 (0)8177 1349

Ⓦ www.studienkreis.org Ⓔ studienkreistourismus@compuserve.com

TODO! AWARDS WINNERS

1998

Aboriginal Art and Culture Centre, Australia
Aboriginal-owned art gallery in Alice Springs which run tours to Aboriginal communities.

Corpomedina CA, Venezuela

A company facilitating a range of community-based tourism projects including guesthouses, tour agencies and micro-credit business support on the Paria peninsula in north-east Venezuela.

1997

Tropic Ecological Adventures (Huaorani tour), Ecuador

Five-day rainforest tours to Ecuador's Amazon, staying with an indigenous Huaorani community.

Shawenequanape Kipichewin (Anishinabe Village), Canada

A First Nations-owned camp, tipi village and cultural tours in Riding Mountain National Park, Manitoba.

Natur und Leben Bregenzerwald, Austria

This tour is not included in our directory.

1996

International Centre of Bethlehem, West Bank

A project to increase local benefit from tourism to Bethlehem.

Toledo Ecotourism Association, Belize

Tours and village stays with Mayan, Garifuna and Kekchi communities in southern Belize.

1995

Sua Bali, Indonesia

A small resort just south of Ubud in Bali that works closely with the local village.

Woodlands Network, Sri Lanka

A women's organization that arranges village stays in (mainly) rural Sri Lanka.

RESPONSIBLE TOURISM CODES

THE RESPONSIBLE TOURIST

People often phone Tourism Concern to ask 'how to behave responsibly' when on holiday. Here we list Tourism Concern's 'responsible travel' guidelines, plus three other codes. Two are for trekkers in the Nepalese Himalayas (or similar mountain regions). The final one is from Survival, an organization campaigning for the rights of tribal people.

These codes lay down broad principles: specific customs and values vary from country to country. On the whole, of course, if you are considerate and respectful to the people you meet, you probably won't go far wrong. That includes learning and observing basic local customs (such as covering bare flesh in religious buildings or not pointing your feet at someone). It means learning a few simple phrases of the local language, even if it's only 'hello' and 'thank you'. It means understanding and respecting the boundary between public and private space.

Leave behind the 'consumer mentality': think of yourself not simply as 'the paying customer', always demanding service. You are also a visitor in someone else's country, village or home. Remember, too, that the people you meet on holiday probably haven't had a say in whether tourists come to their town or village, and that most people you meet probably don't benefit from tourism.

Responsible tourism doesn't mean you can't enjoy yourself. It doesn't mean you can't have a laugh, or share a joke with the people you meet. It doesn't mean you can't simply lie on a beach. It doesn't even mean you can't get drunk or stoned, if that's what you want to do. (In some Mexican cantinas, it would be rude *not* to get drunk!) It simply means treating local people as *people* – not as beggars, nuisances, servants, con men, thieves or exotic photo opportunities.

TOURISM CONCERN GUIDELINES

- **Save precious natural resources.** Try not to waste water and always switch off lights and air-conditioning if you go out.
- **Buy local.** Buy locally made souvenirs where possible. (But avoid souvenirs made from coral, ivory, skins or other wildlife.) Drinking locally produced drinks such as fruit juices gives money to local people: drinking Pepsi or Coke gives money to Western corporations.
- **Support locally owned and operated tourism initiatives.**
- **Recognize tribal land rights** (even if the national government does not – governments are amongst the principal violators of tribal rights). When in tribal lands, behave as you would on private property. (Adapted from Survival's code.)
- If in doubt about whether you are welcome in a tribal community, don't go. **Only visit tribal people on tours that you know they endorse.** Don't accept vague assurances that 'it's OK' from your guide. Tribal people should have the right not to be visited if they choose. With remote tribal communities, you also risk introducing disease.
- **Always ask before photographing people** (or videoing them). If you don't speak the language, a smile and a gesture will be understood.
- **Don't give money or sweets to children.** It encourages begging and demeans the child. A donation to a community project, heath centre or school is more constructive. (If you have a guide, ask for details.)
- **Respect local etiquette.** It will earn you respect. In many countries, loose and lightweight clothes are preferable to revealing shorts, skimpy tops or tight fitting wear. Kissing in public may offend local people.
- **Learn a little of the local language, history and current affairs of a country.** It prevents misunderstandings and frustrations.

Be patient, friendly and sensitive. Remember – you are a guest.

THE HIMALAYAN CODE

The Himalayan Code was drawn up by Tourism Concern with British and Nepalese tour operators and the **Annapurna Conservation Area Project (ACAP)**, a Nepalese NGO. It is designed for trekkers in the Himalayas, but the principles apply to other high mountain environments, such as the Andes.

Protect the natural environment
- **Limit deforestation.** Make no open fires and discourage others from doing so on your behalf. Where water is heated by scarce firewood, use as little as possible. When possible, choose accommodation that uses kerosene or fuel-efficient wood stoves.
- **Remove litter.** Burn or bury paper and carry out all non-degradable litter. Graffiti is a permanent form of environmental pollution.
- **Keep local water clean.** Avoid using pollutants such as detergents in streams or springs. If no toilets are available, make sure you are at least 30 metres away from water sources and bury or cover wastes.
- **Plants** should be left to flourish in their natural environment. Taking cuttings, seeds and roots is illegal in many parts of the Himalayas.
- Help your **guides and porters** to follow conservation measures.

As a guest, respect local traditions and cultures and maintain local pride
- When taking photos, **respect privacy**. Ask permission and use restraint.
- **Respect holy places.** Preserve what you have come to see. Never touch or remove religious objects. Shoes should be removed in temples.
- Giving to children encourages begging. A **donation** to a project, health centre or school is a more constructive way to help.
- You will be accepted and welcomed if you **follow local customs**. Use only your right hand for eating and greeting. Do not share cutlery and cups, etc. It is polite to use both hands when giving or receiving gifts.
- **Respect local etiquette.** Loose, lightweight clothes are preferable to revealing shorts, skimpy tops and tight fitting 'action-wear'. Handholding or kissing in public are disliked by local people.
- **Observe standard food and bed charges** but do not condone over-charging. Remember, when you're shopping, the bargains you buy may only be possible because of low income to others.
- Visitors who **value local traditions** encourage local pride and maintain local cultures. And please help local people gain a realistic view of life in Western countries.

INTERNATIONAL PORTER PROTECTION GROUP

This code covers safety and working conditions for trekking porters in Nepal although, as with the Himalayan Code, it applies to any similar trekking region.

- That **adequate clothing** be available for protection in bad weather and at altitude. This should include adequate footwear, hat, gloves, windproof jacket and trousers, sunglasses, and access to a blanket and pad above the snowline.
- That leaders and trekkers provide the same standard of **medical care** for porters as they would expect for themselves.
- That porters **not be paid off because of illness** without the leader or trekkers being informed.
- That sick porters **never be sent down alone**, but with someone who speaks their language and understands the problem.
- That sufficient **funds** be provided to sick porters to cover the cost of their rescue and treatment.

SURVIVAL

This code is for tourists visiting tribal communities or their territories. It was drawn up by Survival, an organization campaigning for the rights of tribal peoples.

'Tourism need not be a destructive force for tribal peoples, but unfortunately it usually is: any tourism which violates tribal peoples' rights should be opposed. Tourism must be subject to the decisions made by tribal peoples themselves.'

Do...

- **Recognize land rights:** tribal peoples' ownership of the lands they use and occupy is recognized in international law. This should be acknowledged irrespective of whether the national government applies the law or not (governments are amongst the principal violators of tribes' rights). When in tribal lands, tourists should behave as they would on private property.
- **Ask permission:** the lands lived in or used by tribes should not be entered without the free and informed consent of the tribal peoples themselves. Obtaining this consent can be lengthy; it requires respect, tact and honesty. Bribery should never be used.
- **Pay properly:** tribespeople should be properly recompensed for their services and use of their territory. Payment should be agreed in advance with their legitimate representatives. (Bribery should never be used.) Where profits arise from using tribal areas, this should be properly explained to the tribes, who may want a share. Anyone who is not able to accept tribal peoples' own terms for payment should not be there.
- **Be respectful:** tourist companies should insist that their staff and clients behave respectfully towards tribal peoples. (In practice, many tourists who visit tribal areas simply have their false stereotypes reinforced.)

Don't...

- **Bring in disease:** care must be taken in areas where tribal peoples' immunity to outside diseases may be poor. Some contagious diseases (colds, influenza, etc) which affect tourists only mildly can kill tribespeople. Please also remember that AIDS kills.
- **Demean, degrade, insult or patronize:** all tourism and advertising which treat tribal people in an insulting, degrading or patronizing manner (for example, references to 'stone-age cultures', 'untouched by time', etc) should be opposed. They are demeaning and wrong.

GLOSSARY

This glossary defines terms as they are used in this book, which may not be exact dictionary definitions.

ABTA	Association of British Travel Agents. The trade association of large tour operators.
ATOL	Air Travel Organizers Licence. A bonding scheme run by the Civil Aviation Authority. If your tour operator is a member of ATOL, you are guaranteed a refund if the company goes into liquidation.
Aboriginal	refers to the original inhabitants of a country and their descendants. The term is used mainly in Australia and Canada. See also **First Nations**, **indigenous people**.
all-inclusive	a resort providing accommodation, food and all facilities (eg beach and watersports) internally, so that visitors have no need to leave the resort.
backpacker	a (usually young) **independent traveller**; typically carries a rucksack and stays in cheap, locally owned accommodation.
community	a mutually supportive, geographically specific social unit such as a village or tribe.
community tourism	a shorter term for **community-based tourism**.
community-based tourism	tourism that consults, involves and benefits a local **community**, especially in the context of rural villages in **developing countries** and **indigenous peoples**.
customized itineraries	a holiday schedule drawn up by a tour operator specifically for one client or group, usually including flight, accommodation and transport. Sometimes called tailor-made holidays.
developed countries/world	see **the West**.
developing countries/world	the world's less wealthy nations, mostly former colonies: ie most of Asia, Africa, Latin America and the South Pacific. Also sometimes referred to as **the South**.

ecotourism	according to the US-based Ecotourism Society, 'Ecotourism is responsible travel to a natural area that conserves the environment and sustains the well-being of local people'. In the UK, the phrase **green travel** is sometimes preferred.
ethical tourism	see **responsible tourism**.
fair trade	equitable, non-exploitative trade between **developing world** suppliers and **Western** consumers. Tourism Concern is undertaking a three-year Fair Trade in Tourism project to consider whether the concept of fair trade can be applied to tourism.
First Nations	a collective term for the original, pre-European inhabitants of the US, Canada, Hawaii, Australia and New Zealand. In individual countries, different terms are sometimes used: eg **Aboriginal**, **indigenous**, **tribal**, Indian, First Peoples, Native American, AmerIndian.
green travel	a UK alternative to the American term **ecotourism**.
independent traveller	someone who travels without booking a **package tour**.
indigenous people	the original inhabitants of a country and their descendants. Indigenous communities are often, but not always, **tribal peoples** and the two terms are often and easily confused. (Note: there are points in this book that apply particularly to tribal people, others that apply to indigenous people in general, and still others that apply to all rural developing world communities. I've tried to use each term in its correct and precise sense. In the real world, of course, people stubbornly refuse to fit into such simplistic categories, and the distinctions between tribal, indigenous and non-indigenous communities may not always be crystal clear.) See also **First Nations**, **Aboriginal**.
local communities/people	people living in tourist destinations, especially in the rural **developing world**.
multinational corporation	see **transnational corporation**.
NGO	non-governmental organization: an independent pressure group or campaigning organization, usually non-profit.
Native Americans	a collective term for the **indigenous** peoples of the Americas. Also **First Nations**, AmerIndians, American Indians, Indians.

North, the	see **the West**.
package tour	a holiday combining transport and accommodation in an inclusive price.
responsible tourism	tourism that aims to avoid harmful impacts on people and environments. Sometimes referred to as ethical tourism. Other similar concepts include People First Tourism, reality tourism, etc.
South, the	see **developing countries**.
sustainable tourism	tourism that does not degrade the environment or local cultures/societies.
Third World, the	now generally referred to as either **developing countries** or **the South**.
tourists	holiday-makers, generally from the **West**. The term is sometimes used to distinguish **package tourists** from **independent travellers**, but I use it to mean anyone going on holiday.
transnational corporation	correctly, a large company with shareholders in more than one country. I use the term fairly loosely to mean any large, powerful, Western-owned company.
tribal peoples	people living in close-knit social units based on kinship ties and shared belief systems. While most remaining tribal communities are **indigenous**, not all indigenous people are tribal.
West, the	the world's rich nations: ie Western Europe, the US, Canada, Australia, New Zealand and (economically, although perhaps not culturally) Japan. Also referred to as the **North**, the **developed countries/world**.